The Child in Post-Apocalyptic Cinema

The Child in Post-Apocalyptic Cinema

Edited by Debbie Olson

LEXINGTON BOOKS
Lanham • Boulder • New York • London

Published by Lexington Books
An imprint of The Rowman & Littlefield Publishing Group, Inc.
4501 Forbes Boulevard, Suite 200, Lanham, Maryland 20706
www.rowman.com

Unit A, Whitacre Mews, 26-34 Stannary Street, London SE11 4AB

British Library Cataloguing in Publication Information Available

Library of Congress Cataloging-in-Publication Data

The child in post-apocalyptic cinema / edited by Debbie Olson.
pages cm
Includes bibliographical references and index.
ISBN 978-0-7391-9428-7 (cloth : alk. paper) -- ISBN 978-0-7391-9429-4 (electronic)
1. Children in motion pictures. 2. Apocalypse in motion pictures. I. Olson, Debbie C., 1961–
PN1995.9.C45C463 2015
791.43'6523--dc23
2014047775

Printed in the United States of America

To my sons, Rick and Justin—the Good Guys who carry the fire. . . .

Contents

Introduction

Debbie Olson

Nostalgia had beauty because it retained within it the presentiment of what has taken place and what could take place again. It was as beautiful as utopia of which it is the inverted mirror. It was beautiful for never being satisfied, as was utopia for never being achieved. —Jean Baudrillard [1]

For we live under continual threat of two equally fearful, but seemingly opposed, destinies: unremitting banality, and inconceivable terror. —Susan Sontag [2]

Susan Sontag astutely observes in her 1965 seminal article "The Imagination of Disaster," that there is a compelling beauty in the total annihilation of modern physical space, a conscious satisfaction found in an "aesthetics of destruction" that leaves us fascinated by such cinematic images as New York being swallowed by a giant wave in *The Day after Tomorrow* (2004) or crushed by an unknown alien in *Cloverfield* (2008). Such destructive beauty is found in one of Hollywood's most popular cinematic genres, the post-apocalyptic film. [3] The post-apocalyptic film is the quintessential disaster movie that often features total destruction of modern civilization, usually on a planetary scale, with a narrative that follows the survivors as they negotiate the hazards of toxic wastelands, alien invaders, biological threats, environmental decimation, supernatural terrors, or fellow humans in order to survive. The most common apocalyptic destructions occur from divine judgment or the supernatural, alien invasion, environmental disasters, astronomical events, biological pandemics, nuclear annihilation, or destructive technology. Peter Y. Paik observes that post-apocalyptic films offer a "realist depiction of a transformed world . . . that does not omit the horrors that accompany its foundations."[4] Indeed, many such films feature a camera that glides lovingly over wastelands of rubble and death, caressing close-ups of mutant horrors or shell-shocked survivors. Part of the attraction of post-apocalyptic cinema is the voyeuristic pleasure of seeing the destruction of our present reality—the divine sentiment "there but for the Grace of God go I (we)" roots us to our theater seat as we fetishize the visual depiction of the end of human existence as we know it.

One of the most compelling aspects of the post-apocalyptic landscape is that it offers a unique blend of the fear of death with nostalgia for the modern present. The post-apocalyptic film functions as the "mirror" that Baudrillard mentions above, which allows us to view contemporary society (the "now") as a utopia by way of the post-apocalyptic film's nostalgic longing for the imagined lost trappings and conveniences of modern existence; for within the collapse of cities and the destruction of nature lie the failure of memory and the rise of illusory nostalgia. Post-apocalyptic nostalgia for lost modernity is a "beam of memory" that "bends" in such a way as to create a "catastrophic memory failure" so that all the evils of modernity, the things we abhor—crime, racism, hatred, poverty, war, superficiality, isolation, materialism, capitalism—are instead remembered fondly, and we long to return to them.[5] In many ways, post-apocalyptic cinema elides any notion of "the dream of the future" and instead often submerges hope and futurity with a persistent undercurrent of the impossibility of regeneration or renewal, even as the survivors struggle to rebuild what was lost.[6] It is not the future the post-apocalyptic survivors strive to claim, but the past, or rather, the now. And within the cinematic visual struggle to reclaim the past/present there is one character who is inexorably tethered to notions of an idealized past as well as hope and optimism for a future: the child.

Children, and childhood, seem to be an odd pairing with the post-apocalyptic condition and yet, in many post-apocalyptic films, children play a central role in the survival of and hope for humanity. The notion of a dystopian childhood filled with zombies or mutant abominations is disconcerting and functions as a direct challenge to all that adults believe about childhood, innocence, and the resourcefulness and capabilities of children in traumatic situations. And, as often happens, children of the post-apocalypse surprise us. This collection is the result of our fascination with the image of the child within the framework of the end of humanity as we know it. The image of a soft, smiling face of an angelic child who is positioned amidst the horrific destruction of the modern world fills us with a tantalizing brew of dread, voyeuristic fascination, and ultimately, a reason to survive. The essays in this volume explore children and childhood as symbols of past, present, and future notions of humanity, as saviors, destroyers, and finally, as bearers of courage and hope for us all.

CHILDREN OF THE END

In *After the End*, James Berger argues that post-apocalyptic films feature a "discourse that impossibly straddles the boundary between before and after some event that has obliterated what went before yet defines what will come after."[7] The child in such films functions in much the same way—their image, their mythos of innocence and purity, defines the lost past/present and becomes a motivational, almost sacred image to spur on reclamation of the future. In Hollywood post-apocalypse films, this straddling discourse of surviving "the end times" is often the realm of the individual hero or the strong adult group that maneuvers through the flotsam of catastrophe. And while post-apocalyptic films in general tend to interrogate the nature of humanity, democracy and other political, social, and economic conditions or policies, they also feature a specific "straddling" character in the child, who has one foot in the future and one in the past. Images of and references to children are most often used in post-apocalyptic scenarios as symbols of humanity's historical continuance.

The notion of the inherent innocence of the child arose in seventeenth-century Europe, where images of children in art proliferated. The fantasy of "the Child" became a cultural obsession throughout the Renaissance, as Anne Higonnet argues, and visual "fictions about lived experience were more consistent, more convincing, and more beautiful than any lived experience could be."[8] The romantic notion of the "innocent child" did not exist before the modern age.[9] Children are often considered closer to God and therefore spiritually pure, a notion that reflects those cultural changes in the value of a child's life. According to Viviana A. Zelizer, a "new sensitivity toward child loss was part of a broader transformation in the cultural response to death."[10] As Zelizer explains, the eighteenth century saw an explosion of emotional value placed on children, who were sacralized in popular literature and art: "Public sentiment was strongly aroused by twentieth-century conceptions of the uniquely sacred value of child life."[11]

The sacredness of the child, however, takes on a particular significance when positioned within the post-apocalyptic landscape. As Bernard McGinn explains in *Visions of the End*, throughout history apocalyptic beliefs have focused on the intersections of a "*vertical* dimension connecting heaven and earth . . . and a *horizontal* one linking the succession of time and its end."[12] The child, as a symbol of past, present, and future, embodies that intersection. And while most recent post-apocalyptic films are not necessarily based on religious expressions of the "rapture" or the "end times," they almost certainly contain subtextual elements of divine judgment or of evil loosed upon the world. McGinn states that apocalypticism is the "belief that God has revealed the events of the end, both good and bad . . . and that in some way we are now actually living in the midst of these last events."[13] The collision of heaven and earth with time and its end, or the end of history as Baudrillard argues, forms the backbone of the post-apocalyptic film genre. In some post-apocalyptic films, the child is both the image of the divine and the end of history. The nature of the apocalyptic destruction is central to how the survivors will navigate the post-apocalyptic conditions and how, or if, they will rebuild. In *No Future*, Lee Edelman questions the notion of the child as a symbol of futurity: "the Child [is] the emblem of futurity's unquestioned value,"[14] and as some of our authors will explore, the child in the post-apocalyptic film is a key symbolic presence for the survivor's struggle to regain some semblance of hope.

THE CHAPTERS

The collection begins with Aryak Guha's "Monstrous Conceptions: Reading Cronenberg's *The Brood* (1979) and Anton Leader's *Children of the Damned* (1963)." Guha examines *Children of the Damned* (1964) and *The Brood* (1979) and argues that the "wonder-children" or "super-children" in these films are targeted by the state in order for it to retain power. As Guha suggests, the destruction of these "other[ed]" children who are "adult-defying," suggests the move to absolute state power and signals an "emergent apocalypse in the age of democracy." In chapter 2, Jennifer Brown contends that the child character in post-apocalyptic films reveals to us beliefs about our world and our role in it. She examines *Waterworld* (1995), *The Road* (2009), and *Beasts of the Southern Wild* (2012) and argues that in each film the child is a "burden" and a "target," a "mere body to be used by older, stronger forces," but at the same time a "source of incredible strength, joy, and life." She suggests that through the child characters, these films "urge contemporary adults" to take a long hard look at the world they will leave to their children. And in chapter 3, "Perpetual Horizons: Reproductive Futurity in Post-Apocalyptic Films," Mark Heimermann explores issues of futurity in the films *Dawn of the Dead* (2004) and *Daybreakers* (2009). He argues that these films "critique Western capitalism . . . [as] a world hell-bent on consumption." He suggests that in these films, children function, not as symbols of futurity, but "emblematic only of the present" and who "undermine the notion of constant societal progress."

In "The Child Is My Warrant: Virtue, Violence and *The Road*'s Radical Humanism," Joseph Wiinikka-Lydon interrogates the notion of survival in a post-apocalyptic landscape. While "mere survival seems possible," such survival raises the question of "is life worth such toil?" For Wiinikka-Lydon, it is the Boy's compassion and caring that, in the end, reveal the "enduring nature of the moral life and even of hope itself." In chapter 5, Eduardo Barros Grela and María Bobadilla Pérez use theories of space to interrogate the child in a post-apocalyptic landscape. In "Space and Children in Post-Apocalyptic Film: *The Road* and *Les Temp du Loup*," they argue that the children in these films "resignify" the post-apocalyptic space as they "intensely explore and enhance their denial of adult epistemologies" while negotiating their violence-filled, stark dystopian spaces.

Chapter 6 features Eric D. Miller's exploration of the possible connection between the events of 9/11 and the rise in apocalyptic films—particularly apocalyptic films geared toward children. In "When Disney Went Apocalyptic: The Symbolism of Apocalyptic Images in a Post-9/11 World," Miller argues that while such Disney films like *WALL-E* and *9* end with themes of hope and redemption, they also raise important questions about the "appropriateness of apocalyptic imagery in films primarily marketed to children." In chapter 7, "Children of Hope: The Portrayal of Children in Post-Apocalyptic Films after 9/11," Betül Ateşci Koçak examines the ways in which the child in post-9/11 post-apocalyptic films resonates as a particular symbol of hope. Koçak argues that the "true-to-life" experiences of the nation's fear after the apocalyptic events of 9/11 have been replicated in post-apocalyptic films. For Koçak, the child functions as the "one who instigates a new world" and creates new spaces.

In "'Until the World Deserves Them': Representations of Apocalyptic Childhoods in *The Day After*, *Testament*, and *Threads*," Tarah Brookfield observes that these three films explore Cold War anxieties by using children as "powerful conduits for apocalyptic prophecies." Brookfield examines how cultural fears of nuclear war affected children and youth during the Cold War. She argues that despite cinematic "prophecies" of global nuclear catastrophe, children and youth viewers understood that they held the power to prevent the apocalypse they watched on screen. In chapter 9, Frank Jacob examines Japanese director Terayama Shûji's 1971 post-apocalyptic avant-garde film *Emperor Tomato Ketchup*. In "*Emperor Tomato Ketchup*: The Child as the Dictator of Mankind," Jacob explores Terayama's use of children as dictator's to depict his "utopian version of an evil past." While the film has been vilified as child porn, Jacob argues that Terayama's project is instead an intriguingly complex criticism of Japanese postwar society.

In "The Specter of the Postcolonial Child and Faux Long Takes in Cuarón's *Children of Men*," James Hodapp claims the "specter of a potentially postcolonial child dominates the futurity in *Children of Men*." He astutely argues that the filmmaker's use of the long take "amplifies the postcolonial nature of the child." For Hodapp, the film's long takes, and the child, merely "appear as natural extensions of their environment," but instead function as "contested sites of meaning" within the post-apocalyptic landscape. In chapter 11, Glen Donnar exposes how children in "final man" films "make the survival and sacrifices of the 'final men' meaningful." In "Persistently Ambivalent: Race, Sexuality, and a Post-Apocalyptic Hollywood Interracial Future," Donnar offers a richly textured analysis of *The World, The Flesh, and the Devil* (1959), *The Omega Man* (1971), and *I am Legend* (2007). He perceptively argues that the children in these films "expose rather than absolve, reflect rather than salve, American racial anxieties and preoccupations." And in chapter 12, Cassandra L. Jones examines fan reactions to the casting and death of the character Rue in the 2012 film adaptation of the popular post-apocalyptic youth novel, *The Hunger Games*. Jones explains that grief is an act of recognition of each other and our humanity, "marking both a sense of communal identity and individuation within that community." But the casting of African American child actress, Amandla Stenberg, to play Rue in the film resulted in a bevy of negative and racist fan reactions, which as Jones argues, raises disturbing questions about the "cultural inability to associate innocence with black girlhood."

> *The wolf will live with the lamb, the leopard will lie down with the goat, the calf and the lion and the yearling together; and a little child will lead them.*
> —Isaiah 11:6

According to Carl Freedman, Utopia, as we imagine it, is "never fully present in the here-and-now,"[15] and yet, through the visual magic of post-apocalyptic cinema, we experience nostalgia for the present *as* a Utopia-lost. As Claire P. Curtis argues, the "lack of hope" is a "common theme of post-apocalyptic fiction"[16] and of the resulting dystopian societies, a theme that is challenged by the presence of, or promise of, a child. The child in the post-apocalyptic landscape becomes more than just a symbol of the "anxieties and ambivalences attached to the [lost] family"[17] or the ills of modern civilization, but rather, suggests broader cultural anxieties about our loss of innocence in this age of rapid technological development and social media relations, or fears of the end of history, as Baudrillard warns. The child body is the intersection of our past, present, and future, the manifestation of who we were, who we are, and who, or what, humanity can become. And so we examine the special relationship children have to the post-apocalyptic condition, to disaster and fear, to death and decay, to the loss of all that is familiar, and to the desire for a return to our "utopian" now. Rising from the ashes of apocalyptic ruin will be the child—and the child will lead us.

NOTES

1. Jean Baudrillard. *The Illusion of the End*. Stanford: University of California Press, 1994, 120.
2. Susan Sontag. "The Imagination of Disaster." *American Jewish Committee* 40, 4 (1965): 42–48.

3. Sontag, 44.
4. Peter Y. Paik. *From Utopia to Apocalypse: Science Fiction and the Politics of Catastrophe.* Minneapolis: University of Minnesota Press, 2010, 22.
5. Baudrillard, 20.
6. Teresa Heffernan. *Post-Apocalyptic Culture: Modernism, Postmodernism, and the Twentieth-Century Novel.* Toronto: University of Toronto Press, 2008, 7.
7. James Berger. *After the End: Representations of Post-Apocalypse.* Minneapolis: University of Minnesota Press, 1999, 19.
8. Anne Higonnet. *Pictures of Innocence.* London: Thames and Hudson, Ltd., 1998, 8.
9. Higonnet, 15.
10. Vivian A. Zelizer. *Pricing the Priceless Child: The Changing Social Value of Children.* New York: Basic Books, 1998, 26.
11. Zelizer, 48.
12. Bernard McGinn. *Visions of the End: Apocalyptic Traditions in the Middle Ages.* New York: Columbia University Press, 1999, xvi.
13. McGinn, xiv.
14. Lee Edelman. *No Future.* New York: Duke University Press, 2004.
15. Carl Freedman. *Critical Theory and Science Fiction.* Hanover, NH: Wesleyan University Press, 2000, 64.
16. Claire P. Curtis. *Postapocalyptic Fiction and the Social Contract.* Lanham, MD: Lexington Books, 2010, 37.
17. Kirsten Moana Thompson. *Apocalyptic Dread: American Film at the Turn of the Millennium.* New York: State University of New York Press, 2007, 17.

BIBLIOGRAPHY

Baudrillard, Jean. *The Illusion of the End.* Stanford: University of California Press, 1994.
Berger, James. *After the End: Representations of Post-Apocalypse.* Minneapolis: University of Minnesota Press, 1999.
Curtis, Claire P. *Postapocalyptic Fiction and the Social Contract.* Lanham, MD: Lexington Books, 2010.
Edelman, Lee. *No Future.* New York: Duke University Press, 2004.
Freedman, Carl. *Critical Theory and Science Fiction.* Hanover, NH: Wesleyan University Press, 2000.
Heffernan, Teresa. *Post-Apocalyptic Culture: Modernism, Postmodernism, and the Twentieth-Century Novel.* Toronto: University of Toronto Press, 2008.
Higonnet, Anne. *Pictures of Innocence.* London: Thames and Hudson, Ltd., 1998.
McGinn, Bernard. *Visions of the End: Apcalyptic Traditions in the Middle Ages.* New York: Columbia University Press, 1989.
Paik, Peter Y. *From Utopia to Apocalypse: Science Fiction and the Politics of Catastrophe.* Minneapolis: University of Minnesota Press, 2010.
Sontag, Susan. "The Imagination of Disaster." *American Jewish Committee* 40, 4 (1965): 42–48.
Thompson, Kirsten Moana. *Apocalyptic Dread: American Film at the Turn of the Millennium.* New York: State University of New York Press, 2007.
Zelizer, Viviana A. *Pricing the Priceless Child: The Changing Social Value of Children.* New York: Basic Books, 1998.

Chapter One

Monstrous Conceptions

Reading Cronenberg's The Brood *(1979) and Anton
Leader's* Children of the Damned *(1963)*

Aryak Guha

The biological fact of development—growth in individual life that all adults
have gone through and children will—is a miracle so common that it rarely
strikes us anything but "natural." The norm of the modern nuclear family, to
put a different spin on the oft-quoted poem by the British poet laureate
Wordsworth, is well expressed in the epithet: "The child is the father of
man." But can we define what a child is, that is, a child *qua* child? Can we
think of an answer without reference to issues of biological growth, parent-
age, socialization or, indeed, adulthood—taken to be the normal culmination
of a course that has already set in? But is not a person a child insofar as she
has not attained any of these (other than parents)?[1] The odds against locating
the child's agency or voice in her first person are high, because by default the
infant cannot speak (from L. *in-fãns*).[2] Human rights-based documents such
as the one authorized by the United Nations Convention on the Rights of the
Child (UNCRC) of 1989, now a legally incumbent reference point, describe
the child as someone or everyone *who is not eighteen years old*—a rough or
general guideline which is to be interpreted (and frequently is) by supple-
mentary laws regarding sexual maturity/consent, marriage, criminality, labor/
employment, military service, and schooling/education—effectively a variable in different countries or contexts.[3] The emphasis in UNCRC is on children as a hitherto ignored and socially valuable human resource, and the
objective is to treat children's utility (to the benefit of society, state) as
coterminous with their individual developments. Undersocialization is treated as a symptom of exceptionality (on the part of the individual child) and a

1

potential failure (for the society/state which produces such an individual and has to make legal amends).

CHILD AS CULTURAL INVENTION

Scholarly accounts of childhood as a socially significant concept are instructive on this issue. Although written from different perspectives, they seem to agree on a fundamental point.[4] That although the existence of children in different societies is a matter of obvious historical reality, childhood as a focal area of general social concern was a distinct phenomenon of the seventeenth century.[5] It follows, also, that the template called "childhood" is a social construct conceived largely by the educated middle-class, and that its particular histories or configurations are variable according to respective cultural norms. Even a casual look at the Oxford English Dictionary will confirm that our interest in children as "subjects/objects" of care and social responsibility is fairly recent. The words "child," "childish," or "childhood" all occur in Old or Middle English.[6] But terms such as "child-nature," "child-literature," "child-culture," and "child psychology" belong to the last two decades of the nineteenth century, while some others such as "child welfare," "child-mind," "child care," and "child-centered" enter English vocabulary in the early twentieth century. The word "child-faced" to describe a colored person ("negro," actual use) was recorded in 1906.

To return to the point: why does a child appear unique to us, even if s/he is not a direct biological descendant? Nobody puts it better than the German Romantic poet-playwright and philosopher Friedrich Schiller:

> In the child, the *predisposition and determination* is represented, in us the *fulfillment*, which always remains infinitely far behind the former. Hence, the child is to us a vivid representation of the ideal, not indeed of the fulfilled, but of the commissioned, and it is therefore by no means the conception of its poverty and limits, it is quite to the contrary the conception of its pure and free force, its integrity, its infinity, which moves us. To the men of morality and feeling, a child will for that reason be a *sacred* object, an object namely, which through the greatness of an idea annihilates every greatness of experience . . . as we have reason to believe, that the childish simplicity be simultaneously a childlike one, that consequently the source thereof be not want of understanding, no incapacity, but rather a higher *(practical)* strength, a heart full of innocence and truth, which out of inner greatness disdains the help of art, so is the former triumph of the understanding past, and the mockery of simpleness passes over into admiration of simplicity. . . . Our childhood is the single unmutilated nature, which we still encounter in cultivated humanity, hence it is no wonder, when every footprint of nature out of us leads us back to our childhood.[7]

But lest we take what he means by "naïve" and the way a child carries herself as *exactly* synonymous, we are also told that "the actions and conversations of children give us the pure impression of the naïve only so long as we do not remember their inability for art, and in general, only consider the contrast between their naturalness and artificiality in us. The naïve is a *childlikeness, where it is no longer expected,* and precisely for that reason, cannot be attributed to real childhood in the strictest sense. [8]

Behind the inspired appeal and hyperbolic tone of the poet, we get a comprehensive account of the range of ideas associated with childhood (or "the child," a gender-neutral singular) as a canonical idea. Still, Schiller squarely puts his finger on two points (or paradoxes) about children's identity that retains relevance. One, that children appeal to us because they are living representations of human potential (not-yet/would-be), and second, that they are (thought of as being) close to nature because they are still not exposed to culture. The connotation of blissful innocence, a sort of default virtue before the occurrence of the Cartesian break, the *childlikeness* or *naïveté* emphasized by Schiller, follows from here. During the course of the nineteenth century, these bourgeois sentiments more or less permanently replaced the earlier Christian idea of the sinful child or the Puritan idea of the wayward child who needed to be reined in.

The reformist move that started with, say, the Factories Act (1847) or setting up reformatory schools in Britain after 1854[9] has both gained momentum and changed in character since the last three or four decades—since adults have been led to think of the child as a right-bearing individual as they themselves are. This legal conundrum, for one is (at least) a potential adult if she knows and can assert her rights, has accorded the status of exceptionality to children once again. Only this time she is not a blank slate or a naturally naïve and noble creature, but a living bearer of the word of law—a *subject-elect* who must be valued both for what she is, a *minor* who needs protection and care, and what she apparently is not, an *equal* who is entitled to such measures. In other words, the child's very incapacity becomes the moral ground for preferential treatment.

What is lost, arguably, in the present legal-moral framework is a genuine acknowledgment of the child's "other-ness." If the advocates for child rights discourse have urged for socialization as a practical or pragmatic course of wholesome development that all children claim as right, they have, in effect, promoted a standardized content of future adulthood as their goal. In the juridico-political discourse of rights, individual children are denied the possible singularity of their childhood[s] and driven toward a lowest common denomination (the child as adult-in-waiting). Strategic redress for the power imbalance in the adult-child dichotomy is, of course, itself a technique of power in the Foucauldian sense—a regulatory mechanism and a form of political reason. It is an exercise in (what Foucault has famously called) "governmentality" or "conduct of conduct."[10] The two great social sciences to have played important mediating roles in this balancing act, respectively, are (Freudian) psychoanalysis/psychiatry and developmental psychology. The radical quality of the "old-world" vision of children as we saw with Schiller when he calls them "sacred objects," is thus absorbed in anticipation of a basic condition of governmental modality—a new homogeneous entity called (adult) *population*.

Keeping this theoretical framework in mind, we will look at two films where such machinations of power *do not operate*—not straightforwardly anyway, any more than in reality. I do not claim that these portrayals of children, they are fictive representations in any case, are "oppositional" for that reason. On the other hand, to say that these child-figures represent a dystopic vision of the future would be true only as a surface observation. Rather, they might serve as useful reminders of what the usual adult projection or expectations of a growing child belie and repress. That both films are often cited as belonging to the horror genre is significant in this regard.

THE HOLLOW MEN

In Anton M. Leader's *Children of the Damned* (1964, UK, MGM, 1 hour 29 minutes, hereafter *Children*), a rather crude sci-fi and thematic sequel to *Village of the Damned* (dir. Wolf Rilla, 1960, UK, MGM), a group of six precocious children pose a threat to the global order. The opening sequence of the film is particularly haunting, where a boy (who turns out to be the main, and fittingly English, character called Paul) with blonde hair and roundish, angelic but unsmiling, almost grim face, looks straight at the audience. Three jump-cuts, accompanied by an orchestrated score rising in a crescendo, show the boy walking toward and (literally) gaining on us—from a long shot to medium and an extreme close-up—as the credits roll. The still, straight gaze of the boy (as indeed of the rest of these "special" children) is a technique/thematic that is exploited repeatedly, not only to turn the gaze back on those watching but ultimately to churn a typical B-movie formula out of it: the children's eyes light up to signal their telekinetic power at work.[11]

One can hardly recommend the artistic merit of such a thick semiotic code. But importantly, other than the unmistakably uniform (therefore unnatural) tone of their conversation, the glowing eyes are the most obvious visual sign of these non-docile bodies defying adult domination or even solicitations. The eyes of youngsters discharging potent rays are also the highlight of the evidently kitschy theatrical poster for the film. In the beginning of *Children*, two children having extraordinary powers of intellect are identified by a team of UNESCO researchers, led by a biologist (Neville) and a psychologist (Lewellin) in London where the action takes place. Reports soon come in

Figure 1.1. *Children of the Damned*, 1964, Metro-Goldwyn-Mayer.

about another four—making it a total of six children (four boys, two girls) who are all able to complete a difficult puzzle in exactly the same amount of time. Their precocity is explained by Neville as "biological sport" or unforeseeable genetic accident/mutation, comparable to those in elementary plants, rodents, and algae, but the sheer number involved in this (anthropological) coincidence still seems scientifically inexplicable.[12] The additional problem is that they seem to have been born "miraculously," out of biological insemination—all having mothers but none a father—which leads to the speculation among the scientists and a British diplomat/spy/secret service agent called Colin Webster, a character straight out of the murky Cold War era and an evil figure in the film, that they might have the *same father*.

We should note here that both the 1950s and 1960s saw unprecedented advance in genetics and molecular biology. The structure of DNA (the famous "double helix") was discovered in 1953, resulting in subsequent research into the nature and constitution of genetic code which, in turn, had substantive influence on physiology and medicine. Once we add to this the enormous popularity that eugenics had among the advanced nations between 1910 and Word War II—not to speak of the racial selection, warfare and mass genocide that followed—we can appreciate the contemporaneity of *Children* in the peak of Cold War years. And if Neville is the representative of "hard science" in highly bureaucratized, multifarious and intellectually advanced powerhouse of an erstwhile empire—nothing could be a better example of the progressive power-knowledge nexus aided by cutting-edge technology in the age of late capital—Lewellin represents the mediating function of "social science."[13] Perhaps in keeping with popular sentiment,

Lewellin turns out to be more sympathetic of the two toward these mutant children even in the risk of impending disaster.

To return to the plot, the question of unknown fatherhood/fathering poses an important juncture in *Children* since from here the film-plot could turn into a standard [oc]cult horror fantasy with an oblique suggestion and visual evocation of Satanic birth, as in *Rosemary's Baby* (1968) or *The Omen* (1976).[14] Meanwhile, the viewers witness, for the first time in the film, how the main protagonist Paul impels his uncaring, hateful, hysteric mother towards an accident by simply *willing* it. Again the seat of the power lies in the eye/s as he watches over his visibly distressed mother, sends her walking barefoot into a dark alley, as if acting under a spell.

The whole incident is introduced through a *montage*. The device is effective because the superimposition of Paul's eyes is a cinematic rendition of his overwhelming act and it depicts vision/visibility as a pathological condition of authority; additionally, makes room for a disturbing sensation of being under surveillance by turning Paul's eyes into a metonymic analogue of the camera. Later, Paul's aunt Susanne is subjected to similar monitoring by the children.

The biogenetic research is soon intervened by respective countries engaged in "cold war." Paul demonstrates his power by thwarting an attempt to take him in, escapes and makes a decisive move—joining the six "prodigies" who take refuge in a derelict church. Susanne also joins them, now a captive to their combined will, as a nanny-cum-hostage. The actions that follow are evidently in the nature of (diplomatic and direct) warfare between two terri-

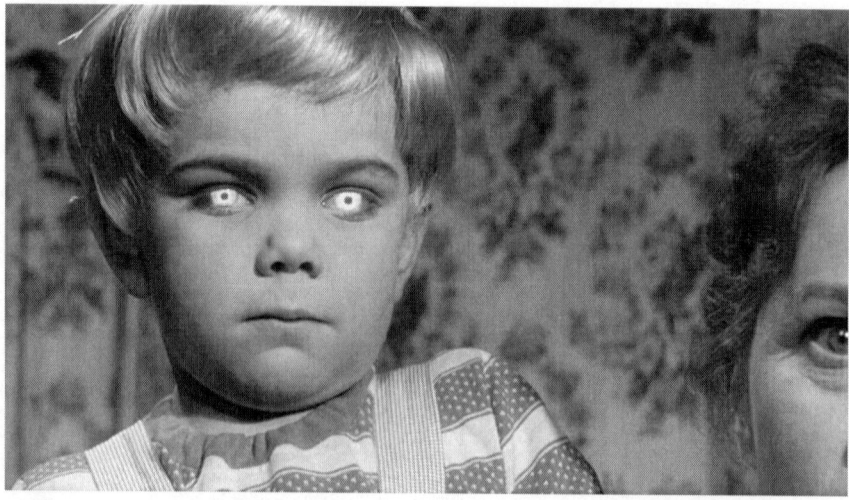

Figure 1.2. *Children of the Damned*, **1964, Metro-Goldwyn-Mayer.**

torially marked sovereign forces. There is a brief moment of possible respite when, at Lewellin's request, the children go back to their respective embassies; only to find out that the (adult) authorities want these "superchildren" to help tilt the arms race in their favor—using them as superior bioweapons of sorts.[15] The authorities' reaction at the embassy, obsessive yet comically clear behind their artful conversation, could remind one of the black humor of the title character in another Cold War film released in the same year, *Dr. Strangelove.*

Attempts to take over the church follow and bullets fly. The "children" design a futuristic weapon out of leftover wires and boxes that emit high-pitch sound waves to ward off the (adult) army. As a result, one child and several soldiers/officials are killed. Everyone but Lewellin, although it is clear that these minors did not attack unless they were attacked, is convinced that these strange creatures must be destroyed to ensure safe passage of the present generation—here the title assumes an ironic twist—themes of damnation and descent become equally applicable to both generations. The scientific diagnosis that these prodigies are after all genetically "human" beings that have arrived accidentally from an unspecified superior future does nothing to curb the perception of threat, more so when the child who succumbed to a gunshot appears alive in full view of a panicky crowd of soldiers, generals, and scientists. Questions directed to these children elicit little response other than that they are here with the same purpose as adults, to *live*. The film takes on a moralist-religious overtone as the children appear resigned to their fate and, though apparently by mistake, are blown to pieces, drawing the antiwar parable to a fittingly tragic end. The generation still trying to recover from the horror of two world wars seems, for all scientific and civilizational progress, morally incapable of facing anything other than a future that upholds a mirror-image of present values and public order. The exceptionality of children becomes an argument in favor of a political emergency where the (otherwise legitimate or moral) question of rights is suspended in order to ensure security or bare survival.

THE (M)OTHER OF ALL MONSTERS

If *Children* is a parable couched in the narrative genre of science fiction, our second film is a much darker tale of intimate violence. David Cronenberg's *The Brood* (Canada, 1 hour 32 minutes, 1979, written and directed by Cronenberg, produced by Claude Heroux, hereafter *Brood*) is more difficult to place in any single genre, straddling the cinematic conventions of an exploitation film, slasher/revenge film, thriller, and horror.[16] Like our first film, though in an extremely bizarre fashion, *Brood* also deals with pathology and genetic mutation. Mental extremities are accompanied by physical deformities and repressed memory—their realist portrayal is an imaginative study of deviant individuals, like Cronenberg's other films: *Shivers* (1975), *Rabid* (1977), *Scanners* (1981), *Dead Ringers* (1988).

The plot of *Brood* centers on the Somafree Institute, a psychotherapy clinic run by Dr. Raglan where he carries out experiments on psychoplasm—a primordial organic substance constituting the human mind.[17] Frank, whose wife Nola is under Raglan's care, confronts Raglan with the threat to stop visitation rights of his wife and accuses him of incorrect treatment after Frank finds bruises on his daughter Candice's back which he believes to have been made by Nola. Candice is then placed under her grandmother Juliana's care. The elderly alcoholic lady is drawn to her kitchen by a dwarf-like humanoid creature who wreaks havoc as she is bludgeoned to death, leaving little Candice traumatized as much as the audience by its abrupt, animal violence, as if the display of infected bodies and diseased minds till now was not enough.

Frank starts mobilizing Raglan's ex-patients against him and the institute, even as Raglan begins to intensify the sessions with Nola. Frank discovers that Nola is known as the "Queen Bee" among the patients.[18] In a parallel development, Raglan suspends all treatment at the institute, sends his patients home, and decides to concentrate on Nola alone. He learns that as a child, Nola was abused by her mother, and her father did little to protect her. Her present obsession and excessive rage, we are given to understand, is a pathological recursion of that distraught childhood.[19] Following that (psychoanalytic) rationalization, Nola's present adulthood is shaped by the persistence of her abused identity as a child—as a waking dream that seeks to make amends for past repression in reality. There is more than a suggestion of Nola's identification with her daughter, physically (Candice has similar red wheals as her mother, as Juliana points out) and emotionally (she suffers most as the result of the violence around her, appears self-absorbed yet helpless, lives through repression of the violence she witnesses) as well as in the structure of the plot—indicating the etiology of neurosis running through generations.

Meanwhile, violence accelerates. Frank's father-in-law who comes back to bury his divorced spouse accosts Raglan, demanding that he be allowed to meet his daughter and deliver the news of her mother's death. Denied, he returns to Juliana's home and suffers the same fate as his wife. The childlike midget then attacks Frank when he arrives at the spot but he manages to throw it off his shoulder, causing its instant death. The autopsy report reveals the *unnatural* biological constitution of the midget-creature: it is asexual, toothless, incapable of speech, color-blind and has no navel, that is, it is not nurtured in a human womb but is born miraculously—the mutant killer comes across as the evil double of Immaculate Conception. Growing in number, a couple of them sneak in Candice's play school, strikes down

Ruth—the teacher who has lately been taking care of the girl personally—with a mallet in front of the whole class as they watch and cry helplessly, and leave with Candice. For the only time in the film, the children walk hand in hand on a bleak landscape, forming a demonic trinity as it were.

THE SHAPE OF RAGE

The union of the children forms the climax in the film's plot for our purpose.[20] The denouement shows the dwarfs as mutant offspring of Nola acting under rage during her intense therapeutic sessions with Dr. Raglan—her "psychoplasm" generated in that condition triggering parthenogenesis. The "talking cure" gone awry denotes, paradoxically, the radical success of Raglan's experiment through Nola. Diminutive, dressed in overalls and occasionally enjoying a ride on the swing in the schoolyard, the dwarfs' affinity to Candice is remarkable from the very beginning and yet, visibly with an ashen, distorted face and pale-white eyebrows, they are her "other." The chief reason why we (as the audience) are deeply disturbed or horrified by the killings is that visual evocation or parallel which suggests that Candice, the frail weakling who lacks parental care and appears to be a victim, is also *an accessory.* This motif of doubling or constant relay is present throughout the film and distributed in different degrees among several pairs of characters—Candice and Nola, Juliana and Nola, Barton and Frank, and the last but most strategically mobilized of them all, Raglan-as-psychiatrist-role-player and Raglan-the-moral-man. We should note, however, that Nola-the-abused-child and Nola-the-pathological-adult do not form a double in this sense;

Figure 1.3. *The Brood,* **1979, Canadian Film Development Corporation.**

they are *causally related* through techniques (or economy) of psychiatry as a modern medical science/practice.

Meanwhile, important developments occur. Frank begins searching frantically for his daughter and is informed by Mike (an ex-patient of Somafree for whom Raglan was the "best daddy") that Raglan has a shed full of "disturbed kids" that Nola looks after. Frank faces Raglan there and demands that his daughter be returned. Raglan's hostile mood changes only when he is told that "they" (that is, the "children"; Frank calls them "freaks," "deformed children," and, earlier, a "bunch of crazies") have killed Ruth before abducting Candice. He reveals the truth about these children's birth and that Nola, after she has unconsciously (that is, telekinetically) driven these kids to enact (her own) vengeance, remains completely unaware of the event.[21] Raglan then advises Frank to pacify Nola by pretending that he has come to make amends with her. That would keep the broods asleep and give Raglan the opportunity to rescue Candice.

In the intense drama that follows, things do not go exactly as planned. Frank can only look on (and away) with horror and disgust as Nola delivers a brood by herself and licks the blood clean off the newborn's body. The scene is gory and spectacular, and consciously stylized. Nola sits in front of a kneeling Frank like a ritual priestess, with her arms raised along with her dress, to display her bulging womb which looks like a big cancerous tumor, and then brings her hands down, resembling a proud, giant bird-mother which spreads and then wraps her wings around her young one. Frank's repulsion arouses Nola's anger, provoking the dwarf-children to pounce upon Raglan who succumbs to them, but not before rescuing Candice to safety. The broods make a last desperate attempt to reclaim their human sister who screams in panic. Understanding that the dwarf-children are trying to kill his daughter, Frank chokes Nola to death. The broods, needing to draw life from their mother, die instantly. Frank then carries his traumatized daughter through a snow-filled backwoods and is seen driving on the way to his apartment. Candice, however, looks hardly relieved; she bears a stern face and fixed stare away from her father. The film closes with a zoom on her right hand. She has developed the same blisters on her skin as her mother Nola when she delivered her "child" before Frank. The cycle of violence has not ended, nor will little Candice ever get away from her demonic siblings— she has internalized them.[22] Unlike *Children*, *The Brood* ends more like a modern-day horror, promising an equally grim afterlife of the film for the audience than offering a resolution.

APOCALYPSE NOW?

We need a grid of possible connotations of the term "(post-)apocalyptic" to situate our interpretation of these films. Within institutional religion or mythology, "apocalypse" is taken to cause an unbridled awe, likened to what the Romantics called the "sublime," about the event in question to a degree that we are stretched to our *human limits*. Even by witnessing it, our understanding of the world, natural phenomena, various institutions and relations that we inhabit, the horizon of subjectivity and human condition, go through a crisis—the whole of our existence and identity is *put at risk*. Through an intuitive appreciation of other, unprecedented or unknown forms of life, values or truth that we cannot fully comprehend, organize, or categorize as experience, the apocalyptic event transforms and becomes constitutive of us. However, there is a second, more *strategic* sense in which the word is used to refer to dystopian narratives set in an unspecified future or historical period marked by general crisis of a large community, such as war, epidemic, genocide, mass expatriation, ecological, or cosmic disaster, and so on.[23]

The films discussed above draw on both connotations along the way, albeit differently. *Children* begins as a drama about the (contemporary) present, referring to recent developments in scientific research and politics, and is suddenly thrown off-balance by the untimely arrival of children from the future. The film stages this particular event and the repercussions it sets off, ending in a provisional resolution of the crisis and the state of affairs reverts back to the status quo. The initial trouble in *Brood* is much more localized and personal (Nola's maladjustment, Frank's problems in raising his daughter as single parent, Candice's alleged torture, which could be summed up as a crisis of the nuclear family) which then spawns into a bigger, general crisis through imaginative deployment of filmic realism, by rendering hysteric fantasy as material phenomena. The dwarf-children not only represent something unrepresentable, namely repression—they function as *figurations of the abnormal*.

The singular apocalyptic event is much easier to define in the case of *Children*—it is simply a disruption of history or *anachronism*. The children of the Cold War era (adults, really) cannot share the planet with children from the future; effectively the gerontological description of these two tribes remain provisional and could be reversed. Hence, I suggest that *Children* could be read either as a fantasy about race or about child abuse. In 1962, Dr. C. Henry Kempe and Dr. Brandt F. Steele published the paper titled "The Battered Child Syndrome" in the *Journal of the American Medical Association* and it has been reprinted several times since. The publishing of this landmark article led to the identification and recognition of child abuse by the Euro-American medical community. Dr. Kempe received his second Nobel Prize nomination as a result and went on to establish an organization to prevent and treat children affected in such cases. What I want to emphasize here is not so much a fortuitous factual link between Kempe's research and this film, but that the midsixties marked an important phase in the congealment of middle-class adult anxieties around the child as an endangered entity. Both statistics and medical research could be assembled to mobilize widespread public awareness about this "social disease" responsible for childhood disability and death. [24] The diagnosis and formal "naming" of child abuse as a problem needing attention/protection is more important here than the incident of abuse. There might be a further subtext to this sad tale of betrayal and ultimate elimination of children, visible especially in the character of Paul's unsympathetic mother—a former model and single woman who both smokes and drinks—an ambivalence expressed in the 1960s disapproval of dictates of daily existence, and subsequent experimentation with institutional spaces such as the monogamous family, patriarchy, educational institutions, or the state. The precocious children in the film arrive (as it were) from this utopia of apocalypse postponed, but only too soon.

Since *Brood* is a complex *auteur* film, it is imperative that we closely follow the narrative strategies as well as the structural logic of the plot, because action and apparent motive often seem to belie each other. The line between characters and phantasms are blurred, the twin drives of death and life become too strong and indistinct, and all characters—including Frank, who tries hard to restore order until at the very end—resort to violence. The diminutive mutants are the embodiment of ids that signal the return of the repressed child-Nola as much as they are born out of her ego in a hysteric state, working against an internal threat. As an adult, mother-Nola has turned herself into a machine that compulsively acts out the originary, internalized trauma through endless repetitions of her violent experience. Only that these retroactive violent attacks (must) fail to achieve their objective—they are actually directed inward. Nola's wish to become an ideal child is illusory because it is unreal, and harmful for Candice because the ideal produces real jealousy and narcissistic violence. Candice's simultaneous attraction and repulsion toward the broods signals the ambivalent nature of instinct as such: their bond is in a sense properly, fundamentally an *infantile* bond—in the pre-discursive, aphasic register of desire. [25] The "wonder children" of *Children* too, we might recall, do not use words to communicate among themselves or assail their opponents but through visual signs and telekinesis.

EPILOGUE: MINOR SPECTERS

How does the crisis posed by the wonder-children or those begotten by a hysteric mother examined here affect us, that is, beyond their immediate narrational-fictional context? How are these aberrational offspring related to the adult norms of subjectivity, of growing up as productive laborer and responsible citizen? Not least of all, why do these children appear as an absolute scourge, so threatening that nothing less than their obliteration is the only solution?

Drawing on Foucault, I offer a speculative thesis instead of providing a comprehensive answer. The "superchildren" from the future in *Children* pose a threat to normal adult order on two counts: by transgressing the code of innocence and the law of growth. Human growth, as we noted in the beginning, is a complex normative network of nature/biology and culture/ideology that determine the initiation of a human being as subject. Following Foucault, we might describe this network as an ensemble of modalities or technologies (scientific discourses, disciplinary institutions, domains of practice, sexuality) of power that produces the thinking-acting individual as members of the social collective. It is an elaborate organization (and regulation) of controlled development—a modality of subjectivation that he famously termed "biopolitics"—exercised via a general extension of neoliberal economics to human behavior and growth through policies of education, health, demography, and other specialized fields of modern knowledge (criminology, psychiatry, etc.). The failure of (individual) states and society (in general) to incorporate the superchildren therefore creates a breakdown of this system of biopolitics and throws the raison d'état into disarray. The subjects of development suddenly appear as authors of destruction.

Notably, in both films it is the glaring presence of recalcitrant or diseased bodies and bodily mechanisms of inflicting paralysis or death that defy the modern state's power to "make live and let die."[26] The nonconversion of human entities/person into human capital—a bio-political transfer of category fundamental to the modern state's economy of governance—produces a *regression* into an earlier modality of dispensing power displayed by absolutist state or monarchy: the state with a single, originary source of power. The eradication of these exceptional political entities, after having defined them as biologically superior freaks or progeny of an adult body in a mentally regressive state (a prototype of the infantile, a failed adult), becomes a necessity for the state power to function. This regression to absolute power signals an emergent apocalypse in the age of democracy. Whereas in *Children* the state-form is more conspicuous in the form of scientific surveillance and the United Nations (UN) as an arbiting body, it is less a territorially marked sovereign power in *Brood* than a form of political rationality operating in the register of psychic normalcy/pathology. The horror, in the end, stems from the momentary return of the "unconscious": the psychopathology of the current rationalization expressed in citizenship as a condition of living. The exceptional children stands (on two accounts, as adult-defying and arriving from the suppressed memory of the *normative present*) for alternative forms of political reason and life—a symbol of what is *made* absent in history—the minority.

NOTES

1. The foundational text of liberal-secular pedagogy, Rousseau's *Emile, or On Education* (1762) that advocates the "natural man" as the ideal of good rearing, puts in a word of caution: "They are always looking for the man in the child, without considering what he is before he becomes a man. It is to *this* study that I have chiefly devoted myself" (trans. B. Foxley; London: J. M. Dent, 1974; italics added).

2. Not that the prospect of finding the "authentic" child's voice should be the objective for historians of childhood or such a pure object can be found, given the cultural, class, ethnic, gender, or other variables that operate in and across history. The term "allochronism" (that subject and object cannot exist on the same temporal plane) used by anthropologist Johannes Fabian retains importance for all ethnographic researchers, and those interested in the socio-cultural construction/constitution of childhood as a modern sentiment.

3. Its antecedents, the Geneva Declaration of 1924, or the Declaration of Rights of the Child adopted by the UN General Assembly in 1959, do not even say as much regarding who is a child (that is, it is taken to be both obvious and consensual). Instead, these documents talk about how we (adult society, individual states, the UN as a confederation) are bound by moral responsibility to save the endangered species called children.

4. Philippe Aries, *Centuries of Childhood: A Social History of Family Life* (trans. R. Baldick; London: Jonathan Cape, 1962)/cultural history, James, Jenks, and Prout, *Theorizing Childhood* (Cambridge: Polity Press, 1998)/sociology, Heywood, Colin, *A History of Child-hood: Children and Childhood in the West from Medieval to Modern Times* (Cambridge: Polity Press, 2001)/history, Joseph Zornado, *Inventing the Child: Culture, Ideology and the Story of Childhood* (New York: Garland Publishing, 2001)/cultural studies, to name a few. I am leaving out psychoanalytic literature, starting with Freud, for the moment because of its distinct under-standing of childhood—less as a social-cultural phenomenon than a latent "presence" or motor of action in all adult individuals.

5. Europe is the primary point of reference in this case. The thesis, now more or less accepted, was proposed by Aries. However, though the timeline has been challenged since. For a useful summary of this historiographic debate, see Adrian Wilson, "The Infancy of the History of Childhood: An Appraisal of Philippe Aries," *History and Theory* 19.2 (Feb. 1980), 132–53, accessed via JSTOR on December 5, 2012.

6. The archaic and literary variant "childe" was used to denote a person of genteel descent, usually belonging to the family of a knight as in Childe Harold or Childe Roland in Lord Byron and Robert Browning's poems, respectively.

7. F. Schiller, "On Naïve and Sentimental Poetry," trans. by William F. Wertz, Jr., 2005, found on www.schillerinstitute.org/transl/schiller_essays/naive_sentimental-1.html. The essay appeared in the journal *Die Horner* in 1795–1796 and the final title was given in 1800. All italics appear in the original.

8. Ibid.

9. It was initiated with the Reformatory Schools Act of 1854 and followed by the Industrial Schools Act three years later. These schools were meant to cater to the poor children, orphans, abandoned children, and delinquents. Soon, these institutions had their own workshops and even brass bands, a complete set of disciplinary mechanisms in place.

10. "The contact point, where individuals are driven by others is tied to the way they conduct themselves, is what we call, I think government. Governing people, in the broad meaning of the word, governing people [*sic*] is not a way to force people to do what the governor wants; it is always a versatile equilibrium, with complementarity and conflicts be-tween techniques which assure coercion and processes through which the self is constructed or modified by himself" (Foucault, 1993: 203–4, cited in Thomas Lemke "Foucault, Governmen-tality, and Critique," *Rethinking Marxism* 14, 3 [2002]: 49–64).

11. I use the word "signal" deliberately: their eyes change color to signify danger in a manner reminiscent of how traffic lights operate, sending clear messages to adults who surround them.

12. The national variety among prodigies looks too well-distributed: one from three superpowers, that is, the Soviet Union, the United States, and China; the home country of the United Kingdom; and one each from Asia and Africa. It is in keeping with the balance of power during the Cold War era and looks almost like a matter of political correctness or fair representation in the General Assembly.

13. For a critical intellectual history of psychology and psychiatric counseling as disciplinary institutions mediating among family as a social unit, education, liberal economics/market and state governance in modern France, see J. Donzelot, *The Policing of Families* (trans. R. Hurley; New York: Pantheon Books, 1997). Gilles Deleuze, in the foreword to this book titled "The Rise of the Social," provides critical insights into the emergence of the "social" as a modern field of knowledge and disciplinary expertise.

14. In the film *Village of the Damned*, a similar situation gives rise to a widespread rumor of sexual scandal. *Children* treats the plot as a sci-fi from the beginning, hinting either toward possible invasions from a different planet or genetic mutation.

15. However, that these children are connected through some telepathic power—a single child's knowledge is instantly shared by the group—defeats any possible diplomatic secrecy.

16. Cronenberg is often considered a unique practitioner of the "body horror" genre, a genre noted for corporeal, gory violence in the realist vein. Cronenberg, however, freely adapts fantasy and psychoanalytic themes for his purpose.

17. Although the substance (psychoplasm) is fictional or quasi-scientific, some followers of the Jungian theories of the unconscious believe that the substance is instrumental in transmitting a genetic/behavioral trait. They consider psychoplasm to be a scientific correlative of the soul. For a brief overview of such opinions or theories, see the website www.reincarnationexperiment.org.

18. Hence the suggestion that Nola, the sexually prolific and dangerous female, would kill the father of her own progeny. The film has been criticized, not without substantive grounds, for its misogynist content.

19. Raglan's impersonation of Nola's parents—a direct cinematic translation of the "talking cure" method—remains somewhat unconvincing, as some critics (Roger Ebert among them) point out. This is despite Oliver Reed's consistently brilliant, restrained intensity and Nola/ Samantha Eggar's spectacular histrionics which capture our attention but does little to absolve the formulaic plot.

20. As visual drama and thriller—explaining who these dwarfs are and how they come about—the climax occurs later, in the remarkably gory scene where Nola sits in a ritual posture with her arms raised and Frank witnesses the birth of a brood, and continues till Nola licks the blood off her newborn's body. The scene, in my opinion intentionally, echoes Francesco Goya's painting of Satan devouring his own child. It is not a mere coincidence that critics have mistaken the scene as Nola reenacting Goya's Satan.

21. This last part, Nola's lack of conscious recall of what her wish-child has done, is a fact that Raglan discovers during his conversation with Nola just before Frank confronts him. The characterization of Raglan as "mad artist"-type resembles Frankenstein.

22. This particular scene showing the broods lurking around the corner is used in a poster; it does not occur as such in the movie.

23. Prophetic literature, whether associated traditionally with religion or civilization or esoteric (Nostradamus), would be primary examples of apocalyptic imagination. As examples of apocalyptic literature in the second sense, we can think of H. G. Wells's *The Time Machine*, Orwell's *Nineteen Eighty-Four*, or Jose Saramago's *Blindness*. Mary Shelley's *The Last Man* which combines a political crisis (republic after monarchy) with a global outbreak of the plague or Wells's *The War of the Worlds* which narrates a fictional account of earth's invasion by Martians are early trendsetters in this genre.

24. For critical accounts that historicize the problem of child abuse, see Ian Hacking, "The Making and Molding of Child Abuse," in *Critical Inquiry* 17, 2 (1991): 253–88, and Chris

Jenks, "Child Abuse in the Postmodern Context: An Issue of Social Identity" in *Childhood* 2 (1994): 111–21.

25. Freud scholars translate the word "trieb" sometimes as "drive," not "instinct." I have followed Laplanche and Pontalis who adopt the word "instinct" generally following the Standard Edition although admitting the applicability of alternatives such as "drive" or "urge" (they suggest a third term: "pulsion"). See Laplanche and Pontalis, *The Language of Psycho-Analysis* (London: The Hogarth Press, 1973), 214 ff. Death-instinct(s) was first proposed (alongwith life-instinct, as a model of deep-seated principles of instinctive dualism) by Freud in 1920.

26. We have noted before that in *Children*, Paul and his cohorts say (when asked about their purpose on earth) that they are here with the same purpose as *you* (that is, "we," the adults, the *natural* or rightful occupants of earth), which effectively implies that the power to "make live" would not rest solely with the adults.

BIBLIOGRAPHY

Aries, Philippe. *Centuries of Childhood: A Social History of Family Life*, trans. R. Baldick (London: Jonathan Cape, 1962). Print.

Cronenberg, David. *The Brood* (Canada and U.S.: New World Pictures, produced by Claude Heroux, written by D. Cronenberg, 1979). Film.

Donzelot, Jacques. *The Policing of Families*, trans. R. Hurley (New York: Pantheon Books, 1997). Print.

Foucault, Michel. *Security, Territory, Population: Lectures at the College de France, 1977–78*, trans. Graham Burchell (Hampshire & New York: Palgrave-Macmillan, N.D.). E-book.

Foucault, Michel. *"Society Must Be Defended": Lectures at the College de France, 1975–76*, trans. David Macey (New York: Picador, 2003). E-book.

Foucault, Michel. *Abnormal: Lectures at the College de France, 1974–75*, trans. Graham Burchell (London & New York: Verso, 2003). E-book.

Foucault, Michel. *The Birth of Biopolitics: Lectures at the College de France, 1978–79*, trans. Graham Burchell (Hampshire & New York: Palgrave-Macmillan, 2008). E-book.

Hacking, Ian. "The Making and Molding of Child Abuse," in *Critical Inquiry* 17, 2 (1991): 253–88.

Heywood, Colin. *A History of Childhood: Children and Childhood in the West from Medieval to Modern Times* (Cambridge: Polity Press, 2001). Print.

James, Allison, Chris Jenks, and Alan Prout. *Theorizing Childhood* (Cambridge: Polity Press, 1998). Print.

Jenks, Chris. "Child Abuse in the Postmodern Context: An Issue of Social Identity," in *Childhood* 2 (1994): 111–121.

Laplanche, Jean, and Jean-Bertrand Pontalis. *The Language of Psycho-Analysis* (London: Hogarth Press & Institute of Psycho-Analysis, 1973). E-book.

Leader, Anton M. *Children of the Damned* (UK: Metro-Goldwyn-Mayor, produced by Ben Arbeid, written by John Briley, 1964). Film.

Lemke, Thomas. "Foucault, Governmentality, and Critique," in *Rethinking Marxism* 14, 3 (2002): 49–64.

Chapter Two

Sustenance for the Body and the Soul

Children as a Vision of the Future of Humanity and a Reflection of Past Sins in Post-Apocalyptic Cinema

Jennifer Brown

INTRODUCTION

It is my contention that the child in post-apocalyptic cinema is the embodiment of the world before its death. Whether the child/world is viewed as a burden in need of rescuing (*World War Z*, Forster 2013); the vessel of our intellect and faith (*The Book of Eli*, Hughes and Hughes 2010); a source of food (*The Road*, Hillcoat 2009); a link in the chain that is humanity's evolution (*Children of Men*, Cuarón 2006); a place of untarnished natural beauty (*Beasts of the Southern Wild*, Zeitlin 2012); or a resource to be used as humanity deems fit (*Waterworld*, Reynolds and Costner 1995), the treatment of the child in post-apocalyptic cinema tells us something about how we view our world itself and how we view our role in it. This is especially the case when, as now, the world as we know it is in danger from climate change and our treatment of it affects the outcome of our future. Based on this contention, I will take three films that feature apocalyptic disasters caused by climate change, *The Road*, *Waterworld*, and *Beasts of the Southern Wild*, and analyze the symbolic role children play in them. I will examine the child as the embodiment of the world in danger in these films in three fundamental ways: the child as the untarnished world, the child as a resource to be used as deemed fit, and the child as the possibility of regeneration. I am not arguing that the child in these films can only embody one of these functions. Rather each child embodies all three of these roles in each film; while the binary lies in the treatment of these children as either something precious, innately good, and worthy of saving or as a consumable, usable commodity. As it is the heroes and villains who treat the children in these ways respectively, it is my assertion that these films, by positioning the former "positive" treatment of children as heroic, are advocating a longer-term view of the world. To put it simply, if we accept the idea that the child embodies our world in danger, choosing to either use that child to fill your belly or to lead him/her to a safe place to continue living, informs the audience of the options we have in our treatment of the environment and the consequences of making those choices. Each child protagonist in these films is a burden, a target for hungry enemies, a mere body to be used as seen fit by older, stronger forces, and a source of incredible strength, joy, life, and optimism. The child in post-apocalyptic cinema is thus the embodiment of our hopes and fears of what we and our world may be becoming in a consumerist, polluted, militaristic world. Before I move on to an analysis of each film, I want to explore some central ideas to my reading of these films: the idea of environmental refugees and associated fears; the philosophical notion of the apocalypse and endings; theories of what the child can mean in popular culture.

THE WALKING DEAD: ENVIRONMENTAL REFUGEES AS ZOMBIES

Because the films I am examining involve environmental disasters as the cause of the end of the world, it is worth considering the idea of environmental refugees and their portrayal in the media. The idea of environmental refugees first appeared in the mid-1980s in United Nations discussions on the environment. According to Gregory White, it has since become a "felicitous catch-all term"[1] that has been couched in philosophies of fear and paranoia. There has been an assertion that population displacement caused by environmental disasters will lead to global refugee crises. White cites Kaplan in terming this dialogue of potential crisis a "coming anarchy" and the "strain that hordes of migrants would pose to the infrastructure of northern countries, to their capacity for absorption, and to their ability to contend with cultural differences."[2] Hyperbolic media reporting fuels this paranoia. Recent disasters such as Hurricane Katrina in 2005, the 2010 earthquake in Haiti, and the 2013 typhoon in the Philippines resulted in round-the-clock reports from the devastated regions. Gerry Canavan explains how the exaggerated reports of looting and stampeding in New Orleans in the wake of the hurricane led doctors and nurses at the Memorial Medical Centre to believe they were in a zombie-like story, that they were beyond help and that outside the walls of the hospital, "roamed monsters."[3] This kind of reporting sets up an "us vs. them" dichotomy with Green Zones and stockpiles of supplies behind fortifications while desperate people become zombie-like threats to security and normalcy.

A number of writers from Marx on have aligned capitalism and consumerism with cannibalism, "zombieism," or vampirism.[4] Beginning with George Romero, many post-apocalyptic films feature zombies on their "virologic march" symbolizing the final stages of the nightmare of overconsumption. Indeed, as Kyle William Bishop notes, scenes of deserted or broken urban areas, abandoned corpses, looting, vigilantes, and chaos have become common as news footage: "Because the aftereffects of war, terrorism, and natural disasters so closely resemble the scenarios depicted by zombie cinema, such images of death and destruction have all the more power to shock and terrify."[5] Anirban Kapil Baishya offers a fascinating reading on post-apocalyptic film by linking it to trauma. He argues that post-apocalyptic films draw on a library of traumatic images and he uses the examples of the Holocaust and Hiroshima to explain how these images disturb audiences because they tap into the "optical unconsciousness" to refer to past and current catastrophes.[6] This effect works on two levels: referring to the past and its related anxieties, usually involving fear of the Other; and evoking an association of that past with present nightmares and current anxieties. Thus, in the films I am considering, images of children bereft of family, shelter, food, and belongings are used to remind the audience of the all too many children around the world already suffering in the aftermath of adults' shortsightedness.

THE END IS NIGH: SYMBOLIC CHILDREN AT THE END OF THE WORLD

In order to understand the symbolic significance of the child on post-apocalyptic cinema it is worth reflecting on Frank Kermode's analysis of the apocalypse in relation to children before noting some theories of the child in popular culture. In *The Sense of an Ending* (2000) Kermode argues apocalypse can be about hope, resolution, and revelation. For Kermode, thinkers who impose the idea of "an end," impose a fictional pattern on history. This habit of imposing paradigms on time is an inherent part of human nature and it reflects the desire to understand ourselves and our relationship to the world around us. As Kermode states, "there is still a need to speak humanly of a life's importance in relation to it—a need in the moment of existence to belong, to be related to a beginning and to an end."[7] Children fulfill this need on some level: they are the embodiment of a beginning in that they are a new generation and they heighten one's sense of belonging to a place and time. As Hanna Arendt argues: "every end in history necessarily contains a new beginning . . . this beginning is guaranteed by each new birth."[8] In post-apocalyptic cinema we can examine this hope for an imagined future time and the notions of what the end of humanity looks like. With current fears of nuclear disasters, terrorism, world wars, environmental catastrophe, and a world population that cannot be fed at current food production rates, popular culture reflects these fears and suggests a zombie or burnt out sun is waiting around every corner. It also, however, asks: what happens next? What kind of new beginning can occur post post-apocalypse and who will the survivors be? Ideas of what the child means, or can mean, influence the answers to these questions.

In Romantic literature and, I will argue, in post-apocalyptic cinema, the child symbolizes the potential for growth and renewal. Jean Jacques Rousseau's writings helped revolutionize concepts of the child when he wrote *Emile* in 1792 and posited ideas of the child as an innocent entity open to the corrupting powers of society.[9] Jacqueline Rose, writing on the child in fiction, sees a common conception of the child's innocence in a close, "mutually dependent relation" with a primary state of language and culture.[10] Rousseau saw "purity and immediacy" in the spoken word in comparison with the "aridity and obtrusiveness of written culture." Rose believes Rousseau sees childhood as the place where an older form of culture survives. This is interesting in relation to the films at hand as they profess an understated celebration of "traditional" skills: making things with your hands, growing food, communicating with nature. Thus, it can be argued that the children, who are devoid of technological know-how, economic greed, and historically based grudges, can lead the survivors to safety and regeneration in a world that was damaged by the adults' unthinking love of modernity's trappings.

Richard Mills posits a Platonic reasoning for the association of the child with goodness: "By virtue of their childhood innocence, their promise of hope, their unalloyed vulnerability, children are somehow a force for good in the world. The concept is probably linked with the Platonic idea of perfection of form, namely, that the outward attractiveness indicates an inner quality of goodness."[11] Certainly, in the films I am discussing the children manage to avoid much of the filth, horrific injuries, and ravaged bodies that one might expect at the end of the world. Their clear-eyed, fresh-faced candor and simplicity is in direct opposition to swarthy, gap-toothed, wheezing villains. Reinhard Kuhn explores the child in culture in *Corruption in Paradise* (1982) and argues that the intrusion of evil into the seemingly innocent universe of childhood is indicative of the "vitality of a benign nature . . . sapped by civilization."[12] Furthermore, the destruction of a child is most commonly viewed as a punishment of its parents as representative of the social order who have abused their privileges. This is also relevant to the idea of children as the untarnished world in post-apocalyptic cinema. In current discussions on climate change, there are often pleas to save the world for the sake of our children. Hence, in films that show what happens when these pleas fall on deaf ears, there is a sense of guilt for both the characters and the audience: we burned the world and our (innocent) children must reap the consequences.

There are, however, more negative views of the role children play in culture. Steven Bruhm sees a startling prevalence of children who kill in contemporary horror (for example, *Omen*, Donner 1976; *Children of the Corn*, Kiersch 1984; *Pet Sematary*, Lambert 1989). In our Freudian world, he argues, sexuality and violence come from the child itself rather than a corrupt adult world. In the physical, psychological, and philosophical devastation of the aftermath of the world wars, children were seen as sites of healing, innocence, and beauty: "The beauties of [the child's] innocence offered us hope that someone could be immune to evil, hope even that all of us may have been born into a state prior to evil and corruption."[13] They were, however, subject to invasion by communism in the 1950s and homosexuality and feminism in the 1960s and 1970s, resulting in a fearsome construction: the Gothic child. Even more terrifying for Bruhm is the idea of the inherently evil child. One needs only to consider *We Need to Talk about Kevin* (Shriver 2003 and Ramsay 2011) or Ben in Doris Lessing's *The Fifth Child* (1988) to grasp Bruhm's terror. Claudia, the child vampire in *Interview with the Vampire* (Jordan 1994), is a suitable example of the Freudian or anti-Rousseauian child; she possesses knowledge, appetite, guile, and power. As Bruhm states, her knowledge is a combination of instinct and embodiment. The reason we fear the Gothic child, Bruhm argues, is that they "not only shatter our identities as adults (and this is frightening enough) but they threaten the collapse of the social order we bred them to maintain."[14] In a post-Freudian psychoanalysis, viewing the child as asexual and nonviolent suggests a false separation between the child and an achieved state of adulthood.[15]

These different representations of the child in culture follow trends in philosophy, cultural norms, and societal fears. Robin Wood argues that the figure of the child in film represents the condition of civilization, "its health or sickness"[16]; thus the child can be viewed as a kind of cipher for the ills and despair in society.[17]

A final concept of the child I want to consider here is the child as resource. We have seen how the child can be used as a political tool to heighten fears and entrench political stances. Likewise, in footage of war zones or terror attacks, children are used as the epitome of the innocent victim. For example, we are all too familiar with footage in which children's broken bodies or corpses are paraded in front of the cameras as if to convey the pain and senseless loss of life all the more acutely. Mills considers the use of children in television advertisements as symbolic of generational continuity or security in a shifting world. He argues that this adult-centric viewpoint of the value of children equates to an idea of them as potential human resources.[18] Likewise, if we consider the use of children in Christmas advertisements to convince parents of the advantages of gaming systems like the Nintendo Wii; child soldiers used to inflict as much horror as possible upon a community; children used as beggars and sex slaves; child workers in sweat shops around the world, there can be no doubt that the child's body is yet another resource in our consumerist world. Thus, be they resources, pure, Rousseauistic angels, or a force from nature, the children in the films I will now examine tell us something about our view of our fragile environment and the actions necessary to save it. I will examine each film in turn and in the examination of each film I will interrogate the child in three ways: as a resource, as a version of the untarnished world, and as an embodiment of regeneration.

WATERWORLD

Waterworld is a film that has been much maligned and mocked for its swollen budget and low ticket sales, its poor plot, and Kevin Costner's acting. I will agree with its critics that there are gaps in the plot and plenty of silliness. Moreover, it reads somewhat like a love letter from Costner to himself; he co-produced the film as well as taking over the direction after difficulties with Kevin Reynolds. On the other hand, it raises some interesting questions on life in a post-apocalyptic world. The film is set a few hundred years after the world has been flooded because the polar ice caps melted, caused by the misbehavior of "the Ancients." Costner plays Mariner, a drifter who has evolved to become a mutant: a human with gills and webbed feet. He sails his trimaran around the waters and trades with other drifters or survivors on atoll communities. Deacon, played by Dennis Hopper, leads a band of pirates called Smokers. He also runs an oil rig and uses the fuel for his bandits' jet skis. Resources are in short supply, especially soil and fresh water; and the small number of people left alive after the flood has led to inbreeding. Mariner comes to an atoll to trade and meets a woman, Helen, looking after a young girl, Enola. Enola is tattooed with a map to Dryland, the only piece of land on earth that was not flooded. As resources are dwindling, Dryland is the only place the people can hope for a future and Deacon hopes he can rule a new society with an iron fist by using the resources there. The difficulty lies in catching Enola and reading the map. I will examine Enola first as a resource in her role as map; secondly as the idea of regeneration in her role as a young, fertile female; and finally as a version of an untarnished world.

Enola's physical body is an invaluable resource in the aquatic lives of the survivors in *Waterworld*. Mariner's heroism arises from his ability, eventually, to see Enola as more than a resource; she is his "friend." By teaching her to swim and encouraging her creative expression, he sees a role for her beyond her functionality as a map. There are very few other children in the film, apart, that is, from a handful of child soldiers in Deacon's gang; their bodies are used as resources too and they are paid in cigarettes and fast cars for their services. These children are unnamed, almost faceless and of inde-terminate race or gender; they amount to little more than mere playthings or workers for the Smokers. Enola, on the other hand, is a more valuable re-source and thus warrants further attention from the various players in *Water-world*. As her body is mapped with the route to salvation, her role as map overrides any role she might have had as a child or individual; therefore, her value lies in her physicality—she is mapped, female, and young. As such, she is in much demand and any tension in the film arises from the battle for ownership of her body. Deacon and Mariner trade blows over her and her body is literally passed back and forth between the two men; she is plucked from the ocean, thrown hither and thither, tossed overboard, manhandled, poked, prodded, tied up, has her hair chopped off, and she is examined in the same way a commodity to be traded is fought over and its value assessed. At one point, Deacon's men suggest skinning her so they can stretch the piece of her skin with the map in order to see it better—the child herself is irrelevant at this stage; she is a piece of parchment.

The idea of the body as a map or a country as a human body and vice versa has a long use in cultural myths and national iconography. For exam-ple, Ireland has long been personified as a woman, Kathleen ní Houlihan, in need of rescuing from the yoke of colonialism; Marianne is the symbol of the French Republic; Brittania is the emblem of empire and unity in Britain; Germania is the robust personification of Germany; Finland is personified by the Maiden of Finland with flowing blond hair to associate the Finns with the Scandinavian rather than Slavic races.[19] J. Douglas Porteous argues that the metaphorical use of body imagery in relation to landscape is fundamental in the Western world. In literature the body as landscape is a frequent occur-rence and he terms the culmination of this metaphor "bodyscape" or "porno-topia," a term borrowed from Steven Marcus.[20] Furthermore, the body in question is generally female, for example, H. Rider Haggard referred to Africa as a reclining woman awaiting invigoration at the hands of imperialist heroes; Pablo Neruda charts Chile's history on his lover's body; Sylvia Plath equates the action of the sea on the rocks with the wounded body. Positive associations between the land and the female body involve notions of fecun-dity, shelter, nutrition, and a sense of home. However, aligning ideas of the "motherland" with the female body, also suggests both are passive entities; there to be taken over, planted, and used as deemed fit by the residents or colonizers.

In *Waterworld*, Enola's mapped body offers the possibility of survival and builds on this long tradition of aligning the female body with the land. Deacon is certain that Enola is the resource that can show him the way to Dryland and, hence, further resources. He lifts Enola in front of the chanting

Figure 2.1.   *Waterworld*, 1995, Universal Pictures.

crowd as an exhibition of his power as he shouts "Dryland is not just our destination. It is our destiny. . . . Behold the instrument of our salvation!" I will explore the religious connotations of Enola's treatment more deeply later but this scene does evoke a swathe of stored images relating to sacrificial ceremonies while the words suggest a biblical significance. Moreover, Enola's body is an item to be revered, envied, and possessed. However, she remains an elusive resource, which in turn heightens both her value and the danger she is in. As a map, Enola is constantly misread because the map is written in a different language and it is viewed upside down. She is a resource from an older age and the skills necessary to "read" her have been all but lost. The child, as Rousseau argued, represents an older, more primal culture that is lost as adulthood and the norms of society take over. Only Mariner and Old Gregor (an elderly survivor) figure out how to decode her tattoo. Both men are outsiders, eccentric, and removed from the savagery of survival in *Waterworld* by their intelligence and their ability to invent, construct, or repair devices that use wind and solar energy. As I mentioned earlier, there is a clear argument being made here about the traditional skills necessary to survive in a changing world.

The attitude toward Enola and her treatment as a resource is reflected in the characters' attitudes toward other resources in *Waterworld*: oil, water, food, soil, and alcohol. Mariner is depicted as a particularly resourceful fellow who does not waste a drop of water or a single leaf. In the opening scenes and Mariner's first encounter with another human, this characteristic is immediately set in the viewer's mind: Mariner's ship is furnished with strange bits of machinery and sails. Everything is sun-bleached and salty except for a small citrus plant, vulnerable but healthy and green in the midst of the greys and browns on the ship. A drifter steals all the limes while Mariner is diving and an enraged Mariner sets a death trap for the thief: in Waterworld food is worth killing for, especially in a seafaring world where vitamins are in short supply and scurvy must be a threat. On the oil rig, Mariner trades all the soil he has for a tomato plant; he uses wind and solar energy to run his boat; he uses a knife instead of guns; and he rubs a final drop of water on Enola's parched lips. Just as his body has evolved gills and webbed feet for an aquatic life, Mariner has honed his skills to value every element of life he is offered and to use the renewable sources of energy around him. These actions, as Mariner is our hero, are deemed to be intelligent, honorable, and right. In contrast, the Smokers (named because of their mode of transport: roaring jet-skis fuelled by Deacon's oil) and the Deacon swill whiskey, ride speedboats, use machine weaponry (guns, rocket launchers, etc.), pay no heed to preserving oil resources, drive cars for fun, and wear showy clothes. One reason for this wastefulness is that it keeps Deacon's army under his control: he indulges his lackeys' whims and desires to consume, thereby maintaining his supremacy and keeping the lackeys wanting more. As the typical villains, glass eye and all, the Smokers are wasteful and this leads to their demise: their oil tankard explodes, their speedboats are trapped in fishing nets, and their own weapons are turned against them. Thus, there is a direct correlation between the treatment of Enola as resource and the treatment of the world's resources. As Enola embodies the fragility of the world, *Waterworld* warns its audience that unless we learn to read/decode the messages of our world in trouble and treat it with care, we are doomed to a life of dwindling resources, warfare, global flooding, and the demise of the human race. I believe the urge to protect a floundering planet is *Waterworld*'s strongest argument and therefore Enola's clearest role is as the symbol of this urgent need. She does, however, also fulfill the idea of a hoped for future.

Enola's physicality has a second advantage to the survivors in *Waterworld*: she is a girl and, as such, will be useful in repopulating the earth. There are undertones throughout the film of the lack of fertile women and how the extreme isolation of each tiny community or drifting individual results in inbreeding. Mariner is offered a young woman on the atoll in an attempt to introduce his outsider's genes into the mix and avoid damaging levels of inbreeding. A further example of the sexual desert that underlies the film is when a drifter trades paper with Mariner so as to have thirty minutes alone with Helen and forty-five minutes alone with Enola. While Mariner later backs out of the deal, he is not surprised by such a request and we are given to understand that this would be normal practice. Enola is scantily clad and is continuously left in enclosed places with mad men. The Smokers' desire to skin her and her smallness in the arms of strong men result in, for this viewer at least, a sense that she is constantly at the mercy of men's whims as to what they want to do with her body. James Kincaid's comparison of our "story of child molesting" to "the literary territory of the Gothic" as we circle in numerous "hopeless encounter[s] with the demon"[21] is applicable here. For Kincaid, the official idea of the child in American culture is that he/she is "adorable," epitomized by Shirley Temple's childish coquetry. He traces Christian iconography of cute babies, eighteenth-century tendencies to value the helpless, and erotic idealizing of children in Victorian culture as sources for this trend culminating in "our culture's central pedophile fantasy."[22] Indeed, there are similarities between *Waterworld* and *Curly Top* (Cummings 1935), which sees a handsome man rescue a young girl and, "after much manhandling" bring her to a safe place where she declares her desire to marry her rescuer.[23] When the clutch of survivors make it to Dryland, Helen and Enola are the women of the future; the mothers of the next generation. The final shot is of them arm in arm watching Mariner leave. The human world of man can continue because Enola-as-map led them to Dryland and Enola-as-female will repopulate the island. This idea of Enola as the mother of future generations also stems from her role as a force of nature from an earlier time. She is a figure from an untarnished world.

Enola can also be read as a messenger sent from Mother Nature, Gaia-like, to allow the resourceful ones to find a home for the continuance of the human race. I use Gaia here in both its mythological sense in viewing Enola as the future mother of all and in its scientific sense as used by James Lovelock in his Gaia hypothesis that argues the earth is self-regulating.[24] Enola is almost a caricature of a semi-feral child reminding one of Mowgli or Peter Pan: wild haired, cheeky, agile, hungry, and grubby, with a deep intelligence and understanding of her surroundings. In the muted palette of the film, the ocean, the aforementioned tomatoes, and Enola's eyes are the only real spots of color. Her eyes are piercingly turquoise, as if they reflect the sea upon which she floated to Helen. The beginning of Mariner's softening toward her is when she points out that they are both freaks: he because he is a mutant and she because of her tattoos. This alignment, along with the positioning of Mariner and Enola as our heroes suggests a combination of ancient knowledge of the earth and ability to adapt to new conditions is the way of our future survival. Text, pictures, and messages play an important role in the film and Enola's sketches of palm trees and equine figures suggest she is a kind of cipher of what the world used to be like or what it may become again. Her honesty and directness, besides providing scant moments of comedy, show an untainted ego. She is driven by what she sees as fair and just. This trait of childhood, the strict interpretation of what is right or wrong and being morally inflexible, is a trait that could help the ailing Waterworld: when Helen apologizes, Enola assumes that means forgiveness; she steals a crayon only in order to create beauty for Mariner; she is not appalled by his mutations, but rather impressed by his strength and valor. Enola's existence and survival also have biblical overtones. Helen recounts how she turned up as a baby in a woven basket with obvious echoes of Moses in the reeds. According to the Bible, Moses was hidden when all the other boy children were to be killed and was set adrift on the Nile in a basket until he was found and adopted. Moses is considered an important prophet in Christianity and Judaism. He brings the Ten Commandments to the people as God's rules for successful living. Enola too is set adrift in a basket in a time of great danger; she floats on water until found, rescued, and adopted; her map is the text that tells the people how to live successfully. At the end of the film, the cabin on Dryland appears to be her ancestral home; it houses the remains of Enola's parents, the Adam and Eve of the story, surrounded by white flowers and soft cobwebs in an Edenic paradise. Thus, Enola can be read as a religious messenger sent to bring the survivor's home and as both the daughter of the original human race and the universal mother of the next.

BEASTS OF THE SOUTHERN WILD

Beasts of the Southern Wild is an adaptation of Lucy Alibar's play *Juicy and Delicious* (2012). It has received much critical acclaim and has been praised for capturing the spirit of the child protagonist, played with breathtaking swagger by Quvenzhané Wallis. Tom Shone praises the film for its sense of magic that is "the lyrical voodoo of childhood"; the result is a film like "Mad Max retold by Gabriel Garcia Marquez."[25] It has also received criticism for ignoring crucial questions on race and class. Much of the hype, be it positive or negative, has focused on the child protagonist and the depiction of her life.

Beasts tells the tale of a little six-year-old girl named Hushpuppy who lives in a community called the Bathtub, a section of the Louisiana bayou cut off from the rest of the mainland by a large levee. While the almost invisible city of New Orleans churns on in its modernity, the Bathtub is moving at a different pace. Hushpuppy lives with her ill and alcoholic father, Wink, and a motley crew of other Bathtub residents. Her mother is absent. Hushpuppy lives in a dilapidated dwelling and is left responsible for her own care most of the time. An utterly devastating flood from an approaching hurricane threatens her fragile community. In the wake of the storm surge, the survivors try to regain their lives but the salt water has damaged everything. They try to blow up the levee in an attempt to drain the flood waters but are subject to a forced evacuation as a result. The levee represents an idea of man manipulating nature to his own ends with later, unforeseen results. Blowing up the levee is an attempt to demodernize and return the land to its natural state.

I feel it may be necessary to argue for the inclusion of *Beasts* in a discussion of post-apocalyptic cinema. I will quote Duncan Wu's analysis of the film to aid me in this: "The film's principal device is synecdoche: southern Louisiana stands at an extreme and in choosing to focus on its environmental problems, Zeitlin attempts to speak to those faced by the wider world."[26] The weakness of the levees (as borne out in Hurricane Katrina) reveals the unpreparedness for the consequences of climate change. Furthermore, the levees block the residents of the Bathtub from the rest of the world. As Wu states, the residents are outsiders in many ways, "comprising an underworld beyond civilization, survivors of the apocalypse before the event."[27] Thus *Beasts* is a concentrated, mini-version of a worldwide apocalypse. Zeitlin chooses to show the plight of some of the earliest victims of climate change in his film. The catastrophes brought about by climate change are many and ongoing; it is not one giant apocalypse but rather a series of community or country-sized endings leading gradually toward more widespread destruction.

The setting of Zeitlin's film is obviously important. The devastation caused by Hurricane Katrina and the resulting floods, coupled with the controversy surrounding the rescue effort and the aftermath whisper through every shot of the character's lives in this film. Tom Shone coined the term "American exotic" to talk about films, including *Beasts of the Southern Wild*, that focus on the hinterlands of America often with the aim of critiquing how broken-down America has become, how divided it is based on class and race, and how "foreign" parts of the country seem, even to Americans.[28] I have written elsewhere on the idea of the regional Gothic and the fear of the edges of society that do not conform to the centers' notions and norms.[29] In films like *Texas Chainsaw Massacre* (Hooper 1974) and *The Hills Have Eyes* (Craven 1977) the edges of America are peopled with cannibalistic rednecks and, I would argue, contain undertones of apocalyptic doom. Because these "edges" are often the site of severe poverty, the effects of climate change can be felt all the more strongly and they, thus, can serve as an early warning system. In *Beasts*, the edges of America are again the site of the end: the end of dry land, civilization, and our future. I will now examine Hushpuppy first as a version of the untarnished world and then as a resource and an embodiment of hope.

In *Beasts* we see the world through Hushpuppy's gaze and the consequences of climate change played out in her imagination and in her daily existence. Hushpuppy learns about extinct aurochs in school and they are reborn in her imagination as heralds of the apocalypse. Her direct communication with the aurochs is a tangible sign of her embodiment of an older world order and her elemental strength is aligned with the mighty beast as she faces them down. The community in the bayou eschews all forms of modern civilization—the dwellings, family structure, health care, and utensils all hark to a time of clans, communal structures, eating what you catch, home remedies, home brew, and communion with nature, that is, a strictly noncapitalist consumerist existence. As bell hooks puts it: "Nature is the most compelling force in the world of the Bathtub . . . [the] complete celebration of their collective feral animal nature binds everyone in sacred contract; they are to resist domestication and civilization at all costs."[30] Of course, I am not for a moment suggesting that Zeitlin's film presents a rosy existence of flower-power happiness in the rural idyll—far from it. As other critics have noted, the loose family structure and lack of education and health care leave Hushpuppy in a precarious position and susceptible to disaster from even the smallest change in the environment. Wink views the trappings of modernity with disdain. He rejects medical treatment and his desire for Hushpuppy to be completely independent of civilization's tools suggests a need for self-reliance in the face of ecological uncertainty and institutional disregard.[31]

At the edge of the bayou lies the city, barricaded and spewing pollution; Shone calls it a "grey Oz."[32] When the residents of the Bathtub are forcibly evacuated, the disparity between the two worlds becomes even clearer: "such has been your immersion in the movie's muck and clutter, that the entire scene, with its bright antiseptic lights, and clean, white orderlies . . . plays like a report from Mars. Actually no. Just America. Which might be the same thing these days."[33] This is not an easy celebration of a simpler way of life, nor is it a voyeuristic gaze on those who dwell beyond the fringes. However, it is undeniable that it is largely the impact of the polluting city that creates much of the negativity in the film: barricades that result in isolation, levees that worsen flooding in some areas, imposed norms, and intrusive health care are depicted as terrifying, alien-like invasions. Tim Kroenert suggests *Beasts* posits an implicit moral argument for the "more privileged citizens of the world to take responsibility for humanity's impact on the environment" and that the movie is an indictment of the prosperous West.[34] As such, Hushpuppy's survival and happiness are symbolically and literally linked with daily decisions made in the viewer's consumerist reality.

Wink's rage against the levee and the city seems to stem in part from his frustrated desire to keep Hushpuppy free from all the damaging trappings of modernity. Indeed, the most electrifying scene hinges on this desire: Hushpuppy struggles to get some crabmeat out of its shell with some kitchen utensils. Wink angrily orders her to eat the crab with her hands and rip the meat out without knife or fork, to "Beast it!" Hushpuppy quietly obeys under her father's gaze and the crowd chanting "Beast it! Beast it!" She is triumphant and leaps onto the table like a mini warrior showing off her imagined biceps and hollering a battle victory cry. Again, one can argue that Wink's parenting skills are far from fine-tuned; nonetheless, it cannot be denied that he is preparing his daughter for a life of difficulty and instilling in her skills necessary for survival as an orphan in a flooded world. It may be the case that inherent in the bayou dwellers' existence is the need to adapt to a rapidly changing environment and this has always been the case. In this sense, they are uniquely evolved to deal with an uncertain and destructive future. As Zeitlin himself suggests, this is why the movie is set where it is. He was inspired to make the movie because he was fascinated by all the roads that "go out into the marsh" in southern Louisiana and how if you follow those roads to the end, you reach places where the land is "falling off into the water." Zeitlin wanted to make a film about the end of the world and saw this location (the Gulf Coast) as a "sort of" glimpse "into the future." More importantly in the context of my argument, he wanted to celebrate the culture of fearlessness in the "hold outs and sort of last stands" in these fragile places.[35]

A positive reading of Hushpuppy as a version of the untarnished world is that she has wisdom, resilience, and a fearlessness beyond her years. She is self-sufficient, alert, and intelligent. I certainly think Zeitlin is a Rousseauist who sees in Hushpuppy the untainted natural world. hooks agrees with other critics that Hushpuppy has a resilient spirit; she sees her as a miniature version "of the strong black female matriarch."[36] However, this is not a positive comparison for hooks, who argues that Hushpuppy's character is a racist and sexist stereotype that has been deployed since the times of slavery. Indeed, hooks states she is "deeply disturbed and militantly outraged" by the film. She sees the film as depicting continuous physical and emotional violation of the body and being of Hushpuppy. Hushpuppy is subject to both romanticization as the strong black child and a "modern primitive" and to eroticization.[37] Wooley too sees this "Gaia-like transcendental ecological interdependence" as a means of avoiding questions of gender, race, and social relations that would undermine its vision of mythic unity. Further-more, while Wooley sees this vision of interdependency and the reevaluation of anthropocentrism as necessary for a sustainable future in the context of a marginalized community living hand-to-mouth, she fears the romanticized localism also invokes Shepard Krech's "ecological Indian"; "the idea that before colonialists arrived, Native Americans lived in perfect ecological har-mony with their environment and other non-human species."[38]

While I agree with hooks and Wooley that an unthinking celebration of anachronistic lifestyles and a suggestion of aligning race and ecological har-mony are facetious and insulting, I do not agree that that is what Zeitlin is doing. By using a child as the lens through which we view the situation in the bayou, we see the world with her reduced but preferable level of knowledge. By preferable I mean that it is pure knowledge untainted by doubt, closed-mindedness, or preconceptions. Rousseau describes the state of childhood, preknowledge of the adult world, as a kind of pure intelligence that later becomes sullied by experience.[39] I believe Zeitlin views Hushpuppy's wis-dom in these terms: it is not because she is black or a girl, but because she is a child untarnished by adulthood's rigidity in terms of race, class, and gender; she is unsullied by the murky grey areas of the morality of adulthood, as a child her morality is absolute. Zeitlin does not suggest that the other black characters are in communion with nature; only Hushpuppy sees and speaks with the aurochs. Like Enola in *Waterworld*, Hushpuppy represents an idealized pre-apocalyptic world. Her ease in her natural surroundings, her bravery, resilience, honesty, and love of animals and people alike are matched by a complete lack of ego, greed, or selfishness. She represents a desire for the post-apocalyptic human to be "better." The beasts of the title can be viewed as the extinct aurochs, come back to warn of the consequences of climate change; they could be the city dwellers who spew poison and consume non-renewable resources at a terrifying rate; they could be the residents of the bayou reduced to animal-like status to eke out existence on the scraps left over by their wealthier neighbors; or Hushpuppy could be the wild beast, untarnished by contemporary norms and desires for comfort, ready to lead her raggle-taggle friends out of the flood and into the next stage of humanity's story. However, as with Enola in *Waterworld*, Hushpuppy is also a resource to be used for one's own ends.

It could be argued that Hushpuppy is most often used as a resource by the filmmakers themselves. As mentioned above, critics have noted the film's avoidance of core questions on race, gender, or class in the film. In Alibar's original play,[40] the child protagonist was a white boy.[41] This, I believe, points to Zeitlin's subtle commentary on race and gender. By making Hushpuppy a young, black, poor, girl, Zeitlin's heroine embodies the political arguments. She stands for the traditionally weak or marginalized members of society. Her defiant strength in the face of faceless institutions that threaten her very existence and her world in the name of profit she will never see is inspiring. I certainly feel gender is a useful lens through which to view *Beasts*. Wooley claims that the film hints that when the effects of climate change begin to reshape the world, the most valuable qualities will be those traditionally associated with masculinity: "repressed emotion, self-sufficiency, aggression and strength." Wink tells Hushpuppy that when he dies she will have to be king of the Bathtub and "the man." The little girls from the Bathtub make their way to a floating brothel called Elysian Fields where they are fed and caressed by women and Hushpuppy meets a woman who could be her mother. For Wooley the marked distinction between the Bathtub and the brothel is significant; "in situating the domesticated female kitchen firmly in the realm of fantasy, the film demonstrates the inadequacy of stereotypical feminine qualities for survival in the wild."[42] However, it is the warmth and nurturing of Hushpuppy's teacher and "mother" in the brothel that instill in Hushpuppy a patient understanding of the world around her. Miss Bathsheba teaches her about the ice age (another era of climate change) and the aurochs; her "mother" teaches about picking up the pieces of life when they have fallen. Thus, Hushpuppy's role as resource is intricately tied up with her gender, as is her role as the embodiment of the future.

Hushpuppy speaks of the universe as being made up of interfitting pieces and how if one piece breaks, the universe breaks. This Gaia hypothesis-like understanding of the world is the core of Hushpuppy's heroism. Her feisty exterior and "masculine" skills learned through hardship are certainly necessary for survival in the flooded world of her future; yet so is the understanding of the balance of the universe; as she herself argues: "The whole universe depends on everything fitting together just right. If one piece busts, even the smallest piece . . . the entire universe will get busted." The final scene shows Hushpuppy leading the people of the Bathtub along a road. She is the resource that needs to fight against the factories and the corporations. As a film about the consequences of climate change induced apocalypse with a child as its protagonist and heroine, *Beasts* posits a child's intelligence and faith in the future as the qualities necessary to a successful post post-apocalyptic reality. The theme of the interconnectedness of the earth in *Beasts* urges viewers to not ignore disasters that are not on their own doorstep but rather to realize that we are all responsible for the consequences of unthinking consumption.

Figure 2.2.   *Beasts of the Southern Wild*, 2012, Cinareach Films.

THE ROAD

The Road is a stark portrayal of humanity on its last legs. Cormac McCarthy's 2006 book won a Pulitzer and was made into a successful film. The novel has been praised for its heartrending tale of father and son love and its sparse, poetic prose, bare bones dialogue, and haunting descriptions of dark, bleak beauty. The film, with direction from Hillcoat, adaptation from Joe Penhall, stunning cinematography from Javier Aguirresarobe, and a resonant soundtrack from Nick Cave and Warren Ellis, provide an intriguing translation of the tale of survival to the screen. *The Road* is a post-apocalyptic tale of a father, known only as Man, and his son, known as Boy, trying to survive the cold and hunger in a desolate America. Their plan for survival is to walk south in search of the ocean, warmth, and the hope of salvation. The cause of the disaster is unknown. We are presented with the current post-disaster reality: ash falling from the sky, intermittent earthquakes, a clouded sun, no animals, no food, and no light. There is no distinction between night and day so temporal markers no longer function. All, it seems, is what Shelly Rambo terms an "eternal middle."[43] This idea of the tenuous middle echoes Kermode's notion of the uncertainty of modern man in the middle leading to a desire for a sense of an ending; what Kermode described as the need for the tock after the tick. In *The Road* the past haunts Man in flashbacks while the future is uncertain; both are threatening and confusing. As Canavan argues, concepts of progress and a future dangle as cruel impossibilities.[44] What few people are left are marauding cannibalistic gangs or desperate, terrified refugees. Along the road, Man and Boy have a series of encounters that test man's humanity and provide moments of powerful tension. Man and Boy journey on the road to reach the sea and to "keep the fire burning." The final scenes depict both the frustrating frailty of the human body and, ultimately, the determination of humanity to hope and love. This echoes the desire in *Beasts* for only the positive traits of human nature to survive the apocalypse. I will now examine Boy as an untarnished version of the world before going on to explore his role as resource and as the embodiment of the hope for regeneration.

I would argue few post-apocalyptic texts have dealt with the theme of the dying earth and our role in its death as subtly and stirringly as *The Road*. The post-apocalyptic world is divided along what appear to be very clear lines: the good guys and the bad guys. The typical obsession with "good guys" and "bad guys" is played out here where the only options left are suicide, cannibalism, or scavenging on the road. This binary is most firmly based on the fact that the good guys are not cannibals, the bad guys are. I will examine this in more detail when I consider Boy as resource. For now, we can content ourselves with the fact that Boy is firmly in the good guy's camp. Man and Boy's identity as good guys and their mission to "carry the fire" are central to maintaining their energy, willpower, and sanity on their seemingly interminable walk. Man rejects suicide yet he teaches the boy how to shoot himself in the mouth should they be captured by cannibals in a disturbing, challenging scene. Boy's untarnished quality largely stems from his ignorance. He is too young to remember the world pre-apocalypse and so he is not devastated by the loss; the loss is all he knows. Again, it is useful to consider Rousseau here and his belief that knowledge leads to corruption. Man and Boy's journey along the road is symbolic in many ways; one such way is that it represents the boy's journey toward knowledge, just as Hushpuppy's journey is. The steps of his education include learning how to shoot himself in the event of being captured by cannibals; tasting Coca Cola; understanding the fragility of goodness; and the need for resilience in the face of horror. Along with the knowledge of his father's love and the skills necessary to survive in a post-apocalyptic world, Boy also learns about avarice, inhumanity, and self-protectionism. All this knowledge leads him to ask the crucial question: "Are we still the good guys?" Man's blind need to protect his son leads him to acts of cruelty. His constant need to demarcate the lines of savagery belies his doubts. As Man's strength wanes and his position in the good guy's camp becomes shaky in his desperation to survive, Boy maintains his hold on "the fire." It is as if Boy is an elemental force, like fire itself, that will persevere no matter how long the road.

In ancient mythology, Cronos, the father of Zeus, having been warned that one of his children might usurp his power, devours them all, and Saturn, his Roman counterpart does likewise. Dante, in *The Inferno*, tells of a father

Figure 2.3.   *The Road*, 2009, Dimension Films.

consuming his dead sons' corpses to put off his death from starvation. In fact, feasting upon the tender flesh of the young is a commonplace in folktales and more contemporary culture.[45] Cannibalism, we soon learn, is "the great fear," and the great division between good and bad guys. Much of the horror and tension in the film come from encounters with this great crime, in particular the cellar scene in which Man and Boy discover men and women awaiting dismemberment and slow death as they are farmed for the cannibals' consumption. The horror of cannibalism is the fact that it reduces humans to animals in an abattoir. Hillcoat's cannibals are a kind of remnant of rural Gothic cannibals found in *Texas Chainsaw Massacre* (1974) or *The Hills Have Eyes* (1977). They are filthy, gap-toothed, overall-wearing savages who ride pick-up trucks, speak in a deep southern drawl and whoop as they chase their prey. The fear in the film comes from the idea that Boy is a resource to fill these savages' bellies. Cannibalism in times of famine or starvation is relatively commonplace in history.[46] In the context of the child in post-apocalyptic cinema, cannibalism functions as a reminder of two things: one, that espousing the notion of indulging the self at all costs means eating children in a world with no food; and continuous consumption of our world's resources in the same unthinking way that a hungry ogre would crunch on a child's bones will result in the metaphor becoming reality. This is not a Darwinian case of the survival of the fittest as might be argued because Darwin would argue for the continuation of one's bloodline; rather it is a short-sighted satisfying of rapacious appetites. Thus the "bad" in these movies is the overconsumption of resources despite the fact that there is a deep-seated knowledge that it is counterproductive—just as we do in the world today. The child in *The Road* is the remnant of innocence and purity in a grey, cruel, dog-eat-dog post-apocalyptic world. He is also, however, tasty flesh and a possible breeder. The father's view of the child and the cannibal gangs' view of the child are the symbolic representations of the view of the future of humanity. Boy is either in possession of hope and life (the "fire" he carries) and must be protected, led to safety, fed, and nurtured so as to preserve the glimmering flame, or he is tasty fresh meat there for the taking in a world of ravenous, self-serving individuals. The message is clear, as it is in *Beasts* and *Waterworld*: what we do to these children is what we do to our world. One option provides a glimmer of hope while the other offers brief satiation followed by interminable doom.

The end of *The Road* can be viewed as conveying a sense of the possibility of hope, of divine presence, even of redemption. Although the father has died, the son will live on and carry on the father's memory.[47] However, some find the idea of a redemptive ending sentimental, unrealistic, and inconsistent with the rest of the film. Thus the boy's survival is at the crux of interpretations of *The Road*. It can be viewed as a testimony to the persistence of hope and regeneration. On the other hand, is redemption possible if the ending has already happened? The literal and moral journey of survival in *The Road* provokes many questions about fatherhood, the innate desire to survive, the possibility of the next generation being better than the current one, the journey to knowledge, and the hope for a better existence at the end of that road. The road itself, long an icon of American popular culture, is, of course, central to the visual aesthetic of the book and the film. The "road" is at the core of American notions of escape, pushing beyond boundaries, freedom to roam, and reinvention of the self. However, as I have argued elsewhere, there are many examples in American horror of "shots of long, empty, dusty roads . . . passages describing the road trip, the irritation and claustrophobia . . . [that] emphasize the notion of moving beyond one's comfort zones to another place."[48] In *The Road*, John Ford-esque wide shots of American landscape and tiny, vulnerable human figures fill the screen; these shots are essential in the conveyance of loneliness and the fragility of humanity. However, rather than the blue skies and lush prairies of the Westerns, these shots are of a muted, grey palette, the land is devoid of life or growth. The tiny figures of Man and Boy standing with their backs to the camera, facing a line of burning forest—facing a veritable hell hole, or bent into the wind pulling their cart as they relentlessly move south, are stunning shots that perfectly capture the bleak beauty of McCarthy's prose and contrast with typical "into the sunset" endings in the classic Western—itself a symbol of hope and rebirth. Again, this image of the struggle to keep moving, to find safety while pulling your entire belongings behind you through horrendous desolation has obvious significance in the light of contemporary environmental disasters and echoes both the images of trauma outlined by Baiysha and the idea of environmental refugees described by White earlier. The desperate need to hope that at the end of the road lies some sort of salvation for our children is exquisitely and poignantly rendered in *The Road* and is all the more powerful in light of these all-too-real disasters.

WATER AND WOMBS

In all three films, there is a move toward or upon the water as if it is the source and mouth of the river of regeneration. This is also the case in other post-apocalyptic films, which, despite the prevalence of great floods as the source of the apocalypse, the move toward the sea is a move toward survival (I am thinking here of *Children of Men* [2006], *The Dark Knight* [2008], and *World War Z* [2013]). There are many myths that use water as a symbol of life or regeneration, so before concluding, I will take a moment to explore how water features in these films. Veronica Strang traces the meaning of water and notes that water worship is ubiquitous in ancient mythology and with "homologous consistency . . . female water gods were responsible for the generation (or regeneration) of human life."[49] Water bodies are the womb of life across cultures and water is a healing substance across religions. Wells and springs symbolize the womb of the Great Mother and are a source of life and regeneration.[50] In *The Road*, the journey is slowly but determinedly made in the direction of the sea as if it is the site of hope, and, assuming one accepts the possibility of redemption in the film, it is. At the end, Boy is embraced by a mother-figure and welcomed into the new beginning of humanity. In *Waterworld*, the sea brings Enola on fortuitous waves to other survivors and in turn back to the womb-space so that humanity can continue. In *Beasts*, the open sea offers freedom from the barricaded bayou and provides fresh resources and food. As the children in these three films survive and gain strength from the ocean around them, there is an obvious correlation between the idea of rebirth and the salty waters of our future world. For Carl Jung, "Water is the commonest symbol for the unconscious."[51] Jung cites numerous mythologies that see water as healing and the sea as the womb and the source of rebirth. Likewise, Freud connects water and birth: "Birth is regularly expressed in dreams by some connection with water; one plunges into the water, or comes out of the water, which means one gives birth to, or is born."[52] Furthermore, Freud cites myths that describe the person who rescues a child from water as the "true" mother. Thus, as the children in these three films move toward the salty brine, there is also a move toward their rebirth and the potential survival of humanity. The ocean is the mother of all life and symbolizes interconnectivity in these films; this is especially powerful as we are dealing here with motherless child protagonists who embody the potential for regeneration.

In a study of the child, it seems worth examining the parents in these films; or rather the lack thereof. The absence of mothers in all three films furthers the sense of the children's isolation and vulnerability. In *Beasts* and *The Road* the children are left in the care of taciturn and severe fathers, while in *Waterworld* Enola's upbringing is in the hands of strangers and substitute parents. In *Beasts* the scenes in the floating brothel are shot in warm reds and oranges with shadows and a sense of warm closeness rendering the scene evocative of womb-like and maternal qualities: warmth, closeness, tactility.[53] In *The Road* the flashbacks to the pre-apocalypse when the mother was alive are shot in warm, suffused, yellow lights in stark contrast to the dim, chilly greys of Man and Boy's current reality. In *Waterworld*, the cabin that houses Enola's parents is drenched in warm sunshine and the sight of warm wood tones, flowers, birds, and cobwebs are like a balm to the eyes as opposed to water, rusting metal, and raw fish. I posit that these womb-like havens are depicted as the sources of warmth and energy, that is, they are the source of life. The move toward these womb-spaces, all located on or near water, is suggestive of an optimism regarding the survival of humanity post post-apocalypse. The atmosphere of comfort depicted in those brief moments are such that the audience can sense the child's safety, happiness, and warmth in these places, further urging viewers to allow for this sense of safety for all children.

CONCLUSION

The films I have explored portray our world in danger of burning or flooding as a direct result of today's actions. The films refer to the "Ancients" or "predecessors" as those who were responsible for the current state of disaster. Of course, these predecessors of disaster are the contemporary audience watching the film. These films, therefore, speak to the need to be aware of the consequences of modern-day levels of consumption. Furthermore, by having child protagonists, these films urge contemporary adults to think about the world they are leaving behind for their children and grandchildren. The films speak to the universal desire to protect one's young.

As I have noted, there have been many negative critiques of the films under discussion as there have been negative readings of their message; that is, as post-apocalyptic films they offer a depressing lesson on the foolishness of humans and the inevitable decline of humanity as a result. However, I posit a more positive reading of these films based on centralizing the children's roles. As resources, the children are most cruelly used and remind the audience of the consequences of unthinking use of nonrenewable resources. As the embodiment of the untarnished world, they call the audience's attention to the danger of losing survival skills and knowledge in the technological age, and they point out the vast beauty that is at stake. As the source of regeneration, the children in these films suggest the possibility of life after the apocalypse, and a glimpse of what that life could be. The children have escaped the rapacious maws of various consumers and their arrival, unscathed at the shores of the future, offer an optimistic vision of the future of humanity.

NOTES

1. White, 21.
2. Ibid., 21.
3. Canavan, 450.
4. Brown, 175–176; Canavan, 431; Shaviro, 288.
5. Bishop, 11.
6. Baiysha.
7. Kermode, 4.
8. Arendt, 478.
9. Rousseau.
10. Rose, 49–50.
11. Mills, 17.
12. Kuhn, 132.

13. Bruhm, 100.
14. Ibid., 103.
15. Hanson, 150.
16. Wood, 189.
17. Hanson, 153.
18. Mills, 17–18.
19. Finland sits between Russia and the rest of Scandinavia. The Russians had control of Finland from 1809 until the Russian Revolution, and more recently during World War II when Stalin invaded and defeated Finland in order to stop Hitler from doing the same. It was a brutal invasion and the Finns held off the Soviets for a surprisingly long time but were eventually crushed. For most of the rest of World War II, the Finns fought on the side of the Axis Powers against the Soviet Union. The Soviets invaded Finland for both resources and as a protective barrier against attacks on Russia. Therefore, the Finns tend to assert the Scandinavian side of their ethnic heritage rather than the Slavic (Russian) side of it.
20. Porteous, 3.
21. Kincaid, 10–11.
22. Ibid., 128.
23. Ibid., 120–121.
24. Lovelock, Preface.
25. Shone.
26. Wu.
27. Ibid.
28. Shone.
29. Brown, 86.
30. hooks.
31. Wooley.
32. Shone.
33. Ibid.
34. Kroenart.
35. Zeitlin.
36. hooks.
37. Ibid.
38. Wooley.
39. Rousseau.
40. Alibar wrote *Juicy and Delicious* when her father was very ill and she was trying to come to terms with his mortality. She made Hushpuppy a boy because she "was too close to the story to make him a girl." As Alibar and Zeitlin adapted the play, she felt stronger and finally able for Hushpuppy to be a girl.
41. Alibar.
42. Wooley.
43. Rambo, 113.
44. Canavan, 440.
45. Kuhn, 173–174; Brown, 131.
46. Brown, 65.
47. Rambo, 113.
48. Brown, 135.
49. Strang, 84.
50. Ibid., 85–86.
51. Jung, 18.
52. Freud, 132–133.
53. Wooley.

BIBLIOGRAPHY

Alibar, Lucy. "Once There Was a Hushpuppy: On the Origins of *Beasts of the Southern Wild.*" *Zoetrope: All-Story* 16, 1 (2012): n.p.

Arendt, Hannah. *Human Condition.* Chicago: University of Chicago Press, 1998.

Baiysha, Anirban Kapil. "Trauma, Post-Apocalyptic Science Fiction and the Post-Human." *Wide Screen* 3, 1 (2011): n.p.

Bishop, Kyle William. *American Zombie Gothic: The Rise and Fall (and Rise) of the Walking Dead in Popular Culture.* Jefferson: McFarland and Company, 2010.

Brown, Jennifer. *Cannibalism in Literature and Film.* Hampshire & New York: Palgrave Macmillan, 2013.

Bruhm, Steven. "Nightmare on Sesame Street; or The Self-Possessed Child." *Gothic Studies* 8, 2 (2006): 98–113.

Canavan, Gerry. "We Are the Walking Dead: Race, Time and Survival in Zombie Narrative." *Extrapolation* 51, 3 (2010): 431–453.

Freud, Sigmund. *A General Introduction to Psychoanalysis.* London: Forgotten Books, 2013.

Hanson, Stuart. "Children in Film." In *Childhood Studies: A Reader in Perspectives of Childhood*, by Jean Mills and Stuart Mills. London: Routledge, 2000, 145–160.

hooks, bell. "No Love in the Wild." *New Black Man (in Exile).* September 5, 2012. newblackman.blogspot.com/2012/09/bell-hooks-no-love-in-wild.html (accessed November 17, 2013).

Jung, Carl. *The Archetypes and the Collective Unconscious.* Princeton: Princeton University Press, 1990.

Kermode, Frank. *The Sense of an Ending: Studies in the Theory of Fiction.* Oxford: Oxford University Press, 2000.

Kincaid, James R. *Erotic Innocence: The Culture of Child Molesting.* Durham, NC: Duke University Press, 1998.

Kroenart, Tim. "Beasts of the Climate Change Apocalypse." *Eureka Street* 22, 18 (2012): n.p.

Kuhn, Reinhard. *Corruption in Paradise: The Child in Western Literature.* Hanover and London: Brown University Press, 1982.

Lovelock, James. *Gaia: A New Look at Life on Earth.* Oxford: Oxford University Press, 2000.

Mills, Richard. "Perspectives of Childhood." In *Childhood Studies: A Reader in Perspectives of Childhood*, by Jean Mills and Richard Mills. London: Routledge, 2000, 7–37.

Porteous, J. Douglas. "Bodyscape: The Body-Landscape Metaphor." *The Canadian Geographer* 30, 1 (1986): 2–12.

Rambo, Shelly L. "Beyond Redemption? Reading Cormac McCarthy's *The Road* after the End of the World." *Studies in the Literary Imagination* 41, 2 (2008): 99–120.

Rousseau, Jean Jacques. *Emile.* Project Gutenberg, 2004.

Shaviro, Steve. "Capitalist Monsters." *Historical Materialism* 10, 4 (2002): 281–290.

Shone, Tom. *More Intelligent Life.* October 1, 2012. moreintelligentlife.com/content/arts/american-exotic (accessed November 23, 2013).

Strang, Veronica. *The Meaning of Water.* New York: Berg, 2003.

White, Gregory. *Climate Change and Migration: Security and Borders in a Warming World.* Oxford: Oxford University Press, 2011.

Wood, Robin. *Personal Views: Explorations in Film.* Michigan: Wayne State University Press, 2006.

Wooley, Agnus. "Politics of Myth Making: Beasts of the Southern Wild." *Open Democracy.* October 29, 2012. www.opendemocracy.net/5050/agnes-woolley/politics-of-myth-making-beasts-of-southern-wild (accessed November 17, 2013).

Wu, Duncan. *Times Higher Education.* October 18, 2012. www.timeshighereducation.co.uk/features/culture/beasts-of-the-southern-wild/421487.article (accessed November 23, 2013).

Zeitlin, Benh. Interview with Adam Conway. July 5, 2012. vimeo.com/45289928 (accessed June 10, 2014).

Chapter Three

Perpetual Horizons

Reproductive Futurity in Post-Apocalyptic Films

Mark Heimermann

INTRODUCTION: POST-APOCALYPSE AND FUTURITY

Post-apocalyptic narratives of all sorts, including film, explore what happens after society is sundered and becomes unrecognizable through apocalypse. Roslyn Weaver defines apocalypse as "a widespread disaster of particularly catastrophic or horrific proportions."[1] Yet apocalypse is often not the end: "Very seldomly . . . does the end of the narrative coincide with the end of the world. Something is left over, and that world after the world, the *post-apocalypse*, is usually the true object of the apocalyptic writer's concern."[2] Although the post-apocalypse necessarily takes place in speculative worlds which often look vastly different from contemporary society, these narratives still deal with current issues. For example, David Ketterer writes, "Apocalyptic literature is concerned with the creation of other worlds which exist, on the literal level, in a credible relationship (whether on the basis of rational extrapolation and analogy or of religious belief) with the 'real' world, thereby causing a metaphoric destruction of that 'real' world in the reader's head."[3] Dealing with "real" issues by placing them in an alternative world may seem counterintuitive, as it has the potential to blunt any sort of social critique by providing estrangement. M. Keith Booker addresses this apparent discrepancy. He argues,

> While the estrangement from reality provided by the projected worlds of sci-
> ence fiction might make the political messages of SF [science fiction] film
> seem less threatening to some, that very estrangement also helps to provide
> new perspectives from which audiences can look at the world in which they

41

live, potentially bringing into focus aspects of that world that might otherwise
be less clear.[4]

While Booker emphasizes science fiction, his argument holds true for all
sorts of speculative fiction. Weaver, who prefers the latter term, writes,
"Speculative fiction denotes the wide array of forms in which apocalypse can
appear, including science fiction, fantasy, magic realism, horror, gothic, sci-
ence-fantasy, and cyberpunk."[5] Booker's rationale—that alternative worlds
may grant transparency to that which is unclear—is present in arguments like
that of Evan Calder William's, who argues, in part, that "zombie films . . . are
the thought of *how real abstractions work on real bodies* . . . they hold out a
way to model and map what happens when seemingly spectral shifts in the
global architecture of a totality (capitalism), which cannot be traced to any
one cause or agent, touch earth and produce real consequences."[6] This type
of thinking exemplifies how post-apocalyptic narratives provide metaphors
for real-world concerns.

Post-apocalyptic narratives often explore how survivors rebuild society
after it has been ripped apart and whether it is possible, or even worthwhile,
to do so. James Berger observes, "The post-apocalypse in fiction provides an
occasion to go 'back to the basics' and to reveal what the writer considers to
be truly of value."[7] These considerations sometimes include children: how
they might be raised, whether constructions of childhood need to change,
whether their present liability offsets their future potential. Furthermore, futurity in a time of limited resources, such as after an apocalypse, resonates
sharply in parts of the contemporary world among concerns over dwindling
resources and the changing nature of our climate and ecosystems. As a result,
futurity in the face of scarcity is a central concern of many post-apocalyptic
films. This essay explores two post-apocalyptic films dealing with issues of
futurity: *Dawn of the Dead* (2004)[8] and *Daybreakers* (2009).[9] These films
critique the implications of a world hell-bent on consumption. They both
depict worlds overrun by monsters, zombies, and vampires, who pass along
their condition through infection. I contend both of these films engage in
critiques of Western capitalism. They are also haunted by children. The films
depict the initial encounter with the monstrous through children before taking
the position that these worlds are unfit for them.

My position is that these films can be understood as an argument for
reproductive futurity, for emphasizing the needs of children in considerations
of the future. Societies locked in short-term thinking become mired in stasis.
According to these films, the failure to consider reproductive futurity and
create a world where children thrive is part of the decline of civilization. For
hope to remain, reproductive futurity must be emphasized in the face of overconsumption and dwindling resources. In fact, reproductive futurity may be
most important to consider when it is hardest to do so. In Anglo, post-

industrialized countries, neoliberalism, the emphasis on market fundamentalism as a way of organizing society, emphasizes short-term, individualistic
thinking. The appeal to the future, as expressed through concerns over children, may be one of the few mobilizing forces left to initiate productive, long
term political, economical, and environmental change without withering in
the face of neoliberal opposition.

NO FUTURE: REJECTING REPRODUCTIVE FUTURITY

The queer theorist Lee Edelman makes a convincing argument against reproductive futurity in his provocative book *No Future: Queer Theory and the
Death Drive.* Edelman rails against how children are used in political discourse in the United States. He convincingly argues that the child is used as
an idealized image: an image which obfuscates what children may actually
want or need, as well as the reality that different children need different
things. Political factions imbue the idealized child with needs, and then these
political factions argue for these needs. In doing so, political factions
strengthen their appeals because they use a rhetoric that emphasizes a marginalized group that has the potential to cut across racial and cultural lines.
Edelman's concern with the use of the idealized child in politics is that it is a
symbol often used to trample on the rights of adults. Edelman finds censorship of actual people in the name of the "perpetual horizon" of the idealized
child ruinous and unfair. [10] Edelman argues,

> On every side, our enjoyment of liberty is eclipsed by the lengthening shadow
> of a Child whose freedom to develop undisturbed by encounters, or even the
> threat of potential encounters, with an "otherness" of which its parents, its
> church, or the state do not approve, uncompromised by any possible access to
> what is painted as alien desire, terroristically holds us all in check and deter-
> mines that political discourse conform to the logic of a narrative wherein
> history unfolds as the future envisioned for a Child who must never grow up. [11]

The idealized child against whom Edelman rails does not grow up because it
is not a real entity. Children grow up, but childhood remains, and the idealized child remains with it. The confrontation Edelman sees between the
idealized child and queerness is prominent because "for contemporary culture . . . [queerness] is understood as bringing children and childhood to an
end." [12]

Other scholars, like Martin Woodhead, discuss the dangers in using the
rhetoric of what children "need" because it can be dangerous for children too,
as it precludes adults from seeing children as actual beings with varying
wants and needs. [13] But Woodhead's concerns differ from Edelman's: Woodhead, with his background in psychology, calls us to recognize the multiple

pathways of development. Like Edelman, Woodhead understands the danger of the universalized, idealized child, but Woodhead comes to an alternate conclusion: children must be cared for by those responsible for them, and children are better cared for when adults recognize their differences. [14] Edelman, however, notes that the idealized child does not accurately represent the "lived experiences" of children, and rejects it completely. [15] Perhaps the answer to Edelman's concerns over the oppositional relationship between the idealized child and the queer community may be found in Woodhead's call to recognize children, in political as well as everyday life, as social agents in need of support, but with varying circumstances and developmental pathways, as opposed to idealized symbols.

Edelman's argument has been quite influential, but it is not without its critics within queer theory. José Esteban Muñoz critiques the "anti-relational" turn in queer studies, of which Edelman is a part: Munoz believes "queerness is primarily about futurity." [16] J. Halberstam is sympathetic toward the "antisocial turn," best exemplified by Leo Bersani and Edelman, but finds the queer history they draw from limiting. Rather than simply rejecting heteronormative discourses, Halberstam wants "to define queerness as a mode of crafting alternatives with others" opposing "global capitalism." [17] Mari Ruti finds much to appreciate in Edelman's antisocial argument, but ultimately finds it limiting because the future is a "way of sustaining the idea that we can participate in an ongoing endlessly renewed process of becoming." [18] Ruti situates this claim in contrast to the stasis of Edelman's focus on the present. Thus, many of the critiques coming from queer scholars emphasize futurity.

But Edelman's argument is persuasive. Children, symbolic or otherwise, should not be used as tools to impose restrictions on others. While certainly some things can be reasonably thought of as unsuitable for children, but not for adults, this does not mean that adults should sacrifice rights at the altar of the idealized child. However, the use of children, and an emphasis on futurity, may be especially important in contemporary debates, because, at least in the United States, political leaders are unwilling or unable to ask that the citizenry make sacrifices. After 9/11, President George W. Bush famously asked for people to continue shopping but never asked for substantial sacrifices on the part of the citizenry to contribute to the subsequent war effort. The unwillingness and inability of politicians to ask the citizenry to make short-term sacrifices makes it difficult to mobilize support for difficult long-term changes or solutions. While it can be problematic determining when and how children may be appropriately used in political discourses, the idealized child provides an important symbol that can still serve as a fruitful call to action, despite Edelman's concerns. It is not Edelman's concern over the misuse of the idealized child with which I argue. Rather, it's the rejection of reproductive futurity as the solution, his argument that "the strategic value" of queerness "lies in its resistance to a Symbolic reality" as represented by the idealized child. [19]

Edelman's argument seems to be an oppositional one. He writes, "Fuck the social order and the child in whose name we're collectively terrorized; fuck Annie; fuck the waif from *Les Mis*; fuck the poor, innocent kids on the net; fuck Laws both with capital ls and with small; fuck the whole network of Symbolic relations and the future that serves as its prop."[20] Despite the polemic, however, Edelman's argument for rejecting images of futurity to focus on the rights of adults in the present actually supports the status quo. Neoliberalism is embraced by a variety of major political parties, both in the United States and around the world. Neoliberalism carries with it a strong streak of individualism, both in its inception and its self-justification. Thinkers like Milton Friedman emphasize the rights of individuals to make economic decisions without government interference as the only way to guarantee freedom. Friedman argues:

> There are few measures we could take that would do more to promote the cause of freedom at home and abroad [then getting rid of market restrictions]. . . . We could say to the rest of the world: We believe in freedom and intend to practice it. No one can force you to be free. That is your business. But we can offer you full co-operation on equal terms to all. Our market is open to you. Sell here what you can and wish to. Use the proceeds to buy what you wish. [21]

Friedman's equation of economic freedom with political freedom seems almost farcical, but it has become the underlying fiction behind neoliberalism: that emphasizing "strong private property rights, free markets, and free trade" leads to improved "human well-being."[22] However, David Harvey, in his detailed account of neoliberalism, demonstrates that neoliberalism always involves the decline of social welfare programs. These cuts to social welfare often hit youth the hardest. Henry Giroux argues for the centrality of children and futurity in political discourse: "Any discourse about the future has to begin with the issue of youth because young people embody the projected dreams, desires, and commitment of a society's obligations to the future."[23] However, he argues that youth are not currently being adequately taken care of: "As the twenty-first century unfolds, it is not clear at all that the American public and government believe any longer in youth, the future, or the social contract, even in its minimalist version" because neoliberalism has caused "institutions committed to public welfare, especially for young people," to disappear."[24] This may seem strange when put into dialogue with Edelman's assertion that the idealized child dominates political discourse. If this is the case, how then is investment in children decreasing? The answer to this may lie in the ideological schizophrenia in politicians who support neoliberal practices and the corresponding deinvestment in social welfare while simultaneously emphasizing long-term reproductive futurity and what's best for the idealized child. This discrepancy lessens the effectiveness of the idealized child. For example, the idealized child may be used when it is politically efficacious, but true investment in institutions that benefit children and adolescents may not be a priority. The cuts in social welfare and institutions benefiting children and adolescents, like head-start programs and all levels of education, continue because neoliberalism is an ideology that emphasizes short-term gain over long-term sustainability. This is a moment of ideological connection with Edelman's argument: both Edelman and neoliberalism emphasize the present over the future. The opposition to futurity from Edelman is related to resisting a structure that marginalizes and impinges upon the rights of certain groups. For neoliberalism, it is the emphasis on short-term spending and profits at the cost of long-term investments in social welfare. Of course, neoliberals believe market fundamentalism will result in long-term stability, but, when proven wrong, the call is not to change course, but to always insist on becoming *more* neoliberal. If initial cuts to social programs do not work, cut more social programs. If tax breaks for businesses are not achieving the desired results, cut their taxes further. This warped logic is famously summed up by Margaret Thatcher: "There is no alternative."[25] Even when neoliberalism emerged, both proponents and opponents "declared there was *no future*: just the eternal present."[26] Therefore, neoliberalism is, ironically enough, also a perpetual horizon: people are told that conditions will improve if given time, and that they must constantly look forward to these improved conditions, even as evidence suggests neoliberalism involves the dismantling of social institutions and services that many people rely on.[27]

The de-emphasis on futurity under neoliberalism is tied to the desire to increase profits and drive consumption ever higher, resources and future stability be damned. In summation, neoliberalism, the dominant economic theory of the Western world, is an ideology of the present bound up in arguments for individualism. It is also an ideology that worsens social conditions now and into the future. But utilizing the idealized child to argue for the future, without using it to impinge on the rights of others, may be beneficial for ameliorating resistance to reproductive futurity and improving resistance to the neoliberal status quo. For example, can a society ever make necessary reforms to combat climate change without thinking about future generations? This may mean the idealized child is necessary, but should be reconfigured so as to provide a way to think about the future without associating children primarily with politicians' present wants. For example, asking what children might need in terms of resources or protections to allow them to chart their own courses and construct their own legacy as they age seems a reasonable consideration.

Dawn of the Dead and *Daybreakers* place neoliberal capitalism in a post-apocalyptic environment. In doing so, they demonstrate the decline of societies or groups when the needs of children are not considered. They show the inability to realize sustainable alternatives when mired in short-term thinking. The critique of capitalism, or aspects of it, in post-apocalyptic narratives is common in such narratives. Berger writes, "Apocalyptic and post-apocalyptic representations serve varied psychological and political purposes. Most prevalently, they put forward a total critique of any existing social order."[28] This critique often involves capitalism, as "The economic logic of advanced capitalism has produced prosperity, but also the absurdity of colossal waste and environmental depletion, as well as the excesses of individual greed and narcissistic self-indulgence."[29] However, I argue that not only are these films critiquing the existing social order, but these critiques also foreground the issue of reproductive futurity. They do not argue that simply reproducing provides the ability to overcome the status quo. Rather, they argue that a future that fails to protect children contains no hope.

STALLED CHILDHOODS: ZOMBIES AND VAMPIRES

Some zombie films, like Zack Snyder's 2004 film, *Dawn of the Dead*, a remake of George Romero's 1978 classic, interrogate the loss of futurity in the face of rampant consumerism. The film follows a nurse, Ana, as she connects with others trying to survive a zombie apocalypse. Ana and a group of survivors bunker down in an abandoned shopping mall before attempting a breakout. They hope to gain access to a survivor's boat and use it to sail to an uninhabited island where they can live in peace. The film can also be classified as apocalyptic, as the viewer sees the catastrophic event which irrevocably alters the world. But the film is also post-apocalyptic in the sense that the survivors begin settling into their routine in the mall and learning how to live in a post-apocalyptic world, eventually coming up with a plan to try and save themselves by leaving the mall for an island. It is their decision, and subsequent attempt, to improve their situation which makes the film post-apocalyptic, which Claire Curtis defines as "any account which takes up how humans start over after the end of life on earth as we understand it.[30] Starting over in the face of catastrophe involves thinking about community, and considerations of community are one of the "essential elements of the *apocalyptic imagination*."[31] The reason that community becomes so important in relation to the apocalypse and its aftermath is because post-apocalyptic worlds emphasize the need to rely on others. These communities are not always successful, nor always altruistic. Many communities, however, beg considerations of reproductive futurity. Because no matter how large or inclusive a post-apocalyptic community is, it will never last without a means of sustaining ongoing growth, without eventually emphasizing reproductive futurity. Communities that seek to survive and prosper, but not grow, may consider futurity to some extent, but risk becoming reactionary.

Early in *Dawn of the Dead*, Ana leaves her shift at the hospital. As Ana drives up to her home she encounters a child, Vivian. They have a brief exchange where they determine their plans for baking cookies the next day, and Ana tells Vivian to be careful as Ana pulls into the driveway. It is an idyllic scene juxtaposed against the horrors to come: future horrors of which the audience are aware, but the characters are not. The next morning Ana and her husband Luis awake and find Vivian in the hallway to their bedroom. After first telling her to go home, they realize she may be injured. Luis goes to pick her up, but she bites him. Ana tosses Vivian into the hallway and locks the door, but it is too late for Luis. He quickly turns into a zombie and Ana is forced to flee her home, setting in motion a chain of events leading to the mall.

Like the rest of the zombie horde, Vivian's life is arrested. All a zombie can do, regardless of age or previous circumstance, is live in the present. They exist solely to consume and pass on their condition: a common reading of zombie narratives since the release of Romero's original *Dawn of the Dead*. Evan Calder Williams critiques this reading. Rather than questioning its accuracy, he instead notes, "To say that *Dawn of the Dead* (1978), with its hordes of blank-eyed shopping mall zombies, is a critique of consumerism is just to describe the surface texture of the film."[32] But in the remake, along with this critique, which the remake retains from the original, is also a critique of the short-sightedness of consumerism and how it relates to an emphasis on the present rather than the future, as demonstrated through considerations of children. Williams observes that the current form of capitalism is an ideology of the present: "The late capitalist present was necessarily staked on the capacity to realize and replicate itself by borrowing against the guaranteed promise of the future as the site of *more of the same* and of the endlessness of reproduction without difference."[33] Williams further suggests that zombie films are a metaphor for the effects of this ideology.

The zombies have no concept of futurity. There is no point when a zombie might think, "Maybe I ought to save some of this flesh for later." In *Dawn of the Dead*, the figure of Vivian is one that, like the vampire child, combines youth and death. When the viewer first sees Vivian in her zombie form, her youthful hair and skin are marred, like her nightgown, with blood and flesh.

Her teeth and gums are exposed, a fitting image for a monster hell-bent on consumption; this image highlights the danger of her teeth, as blood streams down her chest and onto her gown. This little girl, who yesterday was planning to bake cookies, is now a monster with no thought beyond her present, insatiable desire to consume others. Her desire to consume is taken to the

Figure 3.1. *Dawn of the Dead*, **2004, Universal Studios.**

extreme. Her previous desire to bake cookies was one where she would share time with someone else and engage in the creation of her food. Her new desire is one she attempts to partake in alone and comes at the expense of others. Rather than taking satisfaction in a process of creation, Vivian becomes an agent of destruction. As a self-obsessed consumer, she will contribute to the spread of her literal and metaphoric condition. For the characters in the film then, survival is predicated on the ongoing resistance to this condition, and the attempt to reestablish a community safe from the zombie infection. For Williams, the rejection of the zombies, and the capitalist apocalypse they embody, is paramount:

> We do not become post-apocalyptic because the plague swells, the bomb drops, or the earth cools. We become post-apocalyptic when we accept the present as rubbish, as undead, and as under attack. And when we refuse this acceptance, to articulate militant reason out of the obscene persistence of what refuses to die, and to make the apocalyptic not a temporal event but a spatial organization. To be post-apocalyptic is to make a given condition a decision and a commitment. [34]

It is not, then, simply the attempt to live and begin society anew, but to reject completely the way in which society is organized. The refusal to become zombies is not simply a rejection of the zombies, or the fear of the unknown, but also a rejection of the system which produces them. Of course, the remake of the film is not the same as the original. Williams notes that the "*one-to-one* transmission . . . combines the one-to-one logic of the slasher, the subject-turning bite of the vampire/werewolf film, and the fear of the thoughtless rabid masses (although these are now a good deal less concerned with sating hunger than with biting. . . .)."[35] In this way, the reproduction of ideology is obscured. Even films which critique capitalist practices obfuscate how these values are instilled by making it seem as if one can simply avoid, even if circumstances are difficult, infection. It recognizes a society which bombards its people with a consumerist ethos, then shifts the ultimate responsibility onto the individual.

This consumerist ethos is present from the beginning. Sarah and Kenneth, a police officer, initially encounter three other survivors, Andre, Luda, and Michael. Michael tells them that they originally numbered eight, then says, "We're going to the mall," as if no explanation is warranted. Of course, the mall will have supplies, but it's also a shrine to consumerism. The dead can be seen walking toward the mall too. Ana wonders why. Kenneth answers, "Memory, maybe. Instinct. Maybe they're coming for us." Maybe they are coming for them. Yet on the metaphoric level, the idea that they head to the mall in undeath because of memory or instinct is more terrifying. When the survivors first enter the mall, it is immaculately clean and eerily silent. Not eerie because zombies are lurking in its dark recesses, but because it is precisely what a mall is not: empty, every parking space available, with no lines or people to wait for or to brush up against. The quiet emptiness is oppressive. The survivors are able to grow their band by working with some of the people left in the mall and taking in some people trying to get into the mall for protection. There are moments when they all engage in the pleasures of consumerism by utilizing the objects around them. But their illusions of comfort are soon shattered when reproductive futurity meets undeath.

The difficulty in maintaining reproductive futurity in post-apocalyptic conditions such as these is most clearly depicted when the characters Andre and Luda have a baby. Before the baby is born, Andre tells Kenneth, "I feel like I'm here to bring that baby on this Earth. And give it everything I never had. I just want the opportunity to change things." Andre expresses a desire to redeem himself through the future, as exemplified by providing a better life for his child. However, this desire is complicated because Luda is bitten. Andre, knowing this bite will transform Luda, keeps her separate from the others and eventually chains Luda to a bed in a room away from the others, so that she can give birth to their child. A blackout occurs while Luda is delivering the child. Norma, another group member, goes to check on her. She enters a darkened room and sees Andre holding a swaddled child. The child itself is not visible. Luda growls. Norma looks toward her, sees she is a zombie, and then draws her weapon. Andre says, "You wanna kill Luda. You want to kill my family?" A shootout occurs. Norma, Andre, and Luda are all killed. The other survivors hear the gunshots and flock to the scene. Ana investigates the child. When she sees it is a zombie, she raises her gun. There's a close-up of the child's zombie-like, blood-filled eyes. It whimpers. The film cuts to an interior shot of an empty area in the mall, as the gunshot simultaneously takes place off-screen, so as to shield viewers from the death of a child. Even though the child is a zombie, viewers recognize its innocence in what has happened, even as they recognize the danger it represents. Andre and his family are killed not because the survivors do not care about family, but because there is no room in the world for the unstable Andre and his zombie family. The family is unnatural and dangerous because of their zombie status, and they lack the hope common in reproductive futurity. They, minus Andre, can never grow old, and it would be only a matter of time before Andre gets bitten. Andre, Luda, and their child exemplify a desire for a return to a traditional family structure, even as they blend disparate cultures: Andre is African American, Luda is Russian. But the apocalypse created a world wherein the traditional family structure is not feasible. Rather, one's best hope is in the larger community, sacrificing individual and familial desires for communal ones. Reproductive futurity in this scenario must be considered in relation to the community rather than the individual and/or family. Andre's family is not part of a larger community, but seeks to exist on their own terms, even as their proximity to the other survivors helps to protect them. They provide no hope for a better future or escape from the post-apocalyptic condition of stasis.

This moment leads the rest of the survivors to plan an improbable escape from the mall to an island, which they believe will offer protection from the zombies. And although the film ends on a bitter note, with the survivors finding an island already inhabited by zombies, at least these survivors made an attempt at finding a place to build a safer society. They made a decision regarding what would be best for their community and acted on it. Andre, Luda, and the zombie child have no future, just a series of moments existing sequentially—rarely, if ever, would they be able to think ahead to the moments beyond their immediate future. This is where the post-apocalypse intersects with reproductive futurity. The post-apocalypse is partly interested in the communities which form after cataclysmic events. Yet the dangers of these new worlds often make it difficult to think beyond one's immediate future. In this way post-apocalyptic narratives help their audiences consider the world in new ways, but, at the same time, they still struggle to imagine a world vastly different from that which they critique, at least ideologically.

Andre's family could never reproduce further or take part in a larger human community. Andre's decision denies him a future in place of a perpetual present. Had he lived undiscovered with his family, he would have kept them chained in a state of unending imprisonment or risked becoming a zombie himself, at which point the zombie family would only concern themselves with their daily, ravenous desire to consume: a trio of individual zombies tied to each other and other zombies only by their status as consu-mers, with no concern for the future.

Of course, zombies do not provide the only metaphor for a world which fails to emphasize reproductive futurity. Peter and Michael Spierig's 2009 film, *Daybreakers*, also interrogates the loss of futurity in the face of rampant consumerism. Reproductive futurity is threatened as adult vampires consume resources at a dangerous rate and children are denied the possibility of inher-iting a world where they can stake their own claim. In the film, vampires have driven humans to the point of extinction. Blood, the only resource the vampires require, is running dangerously low. Vampires who lack access to human blood become "subsiders," vampires who feed on themselves and other vampires, live in the sewers, and seek only to satisfy their all-consum-ing desire for blood. Because of the lack of new sources of blood and the spread of the subsiders, those in power, led by the vampire Charles Bromley, attempt to create a synthetic alternative; this results in spectacular failure. It is against this post-apocalyptic backdrop that humans, with the help of the vampire Edward Dalton, fight against the vampires and find a cure for vam-pirism.

Characters in post-apocalyptic narratives are often less concerned with futurity and more concerned about the immediate present because they must find a way to survive immediate danger. The intense pressure in post-apoca-lyptic situations to survive sometimes means characters are unable to consid-er how to establish lasting communities which hold the potential for sustain-able growth and development. *Daybreakers* provides an obvious, though important, metaphor for overconsumption, as the vampires have hunted and transformed humans to the point of extinction and now lack blood and are unable to create a sustainable alternative. Overconsumption is necessarily short-term, as it involves the depletion of resources for the sake of the present and thus often connotes a lack of thinking about the future. Yet, the film also demonstrates the effects on children and thus provides a metaphor for the way societies concerned solely with the present sacrifice their youth.

It is a minor character in this film that provides the most interesting insight into the lack of reproductive futurity. The film opens with an image of the early morning sun, interrupted by a bat flying across the screen, and then immediately cuts to a female child. She is writing a letter while sitting in front of a collage of pictures: pictures of her alone and with other children. A calendar gives us the year: 2019. She finishes the letter, places it on her bed, and then steps outside, just before dawn breaks. She sits quietly, expectantly, in her yard; and, as the sun is about to crest a hill, she looks up, giving viewers the first glimpse of her yellow, feral eyes. The film cuts to the letter on the bed, and there are snippets of what she wrote, interspersed with images of the rising sun and its spreading light. The letter reads: "never change," "never grow up!" "can't go on." The child's mouth is slightly open, which gives the viewer a hint of her fangs. As the sun rises fully over the hill, we hear a sizzling and the girl begins screaming. The child is engulfed in flames, one hand raised as if to ward off the sun, as her skin quickly burns away and turns to dust.

In the moment before her body turns to dust, she looks like a child corpse. The youthful flesh becomes burned and desiccated tissue. Her arm breaks and falls, the film segues to the title screen. The film never again shows or discusses the child vampire.

What, then, is one to make of this opening scene? Of a vampire child who conjures up images of Claudia, from *Interview with the Vampire*, but is given much less narrative space? This unnamed vampire child leaves the viewers quickly, with a letter ostensibly meant for someone else, although viewers never see who might read it. This character may function as an idealized, symbolic child: a child who never grows old. Real children grow old, but symbolic ones do not. The vampire child rejects this imposed imprisonment, this unending childhood, and kills herself because she can "never change" or "grow up." This child, in the context of the film, is lashing out at her reality. She cannot grow out of her status as a child. This unaging vampire child can be understood as a critique of those who reject reproductive futurity and are unwilling to consider it within political discourse. She is rejecting the perpetual childhood which Edelman rejects, but she also has no future. She faces a series of days much like the other, where she remains in stasis—an unaging child in a society dominated by unaging adults. She is a child denied a future different from that which already is; she has no apparent possibility of change or growth. To some degree, this is emblematic of what every survivor faces in the post-apocalyptic landscape. For many, it's a monotonous day-to-day survival, filled with the same caution and fears, until they die. But this

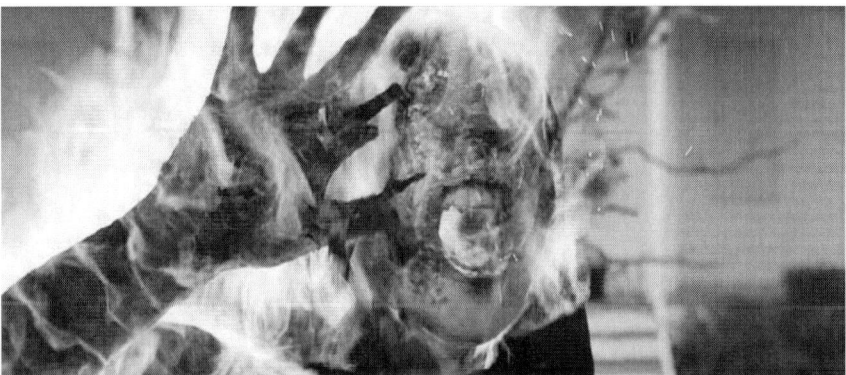

Figure 3.2. *Daybreakers*, 2009, Lionsgate.

child is not a human, she's a vampire. The vampires not only hunt the humans, but they have come to take over their society. They run corporations. They commute to work. They order coffees with blood. They are homeowners. In the film, post-apocalypse is a matter of perspective. For humans, the world is post-apocalyptic. For vampires, it is not. The child's rejection of her perpetual state is a rejection of the society which created her, a society engaged in short-term thinking that fails to consider her long-term needs or desires. Perhaps her vampire creator thought they were doing her a favor, offering her a future as a vampire. But the child's future was a mirage. It only offered more of the same. She tired of it. The vampire society is one wherein reproductive futurity, and childhood, is not considered. Rather, vampirism is passed on or not. Child vampires exist or they do not. Once the child vampire exists, no adults bother to consider if its need or desires may be different from their own.

The unchanging nature of the vampires is what fuels their decline. When the film begins, there are few humans remaining to support the vampires. The vampires rush for a scientific solution to their problems, but they are running out of time. Had the vampires monitored their expansion, they would not have this problem, or, at least, they would have more time to try and solve it. The alluring, immortal aspect of the vampire is one without a future. The unchanging nature of the vampire underscores a neoliberal society's inability to adapt or plan ahead. The vampire adults deny futurity for a constant present, where they can continue to consume limited resources with little thought given to sustainability. In the case of upper-class vampires like Charles Bromley, massive profits are reaped selling these resources.

Because of the vampire leaders' focus on their present circumstances, and their inability to institute long-term solutions, the vampire child takes on a new resonance. It is reasonable to assume that the vampires in power had the responsibility to ration and plan for scenarios such as this. This type of planning is necessary as a matter of survival, if not because of any moral or altruistic motivations. But the vampires have not made these plans. Instead those in charge continue to consume and profit, with the assumption being that if conditions worsen, they, at least, can survive, since they have access to what limited resources remain. Those weaker than them, those who are part of vampire society but lack a voice, like the vampire child, have no means to fend for themselves. The vampire child can be understood as a rejection of the idealized child. She refuses to be a perpetual horizon; instead she is a perpetual child who meets her horizon. She is an unaging child who dies. She also represents frustration over the inability of those in power to consider children's needs. She is an argument for an emphasis on futurity. She is not just critiquing the perpetual child. She is also a critique of ideologies of the present: ideologies that ignore the future or do not allow for consideration of a future much different from the present.

None of this is to say that emphasizing reproductive futurity, whether on behalf of an idealized child or not, is incapable of doing damage to children or of being misused. It is not to say that the vampire girl's problems would automatically be solved by rationing blood and the spread of vampirism more effectively, rather, the vampire child is a girl with no place in the world. She is left abandoned, metaphorically if not literally; the film does not show anyone else in the big home the child resides in. Presumably she is not alone, since she leaves the note, but the viewers see no one else. Instead she pines for her former friends. What, if any, were the considerations when she was made into a vampire? How could she be given a voice in a society that refuses to consider her needs? The answers to these questions are unknowable in the context of the film, but they beg consideration in relation to contemporary society. And this is a film about contemporary society: about resources and their exploitation, about the unsustainable path society has found itself on in relation to the overconsumption of natural resources, about society being made up of metaphoric vampires who consume resources at an unsustainable rate and restrict access to resources based on money and power. This sort of short-term thinking is a recipe for disaster, and it narrows the options of future generations. It may seem reasonable to choose not to consider children when they impinge on adult needs and desires, but what, if anything, is the cost of taking children, even idealized ones, out of the conversation?

The vampire child's rejection is reinforced later in the film. Charles Bromley hunts for his human daughter, Alison, so he might turn her into a vampire. He finds her and has her infected. But she refuses to drink any blood but her own, and attacks her father when he tries convincing her to do otherwise. She becomes a subsider who, along with many others, is chained and placed in the sun to burn. Her refusal to partake in the expected behavior of vampires is a rejection of the corporate and consumerist ideologies her father embodies. Her murder is required by a society that cannot satisfy everyone's desires. Charles's complete misunderstanding of how his daughter will behave as a vampire highlights his tone-deafness toward her desires: to live as she likes, without infection.

The post-apocalyptic nature of this film clearly provides a metaphor for contemporary society. It warns of the dangers of a consumerist ethos under neoliberal capitalism. Under the logic of the film, westerners have become vampires who have left little opportunity for growth to future generations outside of this ravenous ideology. The one-to-one infection and transformation of vampirism obscures the structural dominance of capitalism, across all aspects of society. The humans, living in post-apocalyptic conditions, are fighting for a future. Lionel, nicknamed Elvis, was a vampire who became human again. He was exposed to sunlight and almost burned to death but was immersed in water just before he was incinerated. This baptism by (sun)fire

cured him. He and others now struggle to find a way to create a less dangerous means of delivering the cure. They recruit Edward, a vampire hematolo-
gist who was infected against his will, to help them. Edward asks Elvis what
he wants. Elvis responds: "Same thing you do, a future." For Elvis, this
means a world where humans can expand and thrive. This quote epitomizes
the reasons for many of the communities of survivors which form after
apocalyptic events. Like the survivors in *Dawn of the Dead*, they seek to
create a community and/or environment wherein they can protect each other
and thrive.

In *Daybreakers*, the community of resistance fighters is comprised of
both humans and vampires, but it becomes perilously close to complete
destruction. Everyone is killed except Edward, Elvis, and Audrey (who is the
initial contact between Edward and Lionel). They come up with a way to
cure Edward of vampirism. Furthermore, they find out that vampires who
attempt to feed on a human who has been cured are themselves cured. At one
point, Elvis says, "Vampires think they own this world. . . . That ain't true.
Every day, the sun comes out, and every day, the vamps have to hide. Vampires can never survive." He's right. The vampire community could not
survive even if a cure was not discovered. It's rooted in the type of short-
sighted thinking that makes it difficult to address long-term problems. An
emphasis on reproductive futurity may be necessary, though not enough on
its own, to combat such thinking. This emphasis may not be feasible in a
society of vampires, but it is certainly feasible in the society on which *Daybreakers* is based.

The film ends on a hopeful tone. Edward, Elvis, and Audrey survive an
encounter with Bromley at his company headquarters and ride off into the
sunrise. This is an ironic twist on riding off into the sunset because the
humans are safer, of course, during the day. As they ride off, Edward's voice
narrates: "We have a cure. We can change you back. It's not too late." This
seems to be a hopeful ending as they escape and carry the cure within Edward and Elvis. Yet in the final moments, the camera pans up into the sky,
and, with a shriek, a bat flies across the screen. This shot is reminiscent of the
sunrise and bat which began the film. The shrieking bat and the connection to
the beginning, when vampires still dominated, undercuts the hopeful ending.
This may be because the promise of a cure, "We can change you back," may
mean a return to a human society; but it does not necessarily mean a change
in the structures of said society. After all, the vampires may have massacred
the humans, but they didn't fundamentally change the capitalist society
which the humans founded; they simply took it over. The film imagines a
future wherein the post-apocalyptic tension can be resolved, where vampires
can be transformed back into humans. But it does not imagine a world wherein society can be transformed through the post-apocalypse, instead of settling
for the possibility of the return of humans, without the promise of a corre-

sponding shift in organizational structures. In this way, any critique of the status quo lacks bite, as it does in *Dawn of the Dead*. It remains to be seen whether the vampire child incinerated in the first scene would find a world in which she was offered a true alternative or not.

CONCLUSION: REPRODUCTIVE FUTURITY CONSIDERED

While *Dawn of the Dead* and *Daybreakers* deny their children a future under metaphorical conditions which highlight how societies dominated by short-term ideologies fail to provide the space necessary for considerations of a lasting future, the United States is not quite there yet. But this is precisely why reproductive futurity must not be rejected or forgotten, as Edelman does. While there is room for reorientation in the discussion regarding childhood and what society owes to future generations, rejecting such discussions simply reinforces the short-sighted nature of societies based on consumption and immediate satisfaction. One can reject the politics and images associated with children and childhood that he or she finds damaging or marginalizing in favor of more positive ones, but rejecting images of reproductive futurity outright is problematic.

Children, or images of children, may be especially important today in helping people think about the world they want to leave to subsequent generations. Peter Pufall and Richard Unsworth observe, "The human race continues to set great store by its children's potential, counting on them to restore a measure of the justice and civility that has been eroded from society by their parents' generation."[36] Children provide a powerful symbol for thinking about societal progress. Thinking about children, particularly in the post-apocalyptic setting, may help adults undo some of the deleterious societal effects they have contributed to or caused. John Gillis notes that "childhood has become modern society's myth of both origin and destiny, our explanation of who we are and what we will become."[37]

Dawn of the Dead and *Daybreakers* focus on the children as emblematic only of the present. They cease to be a horizon. Children are stuck in a perpetual state of youth, as either zombies or vampires, and thus undermine the notion of constant societal progress. Children who cannot age are metaphorical representations of contemporary societies that stagnate and become incapable of making long-term decisions. These films complicate Edelman's critique of reproductive futurity by imagining worlds where children cease to function as symbols of the future and, in the process, foreground the disintegration of society.

NOTES

1. Roslyn Weaver, *Apocalypse in Australian Fiction and Film: A Critical Study* (Jefferson, NC: McFarland & Company, Inc., 2011), 8.

2. James Berger, *After the End: Representations of the Post-Apocalypse* (Minneapolis, MN: University of Minnesota Press, 1999), 6.

3. David Ketterer, *New Worlds for Old: The Apocalyptic Imagination, Science Fiction, and American Literature* (Bloomington, IN: Indiana UP, 1974), 13.

4. M. Keith Booker, *Alternate Americas: Science Fiction Film and American Culture* (Westport, CT: Praeger, 2006), 266.

5. Weaver, *Apocalypse in Australian Fiction and Film*, 6.

6. Evan Calder Williams, *Combined and Uneven Apocalypse* (Washington, DC: Zero Books, 2011), 80.

7. Berger, *After the End: Representations of the Post-Apocalypse*, 8.

8. Zack Snyder, *Dawn of the Dead* (Universal Studios, 2004).

9. Michael Spierig and Peter Spierig, *Daybreakers* (Lionsgate, 2009).

10. Lee Edelman, "The Future Is Kid Stuff," in *No Future: Queer Theory and the Death Drive* (Durham, NC: Duke UP, 2004), 3.

11. Ibid., 21.

12. Ibid., 19.

13. Martin Woodhead, "Psychology and the Cultural Construction of Children's Needs," in *Constructing and Reconstructing Childhood*, ed. Allison James and Alan Prout (New York: Routledge Falmer, 2004), 74–75.

14. Ibid., 76.

15. Edelman, "The Future Is Kid Stuff," 11.

16. José Esteban Muñoz, "Thinking Beyond Antirationality and Antiutopianism in Queer Critique," *PMLA* 121, no. 3 (May 2006): 825.

17. J. Halberstam, "The Anti-Social Turn in Queer Studies," *Graduate Journal of Social Science* 5, no. 2 (2008): 154.

18. Mari Ruti, "Why There Is Always a Future in the Future," *Angelaki* 13, no. 1 (April 2008): 124.

19. Edelman, "The Future Is Kid Stuff," 18.

20. Ibid., 29.

21. Milton Friedman, *Capitalism and Freedom* (Chicago: University of Chicago Press, 1962), 74.

22. David Harvey, *A Brief History of Neoliberalism* (New York: Oxford UP, 2005), 2.

23. Henry Giroux, *Disposable Youth, Racialized Memories, and the Culture of Cruelty* (New York: Routledge, 2012), xiii.

24. Ibid., xiii–xiv.

25. Mark Blyth, *Austerity: The History of a Dangerous Idea* (New York: Oxford UP, 2013), 98.

26. Williams, *Combined and Uneven Apocalypse*, 4.

27. Blyth, *Austerity*, xi; Harvey, *A Brief History of Neoliberalism*, 2–3.

28. Berger, *After the End: Representations of the Post-Apocalypse*, 7.

29. James Combs, "Pox-Eclipse Now: The Dystopian Imagination in Contemporary Popular Movies," in *Crisis Cinema: The Apocalyptic Idea in Postmodern Narrative Film*, ed. Christopher Sharrett (Washington, DC: Maisonneuve Press, 1993), 19.

30. Claire P. Curtis, *Postapocalyptic Fiction and the Social Contract* (New York: Lexington Books, 2010), 5.

31. Jerome F. Shapiro, *Atomic Bomb Cinema: The Apocalyptic Imagination on Film* (New York: Routledge, 2002), 17.

32. Williams, *Combined and Uneven Apocalypse*, 78.

33. Ibid., 2.

34. Ibid., 9.

35. Ibid., 141–42.

36. Peter B. Pufall and Richard P. Unsworth, "Introduction," in *Rethinking Childhood*, ed. Peter B. Pufall and Richard P. Unsworth (New Brunswick, NJ: Rutgers UP, 2004), 2.

37. John Gillis, "Transitions to Modernity," in *The Palgrave Handbook of Childhood Studies*, ed. Jens Qvortrup, William A. Corsaro, and Michael-Sebastian Honig (New York: Palgrave Macmillan, 2009), 122.

BIBLIOGRAPHY

Berger, James. *After the End: Representations of the Post-Apocalypse*. Minneapolis, MN: University of Minnesota Press, 1999.

Blyth, Mark. *Austerity: The History of a Dangerous Idea*. New York: Oxford UP, 2013.

Booker, M. Keith. *Alternate Americas: Science Fiction Film and American Culture*. Westport, CT: Praeger, 2006.

Combs, James. "Pox-Eclipse Now: The Dystopian Imagination in Contemporary Popular Movies." In *Crisis Cinema: The Apocalyptic Idea in Postmodern Narrative Film*, edited by Christopher Sharrett, 17–35. Washington, DC: Maisonneuve Press, 1993.

Curtis, Claire P. *Postapocalyptic Fiction and the Social Contract*. New York: Lexington Books, 2010.

Edelman, Lee. "The Future Is Kid Stuff." In *No Future: Queer Theory and the Death Drive*, 1–31. Durham, NC: Duke UP, 2004.

Friedman, Milton. *Capitalism and Freedom*. Chicago: University of Chicago Press, 1962.

Gillis, John. "Transitions to Modernity." In *The Palgrave Handbook of Childhood Studies*, edited by Jens Qvortrup, William A. Corsaro, and Michael-Sebastian Honig, 114–26. New York: Palgrave Macmillan, 2009.

Giroux, Henry. *Disposable Youth, Racialized Memories, and the Culture of Cruelty*. New York: Routledge, 2012.

Halberstam, J. "The Anti-Social Turn in Queer Studies." *Graduate Journal of Social Science* 5, no. 2 (2008): 140–56.

Harvey, David. *A Brief History of Neoliberalism*. New York: Oxford UP, 2005.

Ketterer, David. *New Worlds for Old: The Apocalyptic Imagination, Science Fiction, and American Literature*. Bloomington, IN: Indiana UP, 1974.

Muñoz, José Esteban. "Thinking Beyond Antirationality and Antiutopianism in Queer Critique." *PMLA* 121, no. 3 (May 2006): 825–26.

Pufall, Peter B., and Richard P. Unsworth. "Introduction." In *Rethinking Childhood*, edited by Peter B. Pufall and Richard P. Unsworth, 1–21. New Brunswick, NJ: Rutgers UP, 2004.

Ruti, Mari. "Why There Is Always a Future in the Future." *Angelaki* 13, no. 1 (April 2008): 113–26.

Shapiro, Jerome F. *Atomic Bomb Cinema: The Apocalyptic Imagination on Film*. New York: Routledge, 2002.

Snyder, Zack. *Dawn of the Dead*. Universal Studios, 2004.

Spierig, Michael, and Peter Spierig. *Daybreakers*. Lionsgate, 2009.

Weaver, Roslyn. *Apocalypse in Australian Fiction and Film: A Critical Study*. Jefferson, NC: McFarland & Company, Inc., 2011.

Williams, Evan Calder. *Combined and Uneven Apocalypse*. Washington, DC: Zero Books, 2011.

Woodhead, Martin. "Psychology and the Cultural Construction of Children's Needs." In *Constructing and Reconstructing Childhood*, edited by Allison James and Alan Prout, 63–84. New York: Routledge Falmer, 2004.

Chapter Four

The Child Is My Warrant

Virtue, Violence, and The Road's *Radical Humanism*

Joseph Wiinikka-Lydon

> *Sometimes I tell the boy old stories of courage and justice, difficult as they are to remember. All I know is the child is my warrant. And if he is not the word of God, then God never spoke.* [1]

INTRODUCTION

The post-apocalyptic film, *The Road* (Hillcoat 2009), focuses on the trials of a father and a son navigating the aftermath of a civilizational and ecological catastrophe. What the exact nature of the disaster is, the reader does not know, only that it was total. Everything is dead and dying. The sun hides in a sky of gauze that blocks out light and nutrient. Nights are lathered in pitch. Trees move only to release their grip on the earth and fall. What remains is a remnant: human beings living off the dwindling remains of a spent world. In one scene, the father and son—the *Man* and the *Boy* as the author of the book, Cormac McCarthy, on which the film is based, calls them—awake to see a wall of fire coming toward them, the dead plant matter kindling for the firestorms that rage across the miles. They must rise and run in the dead of night, fleeing from the world's death. As the father and son march south in search of safety, the world has turned to ash and, like the clothes on their backs and the improvised shoes on their feet, is falling apart around them. The viewer is left wondering if survival is possible at all when nature itself has ceased.

Physical survival, however, is not the central theme of this film. Even with its emphasis on the father's daily struggle to keep him and his son from starving to death, the anxiety and conflict at the heart of the film, as well as

61

the novel, is not merely existential. Instead, *The Road* is a dramatic meditation on the fragility of human goodness. It is a deeply moral piece that, through the extreme, fantastical nature of the post-apocalyptic subgenre, brings out this fragility in stark terms. Indeed, it helps us see how critical the moral life is to culture, even as culture is at its end. Specifically, we can see *The Road* asking, what happens when everything you know or have is taken from you? What happens to the moral life, indeed, to one's ability to continue living according to one's moral ideals that, although different, each human being carries?

Both the movie and the novel depart from one another in significant ways, but one important answer to these questions remains at the center of both. Even at the end of everything, the challenges of a moral life still survive. It seems that moral dilemma, dissonance, struggle, and conflict remain as long as human beings remain. And this insight is embodied in the intersubjectivity of the characters, that is, in the relationship between the boy and the man. Their relationship chronicled in the film illustrates the tension between survival, on the one hand, and moral ideals, on the other. With one's survival, and the survival of his or her loved ones as one's main objective, the film and the book probe what a person is willing to sacrifice in order to survive. In other words, the moral life's ends remain imperative even at the end of the world.

It is this tension, and the way the film investigates it, that I will explore in this chapter. I argue that the film demonstrates through its stark topography the tensions that occur between moral ideals and survival when individuals are placed in high stakes, violent situations. Indeed, it helps us explore how the need for survival can displace the need not only to try to lead a moral life, but the very ability to do so. Specifically, I will explore the insights into the moral life that *The Road* affords us. I will focus on the relationship between the man and the boy, what their discussions reveal and the situations they find themselves in, as well as the decisions they must make. Throughout, one can see that the boy, while not having been born in the old world, continually responds to events with an ethic of care, urging compassion on his father. The man, on the other hand, turns his energies toward the seemingly impossible task of keeping his son alive in a world that, from what the film shows, is no longer able to support life. There is little room for compassion in his eyes. Compassion, care, fellow-feeling—these open one to danger and betrayal, in a land where every human has become a desperate animal that sees everything, and everyone, else as a means to the end of their own survival. In this way, it is a radically un-Kantian landscape with a nod to the Hobbesian state of nature, minus the nature. Together, the man and boy, the father and son, at the end of the world, illustrate the tension inherent in the moral life, one that *The Road* shows is so central to being human, that it may survive even when the world is at an end.

THE ROAD'S RADICAL HUMANISM

The film presents the world in the final stages of nature, that is, death. The world has died, and its death is pallid. It is colorless, and the only light that permeates the Earth's shroud is itself tainted by the reigning lifelessness. Ash, grey, and more ash still. When one reads the book, the number of references to ash and grey—more, possibly, than any other work of literature—assaults the imagination in the negative. The film illustrates this grammar, devoid of life, in similar hues, though perhaps the assault of McCarthy's text on one's imagination, its sparing style and fractured organization—the relationship between despairing words and its effect on the reader's mind—can never quite be captured by image. Here, the world is so effectively a negative of the one we live in today that even the old adage, of the worth of images versus the value of words, is turned on its head, and the page renders what even a thousand images could not.

What the film does is to present nature as nonexistent, and the globe itself as a corpse. The only real color presented in the film is in the realm of memory, in the flashbacks that dissolve into the monochrome of the narrative's present. The viewer may feel she is on the brink of experiencing non-being, or at least, coming as close to it as one can. Upon it, humanity, almost gone, clings like bacteria clinging to a corpse, eating what is left, until even the bacteria must expire. Such a simile is graphic, maudlin, but not inaccurate. Except for its death throws—the occasional earthquake, the falling tree—nature is no longer agentive. The viewer is presented with a vision that so many science fiction authors, as well as transhumanists, have dreamed of: a humanity no longer tied to nature, its sufferings and vicissitudes. This freedom, however, is laid bare for the poverty that it is, a revenant humanity for whom the future is no longer the stuff of fantasy and dreams, but of despair and horror.

As I begin to explore *The Road*'s ethic, one can begin by seeing its radical humanism. The only agents left in the world are a few desperate humans, and perhaps the stray dog or animal attached to them, searching for some patch of life-sustaining geography. The natural world, quickly dissolving back into its carbon base, is nearly gone. Food only exists in the cans in which it was sealed before the cataclysm, as well as the few seeds scattered here and there, unable to take root. Being all there is left, the human, to strain Protagoras's original meaning toward the ironic, is now the measure of all things.

The Road, then, is a humanistic text in a profound and profoundly ironic way. It deals squarely with human concerns and lives. Nature and the world have melted away, so that not even color exists. Speaking to his wife in a flashback scene, the Man says, "It's life. It's the only thing left," referring particularly to human life. The world is a background, and poses dangers, but not in the same way as before. No animals can decide to attack. No viruses, it seems, make their way into our bodies. If a falling tree presents a danger, it is not because the tree falls, but because it is fallen. The passive is the only fitting grammatical mood in which to talk about the natural world, and its constituents are now limited to dry reeds, dead trees, burning carbon, and bones. Perhaps one could see in the firestorms and earthquakes some agency, but they strike me more as death throws than agents, one of a series of crises with which the man and boy, and the other remaining humans, must contend. *The Road*'s humanism is ironic, because it shows what a singular emphasis on humanity looks like. The lack of intersubjectivity, if I can extend that term beyond human individuals, between the human and the rest of life, renders the human subject nearly hopeless, and quite desperate, and without the requirements of existence.

The terms of good and bad, of morality itself, are also radicalized. Although one may consider humanity the creator and bearer of ethical horizons, different cultures have had different notions of moral community. These can include gods, rocks, animals, and the wider world.[2] Our relationality with the rest of existence has always been fluid, or at least, alive with fluid possibilities. Yet here, such possibilities are gone. What can humans do, good or bad, to a biology and botany that no longer exist? Goodness now refers only to activities done to another human, and evil follows this paradigm, as well. The worst moral offense, at least for the man and boy, is not killing another, though the boy seems to take killing for almost any reason as a horrible act. The main standard by which one judges their goodness is cannibalism. The father at the very beginning of the film states, "cannibalism is the great fear." But the viewer can see as the movie progresses that this is also a key standard on which goodness is defined.

For example, in one scene, the man and boy find a house, and after searching it, find a cellar full of naked, starving humans. It is obvious that they are food for others, a group that soon returns to the house. After the man and boy escape, the boy questions his father, revealing his moral anxiety.

> BOY: Papa? Papa, we wouldn't ever eat anybody would we?
> MAN: No. Of course not.
> BOY: No matter how hungry we were. Even if we were starving?
> MAN: We're starving now.
> BOY: Because, because we're the good guys?
> MAN: Yes.
> BOY: And we're carrying the fire.[3]

One could see in this anxiety, and in the cannibalism, a violation of Kantian ethics, where the individual, whom Kant refers to as an end in itself, is made totally to be a means to someone else's ends. Yet, the anxiety over cannibalism goes deeper than this. Here, a central moral anxiety the man and boy face, which reflects the radical humanism of *The Road*, is based in the fact that the human being is the only thing left to carry any value at all. As the world withers, human flesh becomes the only source of food, yet the individual also becomes the only moral agent, the only one for whom moral goodness is applicable or who can embody such goodness. They become both food (means) and the reason food is needed (end). Morality, itself, begins to contract until it only occurs within humanity, even as the entire food chain becomes the size and shape of a malnourished, human body. There seems nothing good or defensible about imbibing another's flesh in a world where the pain inflicted will most likely not fend off one's own imminent demise. Indeed, it has become the supreme transgression.

FLOURISHING, SURVIVAL, AND VIRTUE

As the quote that begins this chapter indicates, issues of virtue—courage, justice—run through the film. The father's mission is to keep the boy safe. His worries focus on survival. "Mostly," he says, "I am worried about food, always food. Food and the cold. And our shoes." When they come across an old man—who, the father says, reeked even by the standards of the filthy new world they now inhabit—the boy's father wants to leave him. When a man toward the end steals their food and equipment, the man tracks him down and makes him strip naked and leave all of his clothes. That is a death sentence in a place where "each day is grayer than the one before," and where it is "cold, getting colder." One can see the father's rationale here. The man was a threat; he revealed this in his theft. He could have killed the boy, who lay sleeping as the thief stole their goods strewn all about the boy. This fear must have struck the man hard, and the justice he meets out is one of survival. "I'm going to leave you the way you left us."

Here are issues of virtue, issues of justice, but in a way that refutes the virtue theory and morality that has reigned through a great deal of Western thought. The Aristotelian tradition, for example, views the goal of one's life, one's telos, as flourishing, as the term Aristotle uses, eudaimonia, is often translated.[4] One's life is structurally similar to that of a tree. An acorn has the inherent potential to be a tree, a realization that may or may not occur due to the vicissitudes of life. These vicissitudes, or moral luck (which modern philosophers have further theorized upon) is an inherent part of the moral life, making one's telos not a forgone conclusion. We are meant for flourishing, but the world is too unpredictable, too tragic, to affirm that everyone will flourish. Indeed, if one looks at Aristotle's discussion, she can see that only a small percentage of a political community can have the combination of birth, moral education, friendship, and material resources needed.

What one sees in Aristotle and neo-Aristotelian framings is a coupling of virtue and flourishing, where virtue is required for flourishing, and where flourishing guides the development of virtue.[5] As Alasdair MacIntyre has argued, such a vision requires practices, mentors, a community of support, a tradition with key narratives that embodies a moral vision and in which one can make sense of their life. Even institutions are required, in which virtues can be formed.[6] The world of *The Road*, however, has none of these things. The community that could lend support to maintaining virtues is gone. The practices that build and sustain key virtues individuals can no longer practice, as the material and communal resources needed have become, quite literally, ash.[7]

What has replaced these practices are the practices of survival that the man engages in everyday. Again, as he says, "mostly I am worried about food, always food. Food and the cold. And our shoes." Flourishing is simply not possible in such a world. Even survival may not be possible, and seems improbable, as the film gives the viewer no indication of a safe haven appearing at the end of the movie. Indeed, in the final scene, the boy joins another family after his father dies, and so the film ends not with hope of survival, but a hopeful relief that the boy may not die alone.

Indeed, the virtues the man exhibits are ones born of the need for survival, not flourishing in Aristotle's sense. The virtues he embodies—anger, fear, retributive justice, vigilance—are similar to what feminist philosopher Lisa Tessman calls burdened virtues.[8] Such virtues are decoupled from one's own flourishing and, instead, help drive one to work for social justice. Burdened virtues can be necessary to help alleviate suffering, yet they can also be toxic to the agent. In the case of the man, he is not so much aiming at social justice as the survival of his son, even if the acts he takes toward that goal—theft, murder, lying—betray the moral horizon of his former world.

THE MORAL EDUCATION OF THE BOY

Given the father's desperation at keeping the boy alive, and the seeming lack of support for a moral education, the boy strikes the viewer as an enigma. As Michael Chabon writes in his review of the book, *The Road*, the child's "innocence is literally singular" among the remnants of humanity.[9] And yet, Chabon's comment is not fully correct. It is not his innocence that is singular. Although he may act seemingly out of innocence, both movie and book— each written by Cormac McCarthy—communicate that the boy has witnessed horrors and continues to do so. At the beginning of the film, the man and boy enter a barn to find bodies hung from the rafters—suicides. The boy asks what "committed suicide" means, and the man answers tersely, almost scoldingly, "you know what that means." And later, when the father removes a blanket from a corpse, and his son stares at it, the father tells him, "It's nothing you haven't seen before." In such a world, innocence is the first victim. The father is invoking the child's knowledge, which includes an understanding of life that is too hard or horrific to live in.

At times, the father even seems to forget this; it is that the boy reminds him. It is almost as if they are engaged in a game, one trying to pretend that the boy is still a boy, until the other breaks in and affirms the loss of innocence. Later in the film, when the father tells the boy to look away from corpses, the boy reminds him, he has already seen such things. Such scenes now fill the public sphere in a way that activity and agency once had.

The boy, however, remains young, and does break down at times, even to the point of refusing his father's authority. The reason, however, is often due not to the horror of a scene, but instead, to the moral horror they, themselves, are committing, or that others have committed, that bother him. While the father wanted to leave the seaside thief naked and for dead, the child sits on the ground. The father sees the thief as a threat, even as hateful, as the theft would have killed the boy and the man. The man's son, however, sees it differently. Where the man saw a threat, the boy saw shared desperation. After leaving the thief to die, the boy sits on the side of *The Road*. The man tells him to stop crying, but the boy refuses.

BOY: Oh, papa.
MAN: Stop it!
BOY: I can't stop it.
MAN: What do you think would have happened to him if we hadn't caught him? You've got to learn.
BOY: I don't want to learn! [10]

He pleads with his father, "Just help him, papa, just help him," and they eventually leave him some food and his old clothes. Earlier in the film, the boy responds the same way to the old man, whom the father wanted to pass by. The boy convinces his father to give the old man food, and eventually, dinner.

How, then, did the boy develop such compassion and a way of perceiving dangerous situations with less fear than his father? How did he gain such empathy without the necessary supports that the Aristotelian tradition, at least, argues for? There is little in the movie to tell us this. The boy embodies moral ideals that seem to be in contradiction to those virtues needed to survive. Compassion, as the father reminds him, can get him killed. There is one scene, early on, where the father reads to him from a children's book from the lost world, and gestures toward an education of stories and exemplars that the boy seems to have received. The boy also grew up, at least initially, in a home with father and mother, and perhaps there, too, he could have received a sentimental education.

The boy also does not have a past with which to compare the present. The father dreams of his dead wife. He visits his old home and seems to be haunted by, and wanting to haunt, the remnants of the old world. The boy, on the other hand, seems anxious about such diversions. He tries to convince his father not to enter houses. They seem dangerous places to him, places that attract humans, which represent danger. And he is sometimes right, as they barely escape one house with a basement filled of naked, starving people apparently being stored for future food use. Although to call that world normal to the boy seems not quite right, he probably did not experience a traumatic rupture between worlds as his father and as so many others did. Although the boy was told stories of the old world, he is a child of the new, dying one.

The viewer, however, is left to wonder how such compassion could survive when almost everything else has died. Although this is left an open question, what we can witness is a growing dissonance for the boy as the movie, as well as the book, progress. He starts to question the tales of his father, and notices that his father is not always honest. Even the father says cryptically in a voice over, "Every day is a lie." When his father does not want to help the old man they meet, the boy questions his decision, based on what his father had taught him. "You always say watch out for bad. But the old man wasn't a bad guy. And you can't even tell anymore." He sees the contradiction between what his father's stories teach and his father's actions, between being good and surviving, and the extreme case that the world presents. The boy does not lose his compassion, however. He seems unable to lose empathy, convincing his father to leave the thief his clothes, to give the old, dying man a meal. And at the very end, after his father has died, the boy chooses to trust a stranger offering him a family, rather than shoot him or scare him off, as his father most probably would have done.

THE CHILD SHALL LEAD THEM: AN ETHICS OF *THE ROAD*

The child, and children, represent the only hope that is left in the world. Even to the boy, children are hope. The Boy encounters another child in a burned-out town they visit and, excited at the rare chance encounter with someone his own age, the Boy runs from his father, who chases after him, worried. When the man grabs the Boy and scolds him for running off, the Boy fights and yells, a reaction he gives at no other time in the film. The Boy's desperation to meet the other child is fierce, yet he cannot express why. When his father asks why it is important, his son answers, "I need to see him, I need to!" The man asks, concerned, "why?" His son replies, "I just do!" One could always interpret this as the Boy's need to be with someone else like him, who was also born in this dying world, or just to have company, someone close to his own age with whom to play. It could also be that the other child represents potential community and a life beyond existence on *The Road*, a hope unarticulated in the film but fierce and visceral when it appears in the flesh before the Boy. Revealingly, the son sees the other little boy from the porch of his father's childhood home. While his father is reminiscing about his past, the Boy sees the other little child and runs toward him, toward the future, and away from the house, away from his father's past and the past of that civilization. Afterward, the father reflects, "He yearns for his own friends and imagines how things will be different at the coast; that there will be other children there. When I have nothing else I try to dream the dreams of a child's imaginings." For the Boy, and perhaps any child born in that time, another child may simply spark the hope that there can be hope, that perhaps the only world they have ever known may not be quite as cruel and morally desolate as it seems.

The boy is also hope for the man. He comes to see his successful survival, in part, as a curse, a burden that he wants to lay down. Indeed, without the boy he sees little sense in continuing beyond the world's end. If the boy, he said, was not the voice of god, "then god never spoke."

The film viewer is left at the end of the film, again, possibly with hope, or perhaps in that extreme and traumatic filmscape, simply relieved that the boy lives on with others, that there are children he can be with after all, even if his future is short. At least, the viewer will not see the son die. And at least, one can imagine that they find a place where the world will be renewed. Even as all life dissolves into the carbon from which it came, it puts down layers that, in many thousands or millions of years, could give life again. Perhaps we can dream that the boy and his new family will find a life raft somewhere in that world where they can survive to meet the Earth's renewal. Here, we are reminded of Noah suspended between the end of one world and the creation of the new, but a creation that requires only a few from the old to seed the new world's creation. McCarthy is Biblical in his imagination, after all, and perhaps the child is a seed that will be planted for a new world.

The viewer cannot be sure, because part of McCarthy's success is an economy, in a book and then a film, that gives us just enough information and illustration to build a narrative. Everything else, including the source of the catastrophe, is withheld. In this, it reflects human life in general, as we are caught in moral struggles, working toward happiness, trying to prevent suffering, not knowing why we are called on to live, nor by whom, unsure of our origins and anxious of the end. If McCarthy's vision is Biblical, his testament, though it centers on hope, still challenges one's faith in the final payoff of hope.

One can, however, conclude by sketching some of the insights into the moral life that *The Road* provides us. The first is the difficulty of the moral life, at least as it occurs in the United States culture in which *The Road* takes place. The world of *The Road* is grey. It is ash, and it is ashen. There is no color, no black and white, just nuance and conflict. The viewer can see this as

Figure 4.1.   *The Road*, 2009, Dimension Films.

a metaphor for the moral life, also one that is not easy. The philosopher and novelist, Iris Murdoch, describes the moral life, or moral being, as she calls it, as a field of tension.[11] Individuals are suspended between different loyalties, different areas of value and concern, with the goods and ends of this world often in contradiction. And so, each individual is left trying to negotiate her way through, trying to do the best she can, sometimes succumbing to selfish interest, sometimes finding goodness, even though hard won, and sometimes left with no good options, leaving us with regret.[12]

The greyness of both the book and the novel reflects, in the way the sun cannot, the moral ambiguity that both works embody. That ambiguity— really, a tension—the viewer can find embodied in the relationship of the man and the boy. Both hope, yet they hope toward different things. The man hopes toward a horizon of survival, sacrificing almost everything else, including his life and that of others, to keep the boy alive. The boy, on the other hand, is empathetic, and even if one cannot say that his teleology is to flourish, it is one that reaches out in a shared sense of suffering, instead of contracting inward out of fear for one's survival. He hopes toward a horizon of compassion. The film is a tense pulling, back and forth, between these two poles, these two ends, of survival and compassion. The man toils so that the boy can survive, focusing on this outcome, while the boy is more concerned with how they live. One is more consequentialist, the other, focused on virtue.

It climaxes in the scene, after they leave the thief for dead. The boy cries at what they have done, and finally the father yells in frustration, "You're not the one who has to worry about everything." The boy surprises him by revealing the boy's experience and a hidden truth of the film. He yells, "Yes I am. I am the one!" Until this point, the focus of agency in the film centered around the father. He is the one that most adults probably relate to more, bearing the responsibility to look out for others, for supporting oneself, if not a family. The man is a single father standing at the precipice of the world's doom. The writing and crafting of the film keep the man central and agentive. It is his dreams the viewer sees. It is his voice the viewer hears narrating. One understands his dilemmas, sees his struggle against the coughing and infirmity spreading in his body. It is the man's tale to tell, and for us to see.

This changes, however, when the boy reveals his own point of view, largely occluded up to that point. The boy realizes, to a degree the father does not, what the future holds. Even more, the boy understands, it seems, that not only his future survival is a stake, but also his future soul. The argument occurs over helping another person, a stranger. It happens toward the end of the film, as their food is almost gone, as they have reached the shore and found no haven. It is a critical time, a fulcrum, and the possibility of despair is high. It is at this moment one can understand that the boy sees himself as agentive. The viewer gets no more than his insistence that it is he who worries everyday about making decisions, but perhaps he worries more than worrying about "food, always food," like the father. He is also worried throughout about losing his goodness. At a number of points, the boy asks if they are still the good guys. His anxiety over this persists. At a point when they are particularly hungry, he asks if they will ever eat someone else, a communion that dissolves one's morality. He asks if they will, even if starving. The boy, it seems, is concerned that the need to survive will overrule their morality, and will make them "the bad guys." This, not so much survival—or, we can say, not primarily survival—is what the boy worries over. At this moment, expressing his agency and hinting at his own anxieties, he articulates the need not just to survive, but after he outlives his father, to survive with some of his humanity in tact.

This is an amazing moment, and the boy, an amazing character. At the end of the world, the film viewer sees an individual who, due to his age, will probably be one of the last humans to live, concerned with the moral life and his own integrity. The film turns on the tension between survival, and sacrificing one's moral ideals to that end, and moral character, and the resistance of survival as one's highest end, of existence for existence's sake. This tension resolves with an affirmation of the moral life, even if the days are numbered. The film also affirms, quite boldly, the survival of the moral life, of the concern for goodness, character and integrity, that quite literally survives the end of the world. As long as there are humans, the film seems to be saying, there will be moral dilemma. There will be choices to make of the utmost moral gravity, and individuals, even in such extreme states, will be beleaguered by choice, particularly, that between survival and virtue. The moral life is the human life, and irrevocably so. It also shows that despite the desperation such an environment puts on one, care can still survive when care seems to be a dangerous virtue, even a death wish. Even with utter scarcity, there can be empathy and active compassion.

Finally, the film uses an extreme situation to underline what it is that makes a human, human. It is not, as it turns out, existence. A scene not in the movie, but one in the book, shows the boy and man coming across a settlement, just then vacated, and what seems to be a headless baby on a spit. The text leaves little doubt that it is a pregnant woman's baby, one they had seen only shortly before, and that either she, or the men she was with, or both, had done that deed. The viewer does not know if the child had died first, or whether they killed the infant out of ravenous hunger. Either way, the act is shocking, as much to the man and boy as to the reader. Less graphic, but no less grave, scenes populate the film. They show humans that no longer seem humane, bent over and morally crippled by dire circumstances not of their own making, manipulated by their own bodily needs.

Such scenes dramatically illustrate the moral accomplishment that is the boy. It also shows that, if the man pushed too far in his quest to survive, he could have destroyed the boy's humanity. In that world, the only thing precious left was love, the object of which could not extend much farther than a few yards, and humanity. Everything else was gone, a fact shown in the beginning of the movie where the father steps over money, ignoring it, in the search for seeds. These were the treasures against which the pressing desire to live, to find a place to be human again, were wagered. It seems, however, that survival could take away one's humanity, as the viewer saw in the scene with the infant, in the scene with the humans stored in a basement for food, so that if one ever found such a haven, there would be no humans left, in a moral sense.

CONCLUSION

The man declares at the beginning, that if the boy were not the voice of God, "then God never spoke." Such lines are vague, perplexing, and in keeping with a story that raises more questions than it answers. It resonates Biblically, as does much of McCarthy's works, and reminds one of prophecy, of God speaking through the Hebrew prophets. Maybe McCarthy had in mind Isaiah, who had to be burned at the lips before being able to speak God's word.[13] Perhaps he had the notion of atonement theology in mind, of Christ as the Logos, the Word of God, when he wrote this, gesturing at the boy as a Christ symbol, or perhaps, in a world transformed, its own version of a Messiah. Like so much of this film and book, the viewer or reader does not know, and the lacunae are too rich, and too interesting, to be filled in completely. But the viewer is called upon by this invocation of the father to keep an eye on the child, and that much is embodied in his story.

As others have argued, goodness is fragile, the moral life one of luck as much as of volition.[14] Yet, *The Road* reminds us that moral challenge, and the moral life itself, is enduring, even beyond the world's end. It is central to human life. The choices one has are often not as dire or extreme as one between survival and moral ideals, yet each of us faces such challenges, and perhaps over human history, the dire has outweighed the moderate.

The Road revolves around a binary of survival versus humanity, where any notions of flourishing seem impossible. This situation raises the question: what, then, could someone live for? Mere survival seems possible. I say mere survival, as the extreme lengths many go through in the book to survive raise the further question, is life worth such toil? The film starts with a scene of suicide, as if laying down the fact that, no, for many, perhaps most, survival is not reason enough to live. A life without the possibility of meaning, according to Clifford Geertz, is not really human, and one without any notion of flourishing may be too hard to endure.[15] Indeed, those who survived to the point where the film begins may well be some of the most immoral of humanity. Speaking in another dire situation, which in many ways reflects the apocaplyptic, Viktor Frankl, a famous survivor of the Holocaust, writes of those who survived, and those who did not, in the camps:

> there was a sort of self-selecting process going on the whole time among all of the prisoners. On the average, only those prisoners could keep alive who, after years of trekking from camp to camp, had lost all scruples in their fight for existence; they were prepared to use every means, honest and otherwise, even brutal force, theft and betrayal of their friends, in order to save themselves— the best of us did not return (italics mine).[16]

Survival in such situations often requires violence, both to others, as well as to one's own moral life. It requires sacrifice of those virtues, goods, and relationships which make one feel human, hitting one's moral subjectivity and one's own self regard. This is why the boy's compassion stands out like red against the grey landscape. Juxtaposed to others in the novel, and even his father, he comes across as precious, so much so that his father sacrifices everything to keep him alive. The boy, and in the end, the father, show the possibility of care, even at the end of the world, and even when care seems too dangerous to continue it into the new, dead world. In such a hopeless land, *The Road* focuses on a relationship, perhaps singular, that offers hope where none can be expected. What is amazing is the way such desolation can be used to reveal the enduring nature of the moral life and even of hope itself. *The Road*, then, is one of the more realistically hopeful movies ever made, balancing the reality of the moral life's enduring difficulties and even impossibilities with an affirmation, nevertheless, that love may endure as long as we do, even beyond the end of the world.

NOTES

1. Cormac McCarthy and Joe Penhall, *The Road*, directed by John Hillcoat (California: Dimension Films, 2009), DVD. All quotes and references to *The Road* movie, unless otherwise specified, will refer to this source.
2. Michael Jackson, *Lifeworlds: Essays in Existential Anthropology* (Chicago: University of Chicago Press, 2013), 8.
3. For this dialogue, I used a transcript available online, authored by Joe Penhall. See www.imsdb.com/scripts/Road,-The.html.
4. For a helpful overview article on the relationship between virtue and eudaimonia, see Julia Annas, "Virtue and Eudaimonism," *Social Philosophy and Policy* 15 (1998): 37–55.
5. Lisa Tessman, for example, argues for their decoupling to account for what she calls burdened virtues, needed to fight for social justice. Lisa Tessman, *Burdened Virtues: Virtue Ethics for Liberatory Struggles* (New York: Oxford University Press, 2005).
6. MacIntyre, *After Virtue*, 81.
7. I am referencing here Alasdair MacIntyre's understanding of practice, community, tradition and narrative as it relates to his understanding of virtue. See Alasdair MacIntyre, *After Virtue: A Study in Moral Theory* (Notre Dame, IN: University of Notre Dame Press, 2007).
8. Tessman, *Burdened Virtues*.
9. Michael Chabon, "After the Apocalypse," in *New York Review of Books*, February 15, 2007. www.nybooks.com/articles/archives/2007/feb/15/after-the-apocalypse/.
10. Again, this was adapted from a transcript of *The Road* available online, authored by Joe Penhall. See www.imsdb.com/scripts/Road,-The.html.
11. Iris Murdoch, *Metaphysics as a Guide to Morals* (New York: Penguin, 1992), 492–497.
12. Bernard Williams, "Moral Luck," in *Moral Luck* (New York: Cambridge University Press, 1981).
13. Book of Isaiah 6:6.
14. Martha C. Nussbaum, *The Fragility of Goodness: Luck and Ethics in Greek Tragedy and Philosophy* (New York: Cambridge University Press, 2001).
15. Clifford Geertz, *The Interpretation of Cultures* (New York: Basic Books, 1973), 145, 172.
16. Viktor, Frankl, *Man's Search for Meaning* (Boston: Beacon Press, 2006), 19.

BIBLIOGRAPHY

Annas, Julia. "Virtue and Eudaimonism," *Social Philosophy and Policy* 15 (1998): 37–55.
Chabon, Michael. "After the Apocalypse," *New York Review of Books*. Accessed February 15, 2007. www.nybooks.com/articles/archives/2007/feb/15/after-the-apocalypse/.
Frankl, Viktor. *Man's Search for Meaning*. Boston: Beacon Press, 2006.
Geertz, Clifford. *The Interpretation of Cultures*. New York: Basic Books, 1973.
Jackson, Michael. *Lifeworlds: Essays in Existential Anthropology*. Chicago: University of Chicago Press, 2013.

MacIntyre, Alasdair. *After Virtue: A Study in Moral Theory*. Notre Dame, Indiana: University of Notre Dame Press, 2007.

McCarthy, Cormac and Joe Penhall. *The Road*. Directed by John Hillcoat. California: Dimension Films, 2009, DVD.

Murdoch, Iris. *Metaphysics as a Guide to Morals*. New York: Penguin, 1992.

Nussbaum, Martha C. *The Fragility of Goodness: Luck and Ethics in Greek Tragedy and Philosophy*. New York: Cambridge University Press, 2001.

Tessman, Lisa. *Burdened Virtues: Virtue Ethics for Liberatory Struggles*. New York: Oxford University Press, 2005.

Williams, Bernard. "Moral Luck." *Moral Luck*. New York: Cambridge University Press, 1981.

Chapter Five

Space and Children in Post-Apocalyptic Film

The Road *and* Les temps du loup

Eduardo Barros-Grela and María Bobadilla Pérez

INTRODUCTION

The construction of post-apocalyptic spatialities in recent film has normally been derived from the total destruction of traditional physical spaces. Urban and natural territories are reinterpreted as a common and toxic ground of desolation and despair, and are particularly depicted as the epitome of disintegrated human subjectivity. Cities, for instance, tend to become spaces inhabited by savage animals represented as elements that are dislocated from their logical environment (*12 Monkeys* [1995], *I Am Legend* [2007], etc.). Concurrently, natural sceneries become polluted spaces, flooded with pieces of debris, and dismantled vehicles or industrial devices, all of them being elements that are as well displaced from their corresponding environment (*Mad Max* [1979], *Children of Men* [2006], etc.).

In this chapter, we explore the repercussions of human subjectivity upon space, as well as the dialectic activation of space as a performing agent in the construction of human identifications. In particular, we leave aside the effects of spatiality on adult characters from dystopian films to focus on the role of children in the construction of those new territories. Unlike mature members of the post-apocalyptic "societies," young characters are yet to integrate the new landscapes of the hostile spaces they inhabit into their still unstable epistemologies. Under these conditions, post-apocalyptic children replace reason with emotions, and show clear difficulties in verbally articulating those emotions. In our view, children perform a key role in the cultural

77

production of an allegorical narrative that witnesses the knowledge insecurities of current societies. Emotional aphasia of children opens spaces of dialog with their spatialities in order to deterritorialize the new spaces from their cultural heritance, something that would be rather unapproachable for adults.

The two films we study here clearly show these aspects of children in post-apocalyptic environments. *Les temps du loup* (Michael Haneke 2003) situates children in border spaces of destruction in order to deconstruct human subjectivities and build new epistemologies. This is clearly evidenced in the final scene of Haneke's motion picture, when one of the protagonist children finds himself more likely to give his own body to an improvised pyre rather than surrender to traditional forms of society. He needs to negotiate his own spaces to start building an according epistemology, and considers the remains of preterit social norms as mere obstacles for him to obtain spatial agency. Also, *The Road* (John Hillcoat 2009), a film based on Cormac McCarthy's homonymous novel, presents the topic of the child as wanderer in a set of destroyed landscapes. He will have to internalize those landscapes and make them participant in his construction of identity. Space in this case is signified as an empty place ("terrain vague"),[1] where shadows of past existences still haunt its orography, and constitute a threatening space for children to disidentify from previous epistemologies.

This chapter, therefore, uses the theory of space contained in Henri Lefebvre's, Edward Soja's, and David Harvey's works on urban studies to analyze the aforementioned films. Some specific concepts are of particular interest to develop the articulation of children epistemologies and the theories of space, such as "spatiality," "third space," "non-places," or "empty spaces," which are terms normally used to refer to spaces within the city, but can easily be transferred to nonurban locations. Also, related to the writing of identities in reference to spaces, we take several of Gilles Deleuze's discussions about the epistemological production in postmodernity, and we look at "rhizomes," "territorializations," and "arborescent formations" as starting points in the development—and discussion—of a conflictive spatiality in *Les temps du loup* and *The Road*.

CHILDREN IN PLACES AND NO-PLACES

Let's start with the analysis of a disturbing scene from Haneke's movie. In this film, we know a catastrophe of some kind has happened. We see a family running away from the city, and looking for a fostering place in the formerly-isolated countryside. However, the post-apocalyptic ambience that has resulted from the ignote disaster—at least to the reader—has taken strangers to their safety place, which becomes threatening and violent in nature. The family is attacked and forced to wander about in the desolated environment of the dystopian space looking for help and never getting any. Finally, they reach a train station where many instances of the evil violence of human nature will be portrayed and examined, while they keep waiting for a probably nonexisting train that would take them back to the city. It will be precisely there, in the train station, where this disturbing scene will take place.

The station is a remarkable place in itself. Resembling sceneries of marginal urban environments, the train station portrayed in *Les temps du loup* is depicted according to parameters of subjectification that seem to distance its distinctiveness from other types of transportation terminals. Generally speaking, these types of terminals, such as train stations or airports, could be defined as no-places,[2] as they are just temporary destinations, and individuals passing through never get to establish an identification relationship with these places.[3] However, the train station that is contrarily signified in this motion picture as a place of dwelling, acquires full meaning through the identification of their nomad inhabitants with a perception of contingent domestic familiarity. Occupiers of the station keep their hopes to go back alive to their previous existences, away from the station. At the same time though they melancholically understand that, for them, the only way to survive in this new world is by making of that no-place their own place.

In such a violent environment, spatiality becomes crucial for the survival of this group of stranded citizens, particularly for children. As Jenks and Mitz have argued, today childhood is widely recognized as a social construct, and the aesthetics of *Les temps du loup* require a resignification of the discursivity provided by represented children.

Similar dynamics are common in *The Road*. A father (Viggo Mortensen) and a son (Kodi Smit-McPhee) are forced to wander around the deserted spaces of a post-apocalyptic environment. Destructive forces of unknown origin have devastated the world as we know it today, and have led society to a threatening situation that makes all the remaining inhabitants of a given geographical space run from each other for survival. Cannibalism has replaced both reason and emotion as the motor of human relationships, and nature itself has adopted a vicious significance that has transformed its original—and positive—connotations into forms of menacing against the endurance of humanity. Those two factors of the normal production of identity—human relationships and the relation of humans with nature—are subtracted in this film from their logical meaning, and are resignified as uncontrolled forces that walk toward mutual annihilation. The road, which is normally portrayed as a metaphor of life and progress, is in this film parodied as a never-ending form of dwelling, as if its inhabitants were condemned to a perpetual discovery of the same. The locations the road continuously crosses are but mere shadows of the lively dynamics of former settlements, similar to how the main characters in the film, both father and son, face situations with other participants that would definitely have a different nature in previous times, but have now become polluted and perverse.

The spaces resulting from the events that led the world to turn into a physical and emotional desert are categorically unsuitable for children. The boy in the film reveals himself as a nomadic dweller of the road; one that holds shadows of what once were feelings (toward his father, his gone mother, or even other residents of the dystopian scenarios), but at the same time, his continuous exposure to his overprotective father has transformed his emotions into an aseptic condescendence. The conventional interpretation of becoming an adult through life experiences is decontextualized here as the boy is subjected to empty experiences from his life in the road. He faintly recognizes that his father is actually using the road not to get to a safer place, but to escape from the different perils and from the memories of an idealized past that they will never encounter again. The road they are walking leads to nowhere, and it will be just through the death of the father that the son will be able to reinterpret his path as a new member of his foster family. Indeed, death, that conventionally accepted border between epistemological territories, appears in *The Road* as a desire the boy keeps, as he is willing to reunite with his mother and, implicitly, to leave the world his father has sentenced him to live. The boy's reaction when facing his father's death is surprisingly not one of absolute devastation, but rather a considerably contained manifestation of sadness related to, we suspect, not to the separation from his father, but rather to the boy's inability to follow him away from the space he occupies at the road.

Both space and identity have a very particular way of leaning away from their legitimized connotations in this film. From the very beginning, the

Figure 5.1.   *The Road*, 2009, Dimension Films.

viewers of *The Road* are exposed to a dual formulation of reality: first, through the man's dreams and memories, we can see a world that is very similar to the one any viewer may inhabit, but at the same time a spatial reality that is inflicted with a clear component of idealization. Dreams and memories happen to share the common attribute of being flexible with our exposure to the reality they portray, and that malleability becomes evident in the case of the man in *The Road* as he brings scenes from the past that are perfectly coherent to the need of the particular situation his son and himself live at a given moment. The second reality *The Road* provides for the viewer to witness is the dystopian space of the road. It is this particular space that we find particularly interesting, as it is the space where the child develops the problematic questioning of his identity.

BECOMING EMPTY SPACES

As we mentioned before, the road the boy walks with his father provides a physical itinerary through the desolate spatial conditions triggered by the advent of destructive forces. Several snapshots can be retrieved from significant scenes showing the relation between the boy and the dystopian space he occupies. A significantly graphic view is seen in the first few minutes of this motion picture, when the recurrent voice-over delineates the key factor to be applied to the boy throughout the film. He says, "The clocks stopped at 1:17" (1:36). This short sentence is vital in the development of the remaining occupants of the world and, of course, in understanding the boy's hesitations. What it means is that every human-created reality abruptly ceased its existence at that time, and all that is left is the chaotic and whimsical phenomena that belong to nature. The clocks stopped as the logical evolution of events, and include not only growth and learning evolution, but also result in the apprehended social relations that appertain to the human condition.

The boy drags his teddy bear along the ground as he depressingly walks by his father, unaware of the specific direction of their steps. The space the viewer observes in this scene is a very clear example of an "empty space." The boy lowers his eyes before the horrific scenery he is forced to witness, while remnants of recent battles appear scattered all over the place, joining the images of former social constructions in a mosaic of violent landscapes of emptiness. Such an empty space (terrain vague) would thus be an uninhabited space where one can still feel the specters of previous—and possibly deceased—dwellers. Not only does the boy witness the unsettling set of images provided by these empty spaces, but he becomes—or rather walks the road to become—one of those specters that inhabit the empty space of the road. While he recognizes, internally, maybe unconsciously, the existence of those specters of previous inhabitants, he never gets to see any (in an empty space, a person can *feel* the presence of a lost past, or of former dwellers, but never have an actual visualization). His (lack of?) acknowledgement of the existence of such specters is so significant that he fails to recognize the presence of another boy who hides in the ruins of a town. The boy and his father do not interpret the presence of the other boy as *real*, but as yet another specter. The man's words about the impossibility of that being another boy convince the son and transform his certainty into a questioning of his own capabilities to apprehend reality.

These empty spaces are rather common in contemporary society. As we discussed earlier when we looked at the theoretical significance of the train station in *Les temps du loup*, the representation of these spaces correlates highly with the empty spatiality of the boy. His permanent exposure both to the emptiness of the places the road crosses and the emptiness his father and other human characters in the film produces an alternative progression—or growth—in the child's knowledge of the world. Unable to transcend those relations between humans and spaces, he ends up assimilating his identifications to the (lack of) identities of the human and spatial factors he experiences.

Although the religious relevance of the film is not a central issue in this chapter, there is a particular scene in *The Road* containing a biblical reference that is of interest to this analysis. Earlier in the film, as the empty spaces are introduced, the subjective lens of the camera focuses on a billboard that has the hand-sprayed graffiti "Behold the Valley of Slaughter" written over what seems to be an advertisement of a suburban architectural development. It's interesting to note that director John Hillcoat decided to film the scenes of *The Road* in real-disaster locations, such as post-Katrina New Orleans or the surroundings of active volcanoes. These spaces provide the same feeling of perturbed familiarity as the billboard does. They portray sceneries that are familiar to the audiences, but that have been perverted by apocalyptical signs: the idealized image of the suburban hometown on the billboard has been contaminated with the presence of evil ("Behold the Valley of Slaughter"). Similarly, the abandoned malls, empty stations, unused grocery stores are "no-spaces" that have been filled with the threat of a presence. In the same way as the no-places (malls, airports, etc.) are defined by the unsettling serenity of the multitude, the same type of spaces in *The Road* confer however er a state of horror caused by two relevant factors: physical solitude, and the even more terrifying possibility of aggressive presences.

The child's reactions to these two factors are visibly different to those experienced by adults. An article published by Tim Gill in *The Guardian* in 2005[4] discusses the difficulties children experience when facing the daily routines of making decisions, and confronting complications. Leaving aside the ideological position of his proposal, the general remarks he poses about children are of considerable interest to our discussion. He claims, for instance, that the extreme vigilance that adults exercise on children results in "frustrat[ing] their [children's] natural urge to explore and push boundaries, and it exposes their resultant behavior to the ever more judgmental gaze of adults." While the father's preoccupations circle around the protection of his own understanding of space, meaning the survival of both his son and himself, the child's anxiety obeys the harsh assimilation of his father's containment and possibly excessive precautions, but also to his instinctual necessity of knowing his own space.

There is a particular scene that strikes the viewer as a powerful clash of spaces: the father takes a moment during his son's sleep to go through the belongings the child keeps in a little bag. They are small and with no apparent value. The child, however, is infuriated when he wakes up to find that someone, or even worse, his own father, has observed and touched his belongings. The boy understands those objects as his own private spaces, which have now been violated by the curiosity of his father. His bag and the toys it contains belong to the imagined space of the child, and they are the actual subjects that give physicality to the empty space the child has found himself forced to inhabit, but thanks to these toys, also the space that he is able to create and shape according to his own values. His own spatiality, in short, roots from his relationship with those items, rather than from his inert wandering around an empty space populated by abject beings, both the dehumanized and anthropophagous individuals that threaten his life, and his own father, who lives a nonexistent life from the past, rather than the present one he shares with his son. The innocent incursion of his father into his belongings is, however, translated by the child as an action that the man attempts to reterritorialize the boy's space, something that he radically opposes as the result of the defense of his spatiality. The moment his father gains access to

Figure 5.2.   *The Road*, 2009, Dimension Films.

this space, he deterritorializes it and appropriates its meaning, thus commodifying the value the child has given to the objects and, consequently, to the spaces the objects create.

The aforementioned factors are determining in the creation of a nonplace, which is particular of this narrative through the recurrent emotions produced by a physical solitude, and also by the sempiternal threat of aggressive presences, is therefore established by the clash of spaces epitomized by the situation in the scene we have just explained. This argument coincides with Pufall and Unsworth's claim in their study on the archeology of the language that signifies childhood, in which they explain that,

> [f]rom an organismic perspective, to have voice means to be able to participate in conversation, exchanging thoughts and feelings with others, when some voices are loud and others soft, some are dissonant and other harmonious. For children to have voice is to acquire conversational skills for taking turns, listening, persuading, debating, negotiating, and resolving conflict. With skills such as these, children become able to accommodate others' points of view in conversation without losing sight of their own.[5]

The case of the boy in *The Road* is radically complex in this sense, as he reverses the necessities that are supposed to be expected from a child, and renounces the voice that he knows does not belong to him, but to others' interpretation of how a child's language, voice, body, and space must be. When he experiences the peril of his spatiality being torn, the boy reacts against his father (now seen as a menace) by rejecting to participate in conversations and by denying himself the right to have a voice.

Similarly, the boy in *Les temps du loup* that joins the wandering family is reluctant to let the family know about himself through the use of language—curiously, something very similar to what happens in the final scene of *The Road*, shortly after the boy has lost his father, and is completely alone in his quest to reach the southern regions. Many times the runaway boy in *Les temps du loup* does not provide any personal data about himself—not even his name or origin—in what resembles the elusive behavior of the boy from *The Road*, and in particular in his relationship with his father. Both of these boys feel somehow safer in the spaces they have created for themselves, because they have filled them with voices and meanings that are their own, rather than those belonging to the empty spaces around them. Thus, the hostile environment that provides a post-apocalyptic aesthetic to both films serves as a territory of contrast compared to the safer—yet clearly highly problematic—inner spatialities of the children. Such a reaction from children should be interpreted as following a commonsensical rationale, particularly if we attend to Scheper-Hughes's accounts on how marginal children are treated in certain contemporary locations:

In Brazil, poverty has created an especially dark situation in which society's most vulnerable children are forced to live or work on the streets and fend for their lives on a daily basis. In many societies, poor children are exposed to street life, but Brazil is interesting in that many of its citizens have changed their mentalities from viewing street children as creative "urchins" to viewing them as vermin that must be discarded, often through murder, all while blaming the victim and almost never the perpetrator.[6]

This factor is particularly distinct in Haneke's film. The childhood scenario in *Les temps du loup* is significantly more complex than that from *The Road*. The film directed by Haneke presents a complex epistemological structure defined by three different children who struggle to survive—not only physically, but also in terms of identity production—in the aggressive dystopian proclivity of the post-apocalyptic space. Two of those children belong to the protagonist family in the film, which has been recently destabilized by the assassination of the father. The third child, in turn, travels alone and gets to join the family after a series of emotional events in their pursuit of a safer space. Actually, the approach of this boy to the space of the family should be interpreted as his need to negotiate his own spatiality; rather than a dialectical confrontation with the mother, Ann, he looks to the children for a ratification of an established epistemology of his territories.

The fact that this dialectical clash of spaces takes place in a dystopian scenery is not inconsequential. According to E. Anthony Rotundo,[7] children's perpetual supervision is impossible, but the threatening spaces experienced by the children in *Les temps du loup* precipitate their emancipation from adulthood command. In fact, as the boy and the man from *The Road* did, these three children from Haneke's film negotiate an inversion of roles with the adults around them. In particular, the case of Anne Laurent (Isabelle Huppert) as the children's mother is exceptionally transparent. Coming from an urban space where everything seemed to be under her control,[8] Anne finds herself completely overwhelmed by the deontologized territory she and her family are forced to meander. Again, her children show a much more functional predisposition to adapt to the new circumstances, especially when they become acquainted with the runaway boy. They perceive how natural the relationship of this boy with the dystopian environment has become in a short period of time, while their mother seems to fail to recognize—and adapt to—the new circumstances of their lives. Her son Ben (Lucas Biscombe) responds to the characterization of an extremely weak (epitomized by his spontaneous nose bleeding), dependent (both his mother and her sister feel constantly obliged to be on the lookout for him), and demanding person (sudden disappearances, constant demand for attention, etc.). However, as the story moves forward, he smoothly integrates in the new dystopian scenery of violence. His mother and the people at the train station—as well as many of the adults in the film—find only two opposed methods to interpret their current situation: they either develop a nostalgic desire for a structured past, or they generate an abusing imposition against others. Children, on the other hand, interpret the topical dystopian scenery they are witnessing as just another learning process in their educational process into adulthood.

Ben's reactions to violence against him (actual or potential), for instance, are those of a pusillanimous and fearful individual. However, he spares no expenses at inducing his sister to an act of implicit violence against a little bird that mistakenly enters into the barn the family is using as a temporary shelter. The bird's attempts to find an exit are interpreted by Ben as a cry for help, and in his intentions to free the bird from the hostile environment in which he is trapped, he sends her sister the message that the bird is a metaphor of their own situation, and they must do something to liberate that bird. So he vehemently demands from her sister Eva (Anaïs Demoustier) that she captures the parakeet so that he can rescue the bird and give comfort to it. But then there is an appalling element that is introduced in the scene: as he waits for her sister to seize the bird, Ben has another of his frequent nosebleeds, whose cause Eva attributes to his penchant for becoming overexcited. The final—and powerful—scene in this sequence is a boy who is lying down on the floor, with a bleeding nose and a suffocating bird inside his coat pocket. Haneke excels at creating a disturbing and violent space from a purportedly candid encounter between a child and a domestic animal. The image of the satisfied bleeding boy and the agonizing bird follows the same pattern as the scene from *The Road* when the man tries to peek into his son's belongings. In the case of the sequence from *Les temps du loup*, the underlying conflict is again one of spaces. By providing a safe place for the bird to be protected, the child is appropriating the space of the bird (he is actually creating a spatiality for the bird, which ends up being fatal for the parakeet), and he educates the animal into the *correct* form to produce a certain space.

Naturally, Haneke uses this part of his film to propose a contemplation upon the violent relation between adults and children. The inherent violence that adult individuals exhibit in this dystopian environment is mimicked by Ben both as a physical response to the current situation (through his bleeding nose) and as a voluntary act of passive-aggressive education (through the appropriation of the bird's space as a compassionate action.) The children in *Les temps du loup* are in fact reflections of that bird, trying to fly away from adult normativity out to the open world, but instead being confined to structural patterns of violence and, ultimately, to death.[9]

Eva's epistemology is also portrayed in *Les temps du loup* as one of conflictive spatialities. There are two significant instances to prove Eva's negotiation of spaces in this film, and both take place early in the film, when the characters' personalities are still being introduced. The first case occurs when the runaway boy first appears to the family, after the night Ben disappeared (28:16). Eva starts a conversation with the young boy, trying to convince him to stay with them even though they still contemplate the possibility that it was him who kidnapped Ben. Her mother continually interrupts Eva's interrogation of the boy to ask the boy about Ben's health, but Eva instantaneously reprimands her for being a burden to her more important task of becoming acolyte to a boy who knows how to function in the strenuous space they now inhabit: "—Are you freezing, Ben?—Mom, he is not freezing!" (27:58). Her brother's health is now of negligible importance to her, and similarly to Ben's attitude in the bird scene, she becomes violent against a member of her family in an attempt to conquer the territory she believes essential for their survival.

The most important factor in this scene is that Eva has reversed the hierarchy in her relationship with her mother and, from this moment on, Eva and the young boy will be the ones to decide about the progression of the family. Eva consciously deterritorializes her mother's ability to act in the space of violence they have come to live in, and she assumes the performative responsibility of producing alternative spatialities different from the violent space that has been legitimized by adult epistemologies. [10] Hers, unquestionably, is also a space of violence, but one that has been reterritorialized according to the particular necessities of individual relations in this alternate space.

The second instance that is relevant to perceive the contradictory evolution of Eva's spatial production occurs also in the surroundings of the barn at the beginning of their journey (25:30). After the mother has temporarily left the barn, leaving her children alone, Eva starts a fire with dry hay to keep themselves warm. Just as expected, the flames spread out of control and the mother has to come back to put out the fire. In the middle of the chaotic situation the mother blames Eva and refers to her as "stupid girl," which makes Eva react first violently and then with regret. This scene is identical to the one from *The Road* when the boy stays in charge of his and his father's belongings while the man swims away to explore a run-aground boat, but the exhausted boy falls sleep and all their possessions are stolen. In both cases, the children argue that being in charge of the situation was too much responsibility for them, because they are just children. But the sequences offer a different interpretation. The children pose an obvious indolence about the state of their belongings, because these objects are remains of past spaces that no longer exist, and although their parents refuse to forget about the past, the children demonstrate a much more open flexibility. Eva interprets the coats, the bicycle, or their luggage as items from their past that have no place in their current spaces, and therefore pays no special attention to their maintenance. The boy in *The Road*, similarly, is waiting for his opportunity to start in a new space by leaving behind the past, so he as well has no special motivation to keep dragging the melancholic burden. In *Children at Play*,

Howard P. Chudacoff, paraphrasing Silas Felton, reflects on the education of children in the period between the seventeenth and the nineteenth centuries:

> "People do not pay attention enough to the inclinations of their children," he complained in his autobiography, "but commonly put them to the same kind of business, which they themselves follow, and when they find them [children] not attentive to those particular occupations accuse them of being idle." Such chastisement, Felton continued, "often damps [children's] spirits, which . . . sometimes leads to looseness of manners, whereas if the leading inclinations of the children were sought after, and when found, permitted to follow them, [such inclinations] might prove highly advantageous to themselves, their parents and society." [11]

In our times, relations between parents and children have not changed radically from what Chudacoff explains, at least in what concerns epistemology as interpreted through space.

CONCLUSION

All of the examples provided from *Les temps du loup* are crucial to understanding the use of space proposed by Haneke. In his film, children are the absolute protagonists, as they hold the type of innocent violence that is so disturbing and so appealing to the Austrian director. As we mentioned earlier in this study, the lack of voice or, rather, the aphasic articulation of emotions becomes the only means of communication for the children in these two films. These children intensely explore and enhance their denial of adult epistemologies through their negotiation of spaces, as well as through their production of intimate spatialities. On the other hand, oblivious to the rapid adaptation of the children, the adults in these two films are portrayed as violent and passive parasites unable to recognize the new—dystopian and post-apocalyptic—spaces they inhabit, and instead see themselves stranded to a nostalgic life within past and mostly imagined spaces. The "time of the wolf" Haneke refers to in the title of his film refers to the learning process of children who become violent through the appropriation of spaces, or rather, through their deterritorialization and reterritorialization of legitimized epistemologies. As in the "era" of the wolf a pup's education starts from a point of "innocence" but then they become violently "corrupted" by the spaces around them. In *The Road*, after escaping a house inhabited by an anthropophagous family, the man and the boy have a conversation in which the child asks his father whether they still are the good guys (42:31), and then he adds "and we are carrying the fire." Immediately after his father replies that they are, the boy smiles and extinguishes the fire burning in the embers. The world around them is changing, and so are the children involved in its development, beyond any legitimate supervision by adults, even parents. Children's knowledge of the world is still in the process of constructing its own spaces, rather than being in a situation where they would have to adapt to existing fixed places. Violence is resignified, and acquires open potentialities in its relation with space to produce performed spatialities that will provide new meanings to the children's relation with the dystopian space of both *The Road* and *Les temps du loup*.

NOTES

1. A specific concept coined by Ignasi de Solà-Morales Rubió which refers to "empty [mostly urban] spaces," like an abandoned building or a non-functional airport or subway station.

2. Marc Augé defined these sorts of spaces as places that have not been able to develop an autonomous identity, either because the individuals who normally inhabit them do not spend enough time to identify with them—and therefore provide them with an independent identity— or because their structure and aesthetics is identical to man other places with similar functions all around the globe. Examples of the former would be transportation stations, including airports, which have been traditionally set to be the epitome of this sort of place. As for the latter, shopping centers and malls would conform a clear representation.

3. Exceptions to this definition would be those stations or airports that have become sites of reference because of their particular architecture, characteristic symbolism or historical relevance.

4. Tim Gill. "Licence and Confrontation." *The Guardian*, 13–04–2005. Retrieved on January 15 from http://www.theguardian.com/education/2005/apr/13/schools.uk.

5. Pufall and Unsworth, 75.

6. Scheper-Hughes and Hoffman, 354.

7. E. Anthony Rotundo. "Boy Culture" in Henry Jenkins (ed.), *The Children's Culture Reader*, pp. 337–362. New York: New York University Press, 1998.

8. Right after the unfortunate series of events that end with the assassination of her husband, Anne looks for help in the different rural houses located at the margins of their path, but the only answer she gets from neighbors is advice to keep on walking and a reprimand for having left the city: "You know what the situation is. Why did you come from the city to a place like this?" (7:45).

9. Gerard Jones, in *Killing Monsters: Why Children Need Fantasy, Super-Heroes, and Make-Believe Violence* claims that with certain subjects of analysis, "the violence had helped a timid adolescent tap into her own bottled-up emotionality and discover a feeling of personal power" (5). This is the exact point of rupture Haneke tries to investigate through these children characters.

10. Here, we are also referring to aspects of gender and social class, following William A. Corsaro: Clearly, then, Ariès did not believe that things had gotten better for children. In fact, Ariès saw the progressive separation of children and adults as part of more general cultural changes that have resulted in separations by social class and race in modern society. He argued that the old society "concentrated the maximum number of ways of life into the minimum of space" and in doing so accepted the mixing of widely different social class groups. Modern society, on the other hand, provides "each way of life with a confined space in which it [is] understood that the dominant features should be respected, and that each person [has] to resemble a conventional model, an ideal type" (416).

11. Howard P. Chudacoff, 19.

BIBLIOGRAPHY

Augé, Marc. *Non-Places: Introduction to an Anthropology of Supermodernity*. London and New York: Verso Books, 1995.

Chudacoff, Howard P. *Children at Play*. New York: New York University Press, 2007.

Corsaro, William A. *The Sociology of Childhood*. Thousand Oaks, CA: Pine Forge Press, 2005.

Deleuze, Gilles. *Anti-Oedipus: Capitalism and Schizophrenia*. Minneapolis: University of Minnesota Press, 1983

———. *Thousand Plateaus: Capitalism and Schizophrenia*. Minneapolis: University of Minnesota Press, 1987

Fass, Paula S. *Children of a New World: Society, Culture, and Globalization*. New York: NYU Press, 2007.

Gill, Tim. "Licence and Confrontation." *The Guardian* (London), April 13, 2005.

Harvey, David. *Spaces of Global Capitalism*. London and New York: Verso, 2006.

———. *Social Justice and the City*. Athens, GA: University of Georgia Press, 2010.

———. *Rebel Cities: From the Right to the City to the Urban Revolution*. London and New York: Verso Books, 2012.

Hill, Malcolm. "Children's Voices on Ways of Having a Voice: Children's and Young People's Perspectives on Methods Used in Research and Consultation." *Childhood* 13 (February 2006): 69–89.

Jones, Gerard. *Killing Monsters: Why Children Need Fantasy, Super Heroes, and Make-Believe Violence*. New York: Basic Books, 2002.

Lefèbvre, Henri. *The Production of Space*. Cambridge, MA: Blackwell, 2009.

Mintz, Steven. *Huck's Raft, a History of American Childhood*. Cambridge, MA: Belknap Press of Harvard University Press, 2004.

Les temps du loup. Directed by Michael Haneke. 2003. France: Bavaria Film. DVD.

McCarthy, Cormac. *The Road*. New York: Vintage Books, 2007.

Pufall, Peter B., and Richard P. Unsworth. *Rethinking Childhood*. New Brunswick: Rutgers University Press, 2004.

Rotundo, E. Anthony. "Boy Culture." In *The Children's Culture Reader*, edited by Henry Jenkins, 337–62. New York: New York University Press, 1998.

Scheper-Hughes, Nancy, and Daniel Hoffman. "Brazilian Apartheid: Street Kids and the Struggle for Urban Space." In *Small Wars: The Cultural Politics of Childhood*, edited by Nancy Scheper-Hughes and Carolyn Sargent. Los Angeles: University of California Press, 1998.

Soja, Edward W. *Thirdspace: Journeys to Los Angeles and Other Real-and-Imagined Places*. New York: Wiley-Blackwell, 1996.

———. *Postmodern Geographies: The Reassertion of Space in Critical Social Theory*. London and New York: Verso, 2011.

Solà-Morales Rubió, Ignasi de. Presente y futuros. La arquitectura en las ciudades. Barcelona: Collegi Oficial d'Arquitectes de Catalunya/Centre de Cultura Contemporània, 1996.

The Road. Directed by John Hillcoat. 2009. New York: Dimension Films. DVD.

Chapter Six

When Disney Went Apocalyptic

The Symbolism of Apocalyptic Images in a Post-9/11 World

Eric D. Miller

INTRODUCTION

Time magazine dubbed the first decade of the millennium as "The Decade from Hell."[1] Without a doubt, during this period, America and the world have faced profound challenges, difficulties, and even traumas. The year 2000 began peacefully enough—though there were widespread concerns over a "Y2K crisis" due to the occurrence of possible technological glitches, such as the inability to continue to utilize computers due to computer codes possibly failing to recognize the year "2000." Rapid and profound changes in technological advances—including increasing concerns over potential negative consequences of these advances—grew immensely over the past decade. There were even some vague concerns of terrorism then that proved well-founded given an apparent plot to bomb the Los Angeles airport. Later that year, America faced one of the most controversial and closest presidential election in its history where the popular vote winner, Al Gore, lost via a Supreme Court decision regarding the Florida vote, to George W. Bush.

Months later, America and the world were shocked by the terrorist attacks of September 11, 2001, that left approximately three thousand individuals dead and New York City's World Trade Center in ruins. Arguably, this seminal event not only set the tone for much of the decade but also still significantly colors our perceptions of the world today. These attacks helped to launch the War on Terrorism that ultimately guided America's entry into ongoing wars in Afghanistan and Iraq. Ever since 9/11, the past several years have seen the specter and threat of terrorism and war across various areas of the world (including, but not limited to, the Middle East).

Since 9/11, we have been forced to become aware of rather ghoulish scenarios: biological, chemical, radiological, or nuclear attacks are now stronger possibilities in our world. However, threats to our society need not be completely manmade: we have also witnessed many cataclysmic natural disasters over the past several years. In America, the devastation wrought by Hurricane Katrina (2005) and Superstorm Sandy (2012), among other natural catastrophes, offered some particularly powerful images (although there have been many other global disasters such as the 2010 earthquake in Haiti and the 2011 earthquake and tsunami in Japan). And, of course, America has experienced—and is still struggling with—the greatest economic collapse since the Great Depression. Horrific mass shootings, including the slaughter of twenty first graders at a Newtown, Connecticut, elementary school have highlighted the sobering reality that even our children are not immune from the threats and ills present in society today. Arguably, if one were motivated to consider end-of-the-world thinking, the aforementioned events might signify localized versions of apocalyptic-like behavior.

Interestingly, during this same period, several films have been released containing very strong themes and imagery of Apocalyptic conditions including (but not limited to): *The Road,*[2] *I Am Legend,*[3] *28 Days Later,*[4] *The Dark Knight,*[5] *Star Wars Episode III: The Revenge of the Sith,*[6] *A.I. Artificial Intelligence,*[7] *Cloverfield,*[8] *Apocalypto,*[9] *The Sum of All Fears,*[10] and *2012.*[11] Many of these films also included the use of children as characters (to varying degrees). Amazingly, even some children-themed or animated films, such as *WALL-E*[12] and *9*[13] contain end-of-the-world imagery. The net effects of apocalyptic imagery for both society and the individual have been debated. Some have argued that while such images may reflect an attempt to cope and contend with contemporary problems, including war and terrorism, they may also reflect a yearning to adopt more traditional (including religious) beliefs.[14]

An intriguing basic question to pose is why has there been an influx of these films in recent years—and, also, why have so many of them featured children? Is Hollywood attempting to manufacture—or merely reflect—a perceived social reality of fear about actual societal concerns? While many of these aforesaid films offer messages of hope, one could also wonder whether society has reached an adverse "tipping point" of sorts when such apocalyptic imagery invades films primarily designed for children. This chapter explores these aforementioned and related questions and issues. More generally, the influx of apocalyptic and related horror movies since 9/11 may highlight a need to address the societal and personal traumas not just from that day but also from related ensuing events such as war, terroristic threats, and injustices (such as the Abu Ghraib prison scandal).[15] If we are aiming to come to terms with the horror of 9/11 and its larger global consequences, then a natural corollary would be to consider child characters in these films as well. After all, not only were some children killed in 9/11 (or had loved ones die due to the attacks) but those who were children at the time of the attacks (as well as future generations) may likely try to comprehend these attacks and their aftermath; the use of child characters in film, in part, may be an especially helpful way to illuminate such a perspective.

A central theme of this paper is that many societal events (including the war on terrorism) immediately before and after 9/11 effectively laid the groundwork for potentially greater prevalence of apocalyptic thinking. However, as considered in this paper, the event of 9/11 likely was the single-most critical event driving this effect. An important related argument of this paper is that apocalyptic imagery in post-9/11 films—including in Disney-themed films, like *WALL-E*—is a by-product of these larger societal trends. In that respect, this paper considers that there is a difference between apocalyptic films featuring children versus such films primarily marketed to children and adolescents. Further, while the focus of my paper does not offer an in-depth analysis of any particular film per se, rather (as implied by the chapter title), there ought to be something almost shocking about apocalyptic imagery in Disney (or such related) movies. This paper aims to detail and describe the larger societal landscape that may have contributed to the creation of such films in the first place.

APOCALYPTIC TERROR: HOLLYWOOD'S (PRE- AND) POST-9/11 BOGEYMAN?

Just hours after the September 11, 2001 attacks, while anchoring the breaking news, veteran journalist Tom Brokaw remarked live and on-air that the aforementioned date was "A day unlike any other in the long course of American history."[16] In many ways, Brokaw was correct. The carnage associated with 9/11 truly represents an event that, in many ways, was unique to American history. To date, it represents the most devastating foreign attack on continental America soil in generations and it was nearly the single bloodiest day in American history (second only to the 1862 Civil War battle in Antietam, Maryland).[17] Many psychologists and mental health scholars have studied the longer-term fallout from 9/11 and, in most instances, most Americans have adapted to the trauma of 9/11.[18] Even so, it is difficult to ignore that 9/11 remains a seminal event in contemporary American and world history and culture. Arguably, the ensuing "War on Terrorism"— including military involvement in Afghanistan and Iraq—may not have occurred had 9/11 not happened. Perhaps even more significantly, 9/11 created greater awareness—including, of course, amongst children—of the potential

for mass calamity and casualties and terrifying scenarios involving biological, chemical, radiological, and nuclear attacks. Repeated exposure to war
and trauma notwithstanding, historically, children have shown much resilien-
cy in the wake of other previous existential threats of mass destruction, such
as during the Cold War period. [19]

To some degree, Hollywood has attempted to simply to recreate many of
the critical events either from the actual day of September 11, 2001, or its
immediate aftermath through films such as *United 93*[20] and *World Trade
Center*.[21] Some criticized such films as being released "too soon" after the
trauma of 9/11—while others have contended that such films were released
"too late" in that Americans should have long since been deeply troubled by
the lack of preparedness and military responses to 9/11.[22] The 2003 television movie *D.C. Sniper: 23 Days of Fear*[23] also was a portrayal of another
significant post-9/11 event, the October 2002 Washington, D.C. area sniper
attacks carried out by John Allen Muhammad and (then minor) Lee Boyd
Malvo. The attacks, which killed or wounded over a dozen individuals, ac-
centuated the many terror-related fears that occurred in the wake of the one-
year commemoration of 9/11 and the subsequent anthrax attacks as well as
the military incursion in Afghanistan.[24] The attacks further underscore the
point that, as can be the case in the apocalyptical tales, minors can serve as
central figures in the midst of cataclysmic events.

Even if 9/11 was not explicitly mentioned, its relevance can surely be
inferred in many prominent films in the decade since the terrorist attacks. For
instance, Christopher Nolan's Batman epic *The Dark Knight*[25] can be viewed
as a commentary on both the issues of how shady or hazy teroristic threats
can paralyze communities with fear as well as the post-9/11 counterterrorism
tactics used to address or prevent such threats.[26] The 2009 film *The Road*[27]
was based on Cormac McCarthy's 2006 highly acclaimed novel (with the
same title); it has been argued that it likely incorporated much of the angst
that followed 9/11.[28] McCarthy himself, who fathered a child while in his
mid-sixties, has remarked that much of his inspiration to write *The Road* was
borne out of lingering concern over what America might look like in the
future to his young son.[29] This is relevant to children given that psychologists have long appreciated the myriad of ecological and environmental systems, including familial and societal influences, which influence a child's
development and well-being.[30]

To the degree that early twenty-first-century film has depicted mass carnage, terror, or apocalyptic images, it is arguable how much of a singular
impact the 9/11 terrorist acts have had on this collective psyche of trauma. In
the immediate years following 9/11 and the ensuing military operations in
Afghanistan and Iraq, Americans bore witness to a natural disaster, the 2005
Hurricane Katrina, which morphed into a man-made disaster where nearly
two thousand individuals were killed. This apocalyptic disaster highlighted

another instance of a lack of preparedness not just in terms of anticipating and preventing the mass flooding that took place in New Orleans following Katrina's strike but also the bungled and inept initial governmental response to the disaster.[31] And, of course, just three years later, Americans endured the most punishing economic recession since the Great Depression.[32] One study actually examined whether priming individuals to think and write about the effects of 9/11, Middle East tensions, Hurricane Katrina, and the economic recession would cause an increased belief in apocalyptic thinking, or a belief that one would personally witness the end of the world. Even though this priming exercise (where individuals wrote about their own beliefs regarding the larger societal consequences of these four aforementioned events) did not significantly increase such thinking, a surprising number of subjects were open to the possibility of personally experiencing or witnessing an apocalypse—and, self-described religious individuals were particularly likely to endorse attitudes suggesting that they would personally witness the end of the world.[33] It has also been argued that, to some degree, post-9/11 apocalyptic cinema has explored religious themes in much deeper contexts particularly in terms of religion's more extreme (positive and negative) potentials for humanity. For instance, the 2007 film *I Am Legend* illustrates the ill effects of humankind playing God (by accidentally creating a deadly virus) while ultimately turning to traditional religion and God once humanity has largely been destroyed.[34] Even more significantly, in the wake of 9/11, there appears to have been not just an increased number of apocalyptic films but rather end-of-the-world films that focus on humanity's larger world and societal problems.[35]

The latter point underscores how movies, particularly horror films, can be used to highlight and give greater awareness of larger existential fears.[36] For instance, the 1983 television drama *The Day After*[37] graphically tried to portray the potential effects and consequences of nuclear war,[38] and the 2004 ecological apocalyptic film *The Day after Tomorrow*[39] served as a cautionary tale about global warming.[40] And, indeed, it would be a misnomer to suggest that there were not apocalyptic films prior to 9/11. For instance, select films from the 1950s featured fears about the Cold War (for example, *The Day the Earth Stood Still*[41]) or its potential consequences (for example, *On the Beach*[42]).[43] Moreover, some post-9/11 apocalyptic films, such as *I Am Legend*,[44] are remakes or reworkings of earlier related books or films. However, there are at least two issues that remain unresolved. Even though apocalyptic films had appeared before 9/11, it is unclear if the rate of occurrence of such films has significantly increased since 9/11. The second related issue pertains to the qualitative themes present in such films—and whether pre- and post-9/11 apocalyptic films include different themes. For instance, it is widely believed that the 1996 blockbuster *Independence Day*[45] focused on themes of uncertainty following post–Cold War globalization—but also perhaps more subtle issues of German wartime suffering.[46] If we are to attempt to make any meaningful comparisons of such films, then there should be some way to ascertain the themes present and what precisely portrays an apocalypse. For instance, to classify a motion picture as an apocalyptic film must it presume impending or literal doom, calamities with many deaths or few survivors, disasters with or without clear causes?[47] Relatedly, should we make distinctions amongst films that depict the fall or destruction of a given (real or imagined) civilization or more fantastical possibilities (for example, attacks from space aliens or zombies) versus films that feature more plausible apocalyptic scenarios (for example, the threat of a massive terrorist or military action)? These relatively subtle points can greatly impact how we understand (and label) the possible portrayals of apocalyptic cinema pre- and post-9/11. In terms of understanding the lives and concerns of children in apocalyptic cinema, some of these considerations may be moot insomuch as that simply being able to extract certain themes from such films may be critical. For instance, even though many of the films cited earlier in this paragraph (and indeed throughout this chapter) contain incredibly far-fetched scenarios, the larger issues they imply (for example, nuclear war, climate change) may be fairly palpable not just to adults but even adolescents and younger children.

PORTRAYING VERSUS MARKETING CHILDREN IN APOCALYPTIC FILMS: WHAT'S GOING ON?

In and of itself, the mere presence of children in apocalyptic films should not necessarily be shocking or even troubling. If we assume the premise that apocalyptic films are used (in some form) to portray real or perceived societal ills or calamities, then the inclusion of child or adolescent characters would seem fairly natural to include in such works (since children and adolescents, obviously, are members of society). Moreover, most of the apocalyptic films considered in this paper, at least on the basis of their movie rating (for example, usually a "PG-13" or "R" Motion Picture Association of America rating) were most likely created predominantly for viewing by adults (or older teens).

Clearly, children can be used in film for dramatic effect in order to represent scenes of real (or imagined) atrocities. Even though *Schindler's List*[48] depicts the horrific realities of genocide that occurred during the Holocaust, arguably, one of its most powerful scenes featured the image of a little girl in a red dress (in this black and white film) in order to portray both her innocence and her senseless death.[49] Given the inherent darker nature of apocalyptic films, in theory, it should not be terribly surprising that such films have included select ominous and disturbing scenes featuring children or adolescents. For instance, the 2002 zombie apocalyptic film *28 Days Later*[50] features the hapless search for survivors following a worldwide pandemic which included a scene where the two female protagonists, one of whom was a minor, were on the precipice of being raped.[51] In a lawless, apocalyptic society, it may be fairly easy to imagine a world where antisocial behavior would routinely occur merely out of a need to survive—much like that depicted in McCarthy's *The Road*.[52]

However, it may be somewhat more surprising (or at least somewhat encouraging) that children have been used both literally and symbolically as a reason for hope and to imagine a better future in an apocalyptical world. Consider again McCarthy's *The Road*[53]: It has been argued that this work successfully portrayed a new post-9/11 view of masculinity and fatherhood where the father is determined to protect his son and strive for a better future for him against an incredibly hopeless apocalyptic backdrop.[54] Other recent films with apocalyptic themes further the importance and value of children for both society and the individual. For instance, the 2006 film *Children of Men*[55] depicts the desperation of a society where virtually all humans have become infertile and the dire urgency to protect a rare case of a woman who has successfully achieved pregnancy.[56] Mel Gibson's 2006 *Apocalypto*,[57] which slightly differs from most of the aforementioned films in that it portrays a (Mayan) civilization on the verge of collapse (rather than a potential end of the world or a contemporary world without many humans), also features the theme of children and family as signifying hope for the future juxtaposed against a deeply flawed and troubled society.[58] Instead of considering apocalyptic films that feature children and adolescents, let us consider a couple of apocalyptic films designed to be especially marketed to children and adolescents: The 2008 Disney feature *WALL-E*[59] and the 2009 computer-animated feature *9*.[60]

MARKETING THE APOCALYPSE TO CHILDREN: *WALL-E* AND *9*

There is very little argument over the point that the "G"-rated Disney/Pixar feature *WALL-E*[61] should be construed as an apocalyptic film. This feature depicts an Earth that has been destroyed through years of human pollution where the only hope of returning humans back to Earth, ironically, lies in the hands of robots.[62] This film also highlights the ills associated with overconsumption, gluttony, consumerism, and an overreliance on technology. Even if we assume these to be benevolent themes to portray to children, some have not overlooked the presence of a certain level of irony in that this film (like most other successful Disney films) had many marketing promotions.[63] And yet, others have suggested this film offered a savvy tongue-in-check marketing campaign by unleashing a bogus website for "Buy n Large," which is a corporation depicted in the film that effectively controls the lives of the stranded humans in space; implicit in this satire is that humans (and, by extension, children) are highly susceptible to mass marketing ploys. [64] Unlike WALL-E, [65] the 2009 computer-animated film 9 [66] was rated "PG-13" and, as such, presumably was marketed to older children and teens (although both films did have toys associated with the films). Even so, like WALL-E, [67] 9 [68] was another post-apocalyptic tale where the theme of how excessive reliance and faith in technology has led to societal collapse and ruin was emphasized. [69]

Interestingly, neither film overtly depicts any (human) child characters (though there is a brief scene from WALL-E [70] showing children being educated by a robot). However, many of the characters from these films appear to show childlike behaviors and reactions. In particular, the oafishly obese adults in WALL-E [71] cannot walk or barely care for themselves, much as we might expect from an infant or young toddler. The apocalyptic world featured in 9 [72] features no humans—only machinelike creatures and doll-like figures (created by a deceased scientist who does appear human). However, in his quest to right the ills of this apocalyptic world, one could argue that the title character appears to show adventuresome qualities more representative of a child or adolescent.

Both WALL-E [73] and 9 [74] feature messages of hope and redemption such that they end on a positive note with a possibility of rebirth and renewal following mass calamity and destruction. However, these films should at least cause us to question the appropriateness of apocalyptic imagery in films primarily marketed to children and the more general question of why such films even exist for children (and what sort of commentary can be gleaned from the mere existence of child-themed apocalyptic films). This latter point is particularly important to consider given that children's purchasing power, their ability to persuade their parents to make purchases on their behalf, and the sheer variety and number of products continue to expand whilst the cognitive ability of younger children (and even adolescents) to fully comprehend the persuasive intent of such advertising may not be fully developed. [75]

While the impact that apocalyptic cinematic images has on children has not been fully studied, historically, there have been child-themed movies that have explored other difficult (and somewhat related) issues, including the experience of death. An intriguing study undertook a content-analysis of death-related themes and imagery in ten different Disney films including both classic (for example, Snow White and the Seven Dwarfs [76] and Bambi [77]) and more contemporary motion pictures (for example, Beauty and the Beast [78] and The Lion King [79]); factors such as whether the protagonist or antagonist were killed, the means of death (for example, accidental or purposeful), and subsequent emotional reactions were all coded. The study authors concluded that these films generally allowed children a means to understand and discuss death. However, they also cautioned that such films can send confusing or ambiguous messages, particularly to younger children; likewise, many of these films feature moral messages that some children may not be fully able to appreciate.[80] A similar caution likely bears true in regards to child-themed films containing apocalyptic imagery. That is, on one hand, if such films can promote prosocial values and encourage general well-being in children, then they have likely served a noble purpose. However, just as children may struggle to understand and process death, children and adolescents may find it difficult to fathom the idea that humanity can, in theory, be seriously challenged and even cease to exist. Perhaps this deeper existential question makes such films an even greater challenge for children to process. Social and behavioral science theories about post-apocalyptic thinking remain somewhat limited, particularly in terms of how children consider such thoughts. However, there is some evidence that those who are particularly apt to endorse conspiratorial beliefs (such that others are secretly carrying out behaviors to inflict a certain ideology on society) may also be more likely to espouse apocalyptic beliefs.[81] More generally, though still debated, there is a fairly substantial body of research suggesting that media portrayals of violence—particularly amongst children—do tend to increase both short- and long-term acts of aggression and can serve to desensitize individuals to such acts.[82]

The second question to consider is why have apocalyptic films primarily geared for children even begun to proliferate—and, what social commentary should be presumed due to their mere existence and presence? Writer and essayist Steve Almond attempted to answer this question in a provocative and aptly titled piece, "The Apocalypse Market Is Booming."[83] To some degree, he argued that children and teenagers are sometimes intrigued with the idea of apocalyptic imagery when introduced to science-fiction; traditionally, religious ideology has also offered many apocalyptic themes and images for children to contemplate. However, he suggests a different and more contemporary interpretation as to why apocalyptic film and literature is so prevalent today. He states:

> As a form of disposable entertainment, the apocalypse market is booming. The question is why. The obvious answer is that these narratives tap into anxieties, conscious and otherwise, about the damage we're doing to our species and to the planet. They allow us to safely fantasize about what might be required of us to survive.[84]

Almond likely has a valid point. As discussed earlier, many adults may be searching to make sense of contemporary real and perceived threats. As such, why should we not expect children to develop some of these concerns about such threats—whether they have been formulated by children on their own, through their parents, or due to other forms of social influence? For instance, in the years since 9/11, many parents still struggle to explain the horrors and ramifications associated with the terroristic acts of that day.[85] Once more, it is likely beneficial if a film or related media can help to serve as a means to open dialogue between parents and children about such fears. However, if there truly is an "apocalypse market"—that is, a proliferation of apocalyptic film and literature—then it is unclear as to whether such media, in and of itself, are the source of these fears. Future analyses and investigations would be wise to consider this issue. Consistent with an earlier point, perhaps select "end of the world" fears associated with the turn of the millennium were ultimately realized (to a degree) with society's view that 9/11 was "the" apocalyptic event we all "expected" to happen when we hit 2000.

There is also the larger question of what does the mere presence of apocalyptic films (particularly ones primarily created for children and teenagers) imply about the current state of society. At some level, it might seem downright sobering to think that children should even have the opportunity to be presented with mass media (for example, films) that incorporate apocalyptic-like images or themes—however benign they may be. Naturally, parents and society generally strive to provide an environment where children can develop good feelings about themselves and their world. However, we also live in a world where all of the aforementioned events described in this chapter did (of course) happen. And, we do live in a world where mass calamity and destruction (in theory) could erupt at a moment's notice. While it may not be in anyone's psychological or personal interest to dwell on these points, these are matters that adults—and, at some point, children—need to (or will) acknowledge at some point. Therefore, in some ways, the mere presence of apocalyptic images in child-themed movies may be more illustrative of the social era in which these films were released (for example, a post-9/11 environment). As considered in this chapter, even though some larger societal conditions and events may have contributed to the rise of apocalyptic films— generally speaking—since Y2K and (especially) 9/11, the fact that apocalyptic imagery has crept into children's movies should be viewed as a by-product of this larger societal and social condition.

CONCLUSION

A central thesis of this chapter has been that Hollywood films, particularly since (and perhaps, in part, due to) 9/11 have shown and highlighted much apocalyptic imagery and symbolic content featuring end-of-the-world themes. However, apocalyptic imagery has been featured in films well before 9/11 (though the precise degree to which this has been undertaken remains an unanswered empirical question). To the degree that Hollywood has advanced such imagery, a critical question may be why and what purpose do such films have? There are likely at least four key, equally valid possibilities. First, to some degree, *apocalyptic imagery may be used to depict reality* in that certain films may have very strong parallels to previous disasters or calamities that have occurred; such films may serve to help us make sense of these aforesaid disasters. Another possibility is that *apocalyptic films may fuel fear and paranoia in individuals.* It is unclear if the imagery itself or simply the underlying themes associated with apocalyptic films may foment distress; both of these possibilities (including any possible related negative outcomes for individuals and their well-being) should be further considered. A third (and perhaps more productive) consequence of apocalyptic films is that they *offer true warnings about the future.* Apocalyptic films may provide a vehicle for greater social awareness of select issues and, in doing so, an impetus to try to remedy such problems. Finally, perhaps the uplifting feature of apocalyptic films is that they also may *offer hope about the future.* Consistent with the previous point, apocalyptic films almost serve the same role as "The Ghost of Christmas Future" did for Ebenezer Scrooge in *A Christmas Carol*[86]: That is, it can prime individuals to consider what may be—but does not have to be—in our future in order to better the here and now. Psychological research has found, in select instances, that imagining loss can actually produce positive benefits.[87] Moreover, many apocalyptic films carry a silver lining in that continued goodness of others and the human spirit are often portrayed.

The fact that children may be depicted in apocalyptic films may not be terribly surprising (though there is often much variation in how children are portrayed in such films). However, there are more challenging questions to consider when apocalyptic imagery is used in films primarily meant to be viewed by children or adolescents. Like adults, children and adolescents may share some of the concerns that may have caused individuals to become interested in apocalyptic films in the first place; likewise, such films may have the potential to bestow positive messages to children and adolescents. However, there is also the possibility that such films may also foment confusion, angst, indifference, or aggressive impulses in children and adolescents. Such films also often force us to face difficult moral questions about humanity's worth and our treatment of each other and the world. While these questions may be challenging for adults, they may be especially difficult for children and adolescents to fully process.

The issue of apocalyptic imagery in film appears to have growing resonance and interest amongst the general public and Hollywood alike. Though one could argue that Hollywood may be simply reflecting wider-spread apocalyptic beliefs in the culture, there is some evidence that apocalyptic culture, including Hollywood-produced disaster and apocalyptic films, may foment such apocalyptic beliefs in individuals.[88] Contemporary social science and humanities scholars would be well-advised to continue to address why this may be so and to further explore many of the questions posed in this chapter. There is merit to examining the content of apocalyptic films and the possible underlying societal and political forces and events that may have inspired the creation of such motion pictures. To that end, future historical analyses should help to clarify whether there truly was a unique sort of pervasive angst present in the first decade (or so) of the twenty-first century (and, if so, how much of this angst was specifically due to the 9/11 terrorist acts). Perhaps an even greater challenge involves gaining a clearer understanding of the psychological impact that these films have for individuals (both adults and children) and society.

NOTES

1. Andy Serwer, "The Decade from Hell," *Time*, December 7, 2009, 30–38.
2. *The Road.* Dir. John Hillcoat. Dimension Films, 2009. Film.
3. *I Am Legend.* Dir. Francis Lawrence. Warner Bros. Pictures, 2007. Film.
4. *28 Days Later.* Dir. Danny Boyle. Fox Searchlight Pictures, 2003. Film.
5. *The Dark Knight.* Dir. Christopher Nolan. Warner Bros. Pictures, 2008. Film.
6. *Star Wars: Episode III: Revenge of the Sith.* Dir. George Lucas. 20th Century Fox, 2005. Film.
7. *A.I. Artificial Intelligence.* Dir. Steven Spielberg. Dreamworks, 2001. Film.
8. *Cloverfield.* Dir. Matt Reeves. Paramount Pictures, 2008. Film.
9. *Apocalypto.* Dir. Mel Gibson. Buena Vista, 2006. Film.
10. *The Sum of All Fears.* Dir. Phil Alden Robinson. Paramount Pictures, 2002. Film.
11. *2012.* Dir. Roland Emmerich. Sony Pictures/Columbia, 2009. Film.
12. *WALL-E.* Dir. Andrew Stanton. Walt Disney Pictures, 2008. Film.
13. *9.* Dir. Shane Acker. Focus Features, 2009. Film.
14. Mervyn F. Bendle, "The Apocalyptic Imagination and Popular Culture," *Journal of Religion and Popular Culture* 11, no. 1 (Fall 2005): n.p.
15. Aviva Briefel and Sam J. Miller, "Introduction," in *Horror after 9/11: World of Fear, Cinema of Terror*, eds. Aviva Briefel and Sam J. Miller (Austin, TX: University of Texas Press, 2011), 1–10.
16. Brian A. Monahan, *The Shock of the News: Media Coverage and the Making of 9/11* (New York: New York University, 2010), 90.
17. Eric D. Miller, "Finding Meaning at Ground Zero for Future Generations: Some Reflections a Decade after 9/11," *International Social Science Review* 86, nos. 3 & 4 (Fall-Winter 2011): 113–133.
18. Roxane Cohen Silver, "An Introduction to '9/11: Ten Years Later,'" *American Psychologist* 66, no. 6 (September 2011): 427–428.
19. Milton Schwebel, "How Will the Children Fare?" *The Society for the Study of Peace, Conflict, and Violence*, https://www.clarku.edu/peacepsychology/miltonschwebelop-ed.html (accessed July 1, 2014), 1–2.
20. *United 93.* Dir. Paul Greengrass. Universal Pictures, 2006. Film.
21. *World Trade Center.* Dir. Oliver Stone. Paramount Pictures, 2006. Film.
22. Frank Rich, "Too Soon? It's Too Late for 'United 93,'" *New York Times*, May 7, 2006, http://www.nytimes.com/2006/05/07/opinion/07rich.html (accessed November 1, 2013), 1–3.
23. *D.C. Sniper: 23 Days of Fear.* Dir. Tom McLoughlin. Orly Adelson Productions, 2003. Film.
24. Jack R. Censer and William Miller, *On the Trail of the D.C. Sniper: Fear and the Media* (Charlottesville, VA: University of Virginia Press, 2010), 34–35.
25. *The Dark Knight.*

26. John Ip, "The Dark Knight's War on Terrorism," *Ohio State Journal of Criminal Law* 9, no. 1 (September 2011): 209–229.

27. *The Road.*

28. Aitor Ibarrola-Armendariz, "Cormac McCarthy's *The Road*: Rewriting the Myth of the American West," *European Journal of American Studies* (Special Issue, 2011): 1–13.

29. Tim Adams, "Cormac McCarthy: America's Great Poetic Visionary," *The Guardian/ The Observer*, December 19, 2009, http://www.theguardian.com/theobserver/2009/dec/20/observer-profile-cormac-mccarthy (accessed November 1, 2013), 1–5.

30. Urie Bronfenbrenner, *The Ecology of Human Development: Experiments by Nature and Design* (Cambridge, MA: Harvard University Press, 2010), 3–15.

31. Eric D. Miller, "Can Americans Ever Feel Safe in a Post-9/11 and Hurricane Katrina World?" in *Homeland Security: Protecting America's Targets (Vol. 2)*, ed. J. J. F. Forest (Westport, CT: Praeger, 2006), 350–364.

32. Paul Krugman, *End This Depression Now!* (New York: Norton, 2012).

33. Eric D. Miller, "Apocalypse Now? The Relevance of Religion for Beliefs about the End of the World," *Journal of Beliefs and Values* 33, no. 1 (April 2012): 111–115.

34. Conrad Ostwalt, "Apocalyptic," in *The Routledge Companion to Religion and Film*, ed. John Lyden (New York: Routledge, 2009), 379–380.

35. John Walliss and James Aston, "Doomsday America: The Pessimistic Turn of Post-9/11 Apocalyptic Cinema," *Journal of Religion and Popular Culture* 23, no. 1 (April 2011): 53–64.

36. Briefel and Miller, *op. cit.*, p. 9.

37. *The Day After*. Dir. Nicholas Meyer. ABC Motion Picture Division, 1983. Film.

38. I. Randy Kulman and T. John Akamatsu, "The Effects of Television on Large-Scale Attitude Change: Viewing 'The Day After,'" *Journal of Applied Social Psychology* 18, no. 13 (October 1988): 1121–1132.

39. *The Day after Tomorrow*. Dir. Roland Emmerich. 20th Century Fox, 2004. Film.

40. Anthony A. Leiserowitz, "Before and after the Day after Tomorrow: A U.S. Study of Climate Change Risk Perception," *Environment* 46, no. 9 (November 2004): 22–37.

41. *The Day the Earth Stood Still*. Dir. Robert Wise. 20th Century Fox, 1951. Film.

42. *On the Beach*. Dir. Stanley Kramer. United Artists, 1959. Film.

43. Tony Shaw, *Hollywood's Cold War* (Amherst, MA: University of Massachusetts Press, 2007), 160.

44. *I Am Legend.*

45. *Independence Day*. Dir. Roland Emmerich. 20th Century Fox, 1996. Film.

46. Robert Pirro, "*Luftkrieg* and Alien Invasion: Unacknowledged Themes of German Wartime Suffering in the Hollywood Blockbuster Independence Day," *European Journal of American Culture* 30, no. 1 (May 2011): 19–42.

47. Conrad Ostwalt, "Visions of the End: Secular Apocalypse in Recent Hollywood Film," *Journal of Religion and Film* 2, no. 1 (April 1998): 1–6.

48. *Schindler's List*. Dir. Steven Spielberg. Universal Picture, 1993. Film.

49. David Crowe, *Oskar Schindler: The Untold Account of His Life, Wartime Activities, and the True Story Behind the List* (Cambridge, MA: Westview, 2004), 201–202.

50. *28 Days Later.*

51. Nick Muntean and Matthew Thomas Payne, "Attack of the Livid Dead: Recalibrating Terror in the Post-September 11 Zombie Film," in *The War on Terror and American Popular Culture*, eds. Andrew Schopp and Matthew B. Hill (Cranbury, NJ: Associated University Presses, 2009), 239–258.

52. *The Road.*

53. Ibid.

54. Nell Sullivan, "The Good Guys: McCarthy's *The Road* as Post–9/11 Male Sentimental Novel," *Genre* 46, no. 1 (Spring 2013): 79–101.

55. *Children of Men*. Dir. Alfonso Cuarón. Universal Pictures, 2006. Film.

56. Sarah Schwartzman, "*Children of Men* and a Plural Messianism," *Journal of Religion and Film* 13, no. 1 (April 2009): 1–7.

57. *Apocalypto.*

58. Richard D. Hansen, "Relativism, Revisionism, Aboriginalism, and Emic/Etic Truth," in *The Ethics of Anthropology and Amerindian Research: Reporting on Environmental Degradation and Warfare,* eds. Richard J. Chacon and Rubén G. Mendoza (New York: Springer, 2012): 147–190.

59. *WALL-E.*

60. *9.*

61. *WALL-E.*

62. Robin L. Murray and Joseph K. Heumann, "*WALL-E*: From Environmental Adaptation to Sentimental Nostalgia," *Jump Cut: A Review of Contemporary Media* 51 (Spring 2009): 1–13.

63. Jesse Carey, "WALL*E-Mart: What Are We Teaching Kids?" *The Christian Broadcasting Network,* http://www.cbn.com/entertainment/screen/Carey_Walle_Message.aspx (accessed November 1, 2013), 1–2.

64. Mike P. Williams, "Pixar's marketing campaign for the Buy n Large corporation in WALL-E," *YAHOO! Movies,* https://uk.movies.yahoo.com/pixars-marketing-campaign-buy-n-large-corporation-wall-091900455.html (accessed July 1, 2014), 1–2.

65. *WALL-E.*

66. *9.*

67. *WALL-E.*

68. *9.*

69. Mary Pols, "In the Movie *9,* Technology Ruins the World . . . Again," *Time,* September 10, 2009, http://content.time.com/time/arts/article/0,8599,1921387,00.html (accessed November 1, 2013), 1–2.

70. *WALL-E.*

71. *WALL-E.*

72. *9.*

73. *WALL-E.*

74. *9.*

75. Sandra L. Calvert, "Children as Consumers: Advertising and Marketing," *The Future of Children* 18, no. 1 (Spring 2008): 205–234.

76. *Snow White and the Seven Dwarfs.* Dir. David Hand. Walt Disney Pictures, 1937. Film.

77. *Bambi.* Dir. David Hand. Walt Disney Pictures, 1942. Film.

78. *Beauty and the Beast.* Dirs. Gary Trousdale and Kirk Wise. Walt Disney Pictures, 1991. Film.

79. *The Lion King.* Dirs. Rob Minkoff and Roger Allers. Walt Disney Pictures, 1994. Film.

80. Meredith Cox, Erin Garrett, and James A. Graham, "Death in Disney Films: Implications for Children's Understanding of Death," *Omega* 50, no. 4 (November 2005): 267–280.

81. Michael Barkun, *A Culture of Conspiracy: Apocalyptic Visions in Contemporary America.* 2nd ed. (Berkeley, CA: University of California Pres, 2013), 1–14.

82. Craig A. Anderson, Leonard Berkowitz, Edward Donnerstein, L. Rowell Huesmann, James D. Johnson, Daniel Linz, Neil M. Malamuth, and Ellen Wartella, "The Influence of Media Violence on Youth," *Psychological Science in the Public Interest* 4, no. 3 (December 2003): 81–110.

83. Steve Almond, "The Apocalypse Market Is Booming," *New York Times,* September 27, 2013, mobile.nytimes.com/2013/09/29/magazine/the-apocalypse-market-is-booming.html?from=magazine (accessed November 1, 2013), 1–5.

84. Ibid., 2.

85. Eileen Kennedy-Moore, "Talking with Children about 9/11," *Psychology Today,* September 4, 2011, http://www.psychologytoday.com/blog/growing-friendships/201109/talking-children-about-911 (accessed November 1, 2013), 1–5.

86. Charles Dickens, *A Christmas Carol* (1843; reprint, New York: Tribeca, 2013).

87. Eric D. Miller, "Imagining Partner Loss and Mortality Salience: Consequences for Romantic Relationship Satisfaction," *Social Behavior and Personality* 31, no. 2 (March 2003): 167–80.

88. Matthew Schneider-Mayerson, "Disaster Movies and the 'Peak Oil' Movement: Does Popular Culture Encourage Eco-Apocalyptic Beliefs in the United States?" *Journal for the Study of Religion, Nature and Culture* 7, no. 3 (2013): 289–314.

BIBLIOGRAPHY

Adams, Tim. "Cormac McCarthy: America's Great Poetic Visionary," *The Guardian/The Observer* (2009). http://www.theguardian.com/theobserver/2009/dec/20/observer-profile-cormac-mccarthy.

Almond, Steve. "The Apocalypse Market Is Booming," *New York Times* (2013). http://mobile.nytimes.com/2013/09/29/magazine/the-apocalypse-market-is-booming.html?from=magazine.

Anderson, Craig, A. Leonard Berkowitz, Edward Donnerstein, L. Rowell Huesmann, James D. Johnson, Daniel Linz, Neil M. Malamuth, and Ellen Wartella. "The Influence of Media Violence on Youth," *Psychological Science in the Public Interest* 4, no. 3 (December 2003): 81–110.

Barkun, Michael. *A Culture of Conspiracy: Apocalyptic Visions in Contemporary America*. 2nd ed. Berkeley, CA: University of California Press, 2013.

Bendle, Mervyn F. "The Apocalyptic Imagination and Popular Culture," *Journal of Religion and Popular Culture* 11, no. 1 (Fall 2005): n.p.

Briefel, Aviva and Sam J. Miller. "Introduction," in *Horror after 9/11: World of Fear, Cinema of Terror*, edited by Aviva Briefel and Sam J. Miller, 1–10. Austin, TX: University of Texas Press, 2011.

Bronfenbrenner, Urie. *The Ecology of Human Development: Experiments by Nature and Design*. Cambridge, MA: Harvard University Press, 2010.

Calvert, Sandra L. "Children as Consumers: Advertising and Marketing," *The Future of Children* 18, no. 1 (Spring 2008): 205–234.

Carey, Jesse. "WALL*E-Mart: What Are We Teaching Kids?" *The Christian Broadcasting Network* (2013). http://www.cbn.com/entertainment/screen/Carey_Walle_Message.aspx.

Censer, Jack R. and William Miller, *On the Trail of the D.C. Sniper: Fear and the Media*. Charlottesville, VA: University of Virginia Press, 2010.

Cohen Silver, Roxane. "An Introduction to '9/11: Ten Years Later,'" *American Psychologist* 66, no. 6 (September 2011): 427–428.

Cox, Meredith, Erin Garrett, and James A. Graham. "Death in Disney Films: Implications for Children's Understanding of Death," *Omega* 50, no. 4 (November 2005): 267–280.

Crowe, David. *Oskar Schindler: The Untold Account of His Life, Wartime Activities, and the True Story Behind the List*. Cambridge, MA: Westview, 2004.

Dickens, Charles. *A Christmas Carol*. New York: Tribeca, 1843/2013.

Hansen, Richard D. "Relativism, Revisionism, Aboriginalism, and Emic/Etic Truth," in *The Ethics of Anthropology and Amerindian Research: Reporting on Environmental Degradation and Warfare*, edited by Richard J. Chacon and Rubén G. Mendoza, 147–190. New York: Springer, 2012.

Ibarrola-Armendariz, Aitor. "Cormac McCarthy's *The Road*: Rewriting the Myth of the American West," *European Journal of American Studies* (Special Issue 2011): 1–13.

Ip, John. "The Dark Knight's War on Terrorism," *Ohio State Journal of Criminal Law* 9, no. 1 (September 2011): 209–229.

Kennedy-Moore, Eileen. "Talking with Children about 9/11," *Psychology Today* (2011). http://www.psychologytoday.com/blog/growing-friendships/201109/talking-children-about-911.

Krugman, Paul. *End This Depression Now!* New York: Norton, 2012.

Kulman, I. Randy and T. John Akamatsu, "The Effects of Television on Large-Scale Attitude Change: Viewing 'The Day After,'" *Journal of Applied Social Psychology* 18, no. 13 (October 1988): 1121–1132.

Leiserowitz, Anthony A. "Before and after the Day after Tomorrow: A U.S. Study of Climate Change Risk Perception," *Environment* 46, no. 9 (November 2004): 22–37.

Miller, Eric D. "Imagining Partner Loss and Mortality Salience: Consequences for Romantic Relationship Satisfaction," *Social Behavior and Personality* 31, no. 2 (March 2003): 167–180.

———. "Can Americans Ever Feel Safe In a Post-9/11 and Hurricane Katrina World?" in *Homeland Security: Protecting America's Targets (Volume 2)*, edited by J. J. F, Forest, 350–364. Westport, CT: Praeger, 2006.

———. "Finding Meaning at Ground Zero for Future Generations: Some Reflections a Decade after 9/11," *International Social Science Review* 86, nos. 3 & 4 (Fall-Winter 2011): 113–133.

———. "Apocalypse Now? The Relevance of Religion for Beliefs about the End of the World," *Journal of Beliefs and Values* 33, no. 1 (April 2012): 111–115.

Murray, Robin L. and Joseph K. Heumann, "*WALL-E*: From Environmental Adaptation to Sentimental Nostalgia," *Jump Cut: A Review of Contemporary Media* 51 (Spring 2009): 1–13.

Monahan, Brian A. *The Shock of the News: Media Coverage and the Making of 9/11*. New York: New York University, 2010.

Muntean, Nick and Matthew Thomas Payne, "Attack of the Livid Dead: Recalibrating Terror in the Post-September 11 Zombie Film," in *The War on Terror and American Popular Culture*, edited by Andrew Schopp and Matthew B. Hill. Cranbury, NJ: Associated University Presses, 2009.

Ostwalt, Conrad. "Visions of the End: Secular Apocalypse in Recent Hollywood Film," *Journal of Religion and Film* 2, no. 1 (April 1998): 1–6.

———. "Apocalyptic," in *The Routledge Companion to Religion and Film*, edited by John Lyden. New York: Routledge, 2009.

Pirro, Robert. "*Luftkrieg* and Alien Invasion: Unacknowledged Themes of German Wartime Suffering in the Hollywood Blockbuster Independence Day," *European Journal of American Culture* 30, no. 1 (May 2011): 19–42.

Pols, Mary. "In the Movie *9*, Technology Ruins the World . . . Again," *Time* (2009). http://content.time.com/time/arts/article/0,8599,1921387,00.html.

Rich, Frank. "Too Soon? It's Too Late for 'United 93,'" *New York Times* (2006). http://www.nytimes.com/2006/05/07/opinion/07rich.html.

Serwer, Andy. "The Decade from Hell," *Time* (December 2009): 30–38.

Schneider-Mayerson, Matthew. "Disaster Movies and the 'Peak Oil' Movement: Does Popular Culture Encourage Eco-Apocalyptic Beliefs in the United States?" *Journal for the Study of Religion, Nature and Culture* 7, no. 3 (2013): 289–314.

Schwartzman, Sarah. "*Children of Men* and a Plural Messianism," *Journal of Religion and Film* 13, no. 1 (April 2009): 1–7.

Schwebel, Milton. "How Will the Children Fare?" *The Society for the Study of Peace, Conflict, and Violence* (n.d.) https://www.clarku.edu/peacepsychology/miltonschwebelop-ed.html.

Shaw, Tony. *Hollywood's Cold War*. Amherst, MA: University of Massachusetts Press, 2007.

Sullivan, Nell. "The Good Guys: McCarthy's *The Road* as Post–9/11 Male Sentimental Novel," *Genre* 46, no. 1 (Spring 2013): 79–101.

Walliss, John and James Aston. "Doomsday America: The Pessimistic Turn of Post-9/11 Apocalyptic Cinema," *Journal of Religion and Popular Culture* 23, no. 1 (April 2011): 53–64.

Williams, Mike P. "Pixar's marketing campaign for the Buy n Large corporation in WALL-E," *YAHOO! Movies* (2013). https://uk.movies.yahoo.com/pixars-marketing-campaign-buy-n-large-corporation-wall-091900455.html.

Chapter Seven

Children of Hope

The Portrayal of Children in Post-Apocalyptic Films after 9/11

Betül Ateşci Koçak

INTRODUCTION

In a recent BBC documentary called *Wild Burma: Nature's Lost Kingdom*, the documentary crew aimed to find an elephant herd with their babies so that they could prove the continuity of the life of elephants. The presence of the baby elephants with families would show that the species is not endangered. A search such as this implies the researchers' expectation of the continuity of elephants' lives. It is obvious that the only way to see evidence of this continuity is through the baby elephants as the birth of more baby elephants proves that they are not extinct. While watching the documentary, one can easily feel the excitement and happiness of the group of researchers. They get excited and happy seeing that the baby elephants still exist and that gives them hope to protect the species from extinction. This hope of the scientists in the documentary for the continuity of this species also raises questions about the notion of hope in relation to the survival of human species.

The notion of hope, looking initially in a wider aspect, is scattered throughout many areas and moments in life. As Joseph Godfrey states, hope is seen in several things:

> Hope shows up in our song and poetry, in our politics and religion, and in our very ordinary speech. Sometimes it is plainly expressed; more often it is veiled in images: to be a winner, a lover, to be saved, to build a just society. And, often as words and images are used for hopes, more often still hope comes

across quite wordlessly; only a manner of being silent seems to fit the hope of
some people. [1]

Godfrey's explanation reveals that hope is almost in everything in our daily
life. And Maria Lisboa explains hope's effect at times when life becomes
grim:

> In the myth of Pandora's Box, once all evils had been released into the world
> the only thing left inside the box was hope, and even hope, like fire, turns out
> to be a mixed blessing. It is because of hope that we keep going when all
> seems lost . . . , keep attempting to fulfil desire because it might just be
> possible. [2]

As the quotations may suggest, either explicitly or metaphorically, hope is
multifaceted. It appears in the flow of everyday living in conversations,
images, songs, and prayers or in our future plans as well as at the times of
great difficulties one is exposed to.

In these earthly affairs, children stand as important agents with regard to
hope. Defined as "a young human being below the age of puberty or below
the legal age of humanity," [3] children have generally been considered to
spread positive ideas for humanity. However, this case for children has not
always been the same. For instance, "in medieval society the idea of childhood did not exist" [4] and belief in the child's innocence and that it could be a
promising agent for the future was almost out of the question. As Robin
Bernstein said,

> Three hundred years ago, there was no assumption that children were inno-
> cent. That idea only became common sense in the United States in the early
> nineteenth century. Once the idea of childhood became laminated to the idea
> of innocence, children could be used strategically in political arguments. Chil-
> dren made these arguments appear to be apolitical, or simply evocations of
> truth. [5]

Contemporarily, this past approach to children has altered a great deal and in
the twentieth and twenty-first centuries, the general tendency is to approach a
baby or a child with notions of innocence and purity. Over time, either
politically or sociologically, the symbol of the innocent child became linked
with the notion of hope. Even in daily life, for instance, there are people in
several cultures who suggest couples have a baby in order to overcome their
marital problems. Or, when a child survives a disaster or a severe accident,
his/her survival is generally linked to hope and miracles. Similarly, when a
parent survives from a cataclysm, it is said that the presence of their baby or
child is a great power to help them at the edge of their experience between
life and death. [6] And in some cases there are couples who do not want to end
their marriages for the sake of their children. While these brief examples

suggest the child-based notion of hope that is evident on a daily basis, there are also revelations of hope after massive disastrous happenings such as September 11, 2001, in New York City. Peter Pufall and Richard Unsworth remark that there is a growing interest in children in media after the attacks:

> Mass media now reach into children's lives in an unanticipated way. . . . This public tragedy has alerted us all—scholars, parents, public policymakers, and politicians alike—to the reality that the lives of children are no longer bounded by their homes, schools, or neighbourhoods. [7]

That day of the ashes has caused devastating changes in many people's lives in the aftermath. Even years later, Ground Zero's debris area reminds some people of "end-of-the-world scenes" [8] that were evident on that day or of "an apocalyptic vista." [9] Andreas Huyssen tells that on that day "a whole part of Manhattan had been turned into a cemetery . . . a death zone in which the work of clean up and removal went on day and night." [10] Such an atmosphere resulted in American society's close ties in order to lessen and soothe the shock and fear of the unimaginable.

The apocalyptic face of the city after 9/11 resulted in a changing attitude in terms of space and place in America and the representations of it have widely taken place especially in literature and film. In this chapter, I will discuss the issues and symbols in some post-apocalyptic movies and the correlating relationship of society's responses to 9/11 attacks. In both cases, the child figure is analyzed among the most important sources of hope or reasons to cling to life. I also aim to show that by undertaking the study of spatial processes in the context of post-apocalyptic films post-9/11, the terms space, place, and heterotopias become tinged by the overlapping ideas of hope after the events.

FACES OF HOPE AFTER APOCALYPSE

Individuals gradually grow a sense of attachment to a city sometime after their residing in it. The time of becoming accustomed to that new city often results in the individual's feelings of belonging to that place that was once an unknown space. Due to the busy flow of life, the person generally continues unaware of this attachment until it is challenged, threatened, or exposed to natural or man-made disasters. 9/11 is a bitter example showing this mutual interplay between the individual and attachment to the city. According to Elizabeth Grosz's summary of Henri Lefebvre and De Certeau's approach to the formation of the society:

> Humans make cities. Cities are reflections, projections, or expressions of human endeavour. On such views, bodies are usually subordinated to and seen as

merely a "tool" of subjectivity, self-given consciousness. The city is a product not simply of the muscles and energy of the body, but of the conceptual and reflective possibilities of consciousness itself. [11]

The individual gains experience and knowledge within time and starts to get familiar with the surrounding space in the city. Tuan similarly states this case as follows:

> Human beings not only discern geometric patterns in nature and create abstract spaces in the mind, they also try to embody their feelings, images, and thoughts in tangible material. The result is sculptural and architectural space, and on a large scale, the planned city. Progress here is from the inchoate feelings for space and fleeting discernments of it in nature to their public and material reification. [12]

Tuan here draws a line from general to specific by highlighting the move from space to place. The framing of the spatial transition from space to place hints at the personal awareness obtained during the transition period. As the feeling of place does not happen very easily, it may take a long time for one to get to know and become accustomed to their surroundings until s/he can call it a place and internalize it.

The disappearance of the Twin Towers poses a tragic case in spatial terms. The absence of the iconic towers in the city caused a grand change in the face of Manhattan and it led not only New Yorkers, but also the Americans in the surrounding provinces and other nations to question the meaning of American space and American place. In other words, "it irrevocably altered the spaces and consciousness of New York City and Washington, D.C., disrupting everyday lives, place attachment, and place identity for thousands." [13] After the destruction, the usual face and meaning of Manhattan eroded enormously and the New Yorkers suddenly started to witness the space of ruins named Ground Zero instead of the Twin Towers they were used to. In a broader approach, John Agnew and Jonathan Smith explain that the attacks

> encouraged both a sense of the limits of American power and rallying around the flag. . . . There were also unsettling changes in the nation itself. Deep, disruptive, and highly controversial changes were underway in social structure (especially the family) . . . , culture . . . and the economy. [14]

Combining these notions of solidarity with the psychological studies in the aftermath of 9/11 has shown that the events will never be totally erased from the minds of many individuals throughout the country. Post-9/11, there naturally emerged a traumatic essence upon seeing the absence of these iconic buildings in the following days of the attacks considering the importance and enormity of the buildings, and their vast destruction afterward. Additionally, the large number of people who lost their lives and the ones who were missing caused several people in America and around the world to think that the later moments and the consequences were deteriorating instead of the expectations for the news of recuperation. There were changes of attitude in people's communication in their neighborhood, making the shared and hurtful experience result in "a renewed sense of New Yorkers"[15] identity.

Following the tragedy, a sense of hope has been a dominant idea reflected in several areas during the nation's period of healing. American popular culture at the time was also saturated with news items like "American Musician turns 9/11 grief into musical hope,"[16] books with titles like *Faces of Hope: Babies Born on 9/11*, by Christine Naman,[17] a documentary film named *Reclaiming Hope in a Changed World*,[18] all of which reflect the increasing desire of hope after the attacks. Significantly, the note on the back cover of Naman's book, *Faces of Hope*, features Carl Sandburg's verse which uses the baby as a hope-inspiring symbol: "A baby is God's opinion that the world should go on." There are also families who (middle) named their children "Hope"[19] after the attacks or decided to have a child with the expectation of a new beginning together with a survival motivation that makes them cling to life more strongly.[20] Some families who hesitated to have a child totally changed their minds after the attacks. One New York woman's altered idea about having a baby is expressed as she likens the zone of the attacks to a post-apocalyptic place:

> As I stand on line at the morgue, . . . I can't stop envisioning myself with a child—with my child by my side, my child whom I will nurture, comfort, mentor, love, and protect, who will inspire me to work harder to make the world a safer and better place, a world in which such a terrible thing won't happen again. . . . I promise myself that when things have settled down a bit, when John and I can open our apartment windows without breathing in thick, overwhelmingly putrid smoke, when the National Guard ceases patrolling our block, when he and I can walk freely in our neighbourhood without having to show I.D., . . . the subject of our becoming parents hasn't been put to bed, after all. And I feel hopeful—confident.[21]

Janice Eidus's expression above is like the common voice of many people who somehow witnessed the same unexpected grief and later chose to believe in the power of a newborn to somehow remove and heal the horror of the post-apocalyptic landscape they witnessed.

In addition to these reflections of hope after 9/11, Internet communities such as *9/11 Families*, *Remembering 9/11*, and *9/11 Day* became one avenue for survivors, for people who lost a beloved one or for the volunteers. Among them, a society page called *Meetup* was founded with the aim of connecting people in New York City nine months after the collapse of the towers. Thanks to this organization, several Americans started to construct a community to share and overcome their common grief. *Meetup* is "directly a result of 9/11,"[22] and significant in the sense that it has evoked new relations in the local community of New York with massive behavioral differences compared to pre-9/11. Following the cataclysm, "New Yorkers now felt the necessity to salute their neighbours who they would normally have ignored before the attacks."[23] Obviously, one of the main reasons for such a change of behavior was to reach out to others and unite after the shocking event to bind up wounds together. It is also interesting and worth mentioning that *Meetup* "was launched nine months after the attacks."[24] This nine-month-period before the *Meetup* team appeared is crucial as it evokes the pregnancy period for human babies. Apparently, as "a 9/11 baby,"[25] *Meetup* followed the aim of having a baby as a means of healing the wound and bringing hopefulness to the nation after the tragedy.

HOPE AND POST-APOCALYPTIC MOVIES

According to the common definition, post-apocalypse is the period following a large-scale disaster in which civilization has been destroyed or has regressed to a more primitive level. Both post-apocalyptic novels and films have nearly similar endings which make "possible the post-apocalyptic paradise or wasteland. . . . The study of post-apocalypse is a study of what disappears and what remains, and of how the remainder has been transformed."[26] Therefore, the surviving residents who make a restart in a post-apocalyptic world gradually discover new means to stay alive and continue. During this transformation process, the individual is caught in the interstitial space between nostalgia for the old and the unfamiliarly new post-apocalyptic one that awaits him/her. Hence, in this post-apocalyptic space, survivors hover between these two abruptly different lives. Homes, streets, and buildings that were once called places turn into spaces as they are now almost unknown and foreign to the survivor.

It did not take long for the Hollywood film industry to deal with the apocalyptic facet of 9/11 attacks, and since the events there have been more than fifty post-apocalyptic films released[27]: *28 Days Later* (2002), *Children of Men* (2006), *I Am Legend* (2007), *The Road* (2009), *Book of Eli* (2010), and *Hunger Games* (2012), to name just a few. Several explanations about the relationship between these post-apocalyptic works and September 11 focus on fear due to the end of the world impression it has left on many people. According to Karen Springen, "After 9/11, it seemed that people started thinking about the destruction of the world."[28] Similarly, as a practicing psychoanalyst in Manhattan, Charles Strozier asserts that "after 9/11 many New Yorkers returned often to apocalyptic images to try and make sense out of their experiences."[29] Seeing the sudden destruction of the towers was so hard to perceive for many individuals. Thus, films following the destruction have been a means to convey the shock and fright of many people who somehow witnessed the attacks. And among the genre, post-apocalyptic films have reflected the further visualizing of the attacks and asking what would have happened if we had experienced the aftermath of the end of the world.

In many recent post-apocalyptic films, the child has been a prominent figure and thus has fostered new critical analysis. Films such as *I Am Legend*, *Children of Men*, and *The Road* present a created space where the child is illustrated as the most significant and protected figure, implying resilience, a new beginning, innocence, and a better life. These examples demonstrate that the child symbolizes an intersecting role between the real disastrous events and imagined visual representations of post-disaster scenes in post-apocalyptic films. The true-to-life examples stated above support this chapter's thesis that these post-apocalyptic films highlight America's fear of *the end* following the World Trade Center attacks and reflect the country's imaginative perception of the child as the representative of hope in the aftermath of the events. The general tendency of the nation to see the child as the one who instigates a new world will also be explained in spatial terms, as hope involves the potential to proceed and gives way to new spaces.

"DESPAIR GREW AS THE NOISE FROM THE PLAYGROUNDS FADED"

Alfonso Cuarón's *Children of Men*, set in post-apocalyptic London of 2027, focuses on human infertility for two decades that have left mankind under the threat of extinction. The film directed by Alfonso Cuarón is based on P. D. James's same titled dystopian novel published in 1992. Though the novel is set nine years before the September 11 attacks, the film version has been adapted to the concerns and debates of the post-attacks era within a globalized view highlighting a wide range of problems from global warming to migration. Within the chaos of migration problems in London, the film visualizes a world where there are no births and the news of pregnancy leads to the hope for the future while raising conflicts, despair, and fear at the same time. The idea of a newborn is not believable in a place where there are posters on the roads that say "no hope of baby."

In its closer concerns to 9/11, there are several criticisms that place the film in post-9/11 frame due to the anxiety and shock felt from the attacks and the later war period, leaving many with hardly defined feelings about the future of the world. One of the critics highlights that

> Though the source material is P. D. James's novel *The Children of Men*, Cuarón's film is a distinctly post-9/11 creation, brimming with not-so-subtle

allusions to Fox News jingoism, xenophobia, environmental disaster, mad cow disease, "democratic" police states, and capitalism run amok. If Occupy Wall Street made a movie, "Children of Men" would be it.[30]

In addition to reflecting political criticism that has kept the world busy since 9/11, the film has a significant role in voicing the anxiety of individuals toward babies. Though the dominant theme of infertility is loaded on the baby, it is also a metaphor of the quandary of the individuals who somehow experienced the apocalypse of their lives post-9/11.

Before starting with a deep analysis of the film, it is necessary to conduct Edelman's reflections on the child and the future. In broad analysis, Edelman states that the child, who is "indeed as the living promise of a natural transcendence of the limits of nature itself,"[31] is generally seen as the symbol of the future yet has been symbolized within the limits and stereotypes of the political framework that is in favor of the continuity of the generations. Standing against the idea of the substantializing of both the child and identities he believes that the novel *Children of Men*, "gives voice to the ideological truism that governs our investment in the child as the obligatory token of futurity."[32] As for Edelman's ideas on the child, baby Dylan stands against the stereotypical formation of a family. That is, she does not have a certain father to be next to her and also the protagonist Theo, Clive Owen, does not try to fit himself as a volunteering father. As a former father who lost his child, he just clings to the hope of a newborn and helps the young refugee mother Kee. However, in an atmosphere where the society is on the verge of extinction, there emerge some groups who want to utilize the child and the fertile woman for their own salvation. These are mostly people who belong to militant groups and want to use the baby as their political tool. Therefore, their action posits an example to Edelman's theory that politics and the baby symbol go hand in hand and, as a result, the child has become the "telos of the social order and been enshrined as the figure for whom that order must be held in perpetual trust."[33]

As regards to spatial terms, the Foucauldian term "heterotopia" becomes significant in some parts of the film. One of them is the symbol of the baby. The existence of the baby serves as the heterotopia for almost everyone in the film regardless of the differing approaches of the people to baby Dylan. It is at this point that Foucault's notion of heterotopia comes to mind with its "power to juxtapose in a single real place several spaces, several emplacements that are in themselves incompatible."[34] With the word "incompatible" it is understood that the baby will have the potential to connect numerous people from different nationalities, professions, ages, or ideologies. After overcoming very harsh conditions, Theo, Kee, and her baby Dylan manage to take a rowboat to wait for the ship in the harbor. Though Theo dies on the rowboat, the film ends giving the message that the baby and mother have managed to board the ship. The ship in this scene becomes the other heterotopia according to the following principles:

> It is a floating part of space, a placeless place, that lives by itself, closed in on itself and at the same time poised in the infinite ocean, and yet, from port to port, tack by tack . . . looking for the most precious things hidden in their gardens. . . . [It is] at the same time the greatest reserve of imagination for our civilization from the sixteenth century down to the present day. The ship is the heterotopia par excellence. In civilizations where it is lacking, dreams dry up, adventure is replaced by espionage, and privateers by the police.[35]

With her birth, baby Dylan will fill the space of void the society has longed for. As the most precious "reserve" of that time, baby Dylan will suggest the power to light up the darkness at the time of despair and chaos in 2027. Though she will be on the ship that does not belong anywhere, her innocence and purity will encourage the society in which all the hopes are on the verge of being lost.

Figure 7.1. *Children of Men*, 2006, Universal.

Therefore, from the idea of the "infant," this baby suggests the potency to bear another society as infant and innocent as the baby.

"THIS IS GROUND ZERO, THIS IS MY SITE"

I Am Legend is an adaptation from the novel that was written by Richard Matheson in 1954. The film is directed by Francis Lawrence and was released in 2007. As listed among the post-apocalyptic films post-9/11, the film reflects the worst-case scenario of the attacks in New York. The fictionalized form of the event in this film is another example to how the attacks have indeed been perceived. It is stated that after the attacks, "the first films to return to the familiar images of New York City under attack were well received. According to the Internet Movie Database, *The Day after Tomorrow* and *I Am Legend* both made the list of the top ten grossing movies for the years they were released."[36]

I Am Legend opens up in New York City with its only resident, Robert Neville, starring Will Smith, who is a former military virologist having lost his family due to the contagious virus that erased a high percentage of the world's population due to the infected blood-drinking mutants that appear in the dark. Neville is immune to the virus and stays as the only uninfected survivor in New York. Knowing the reason for the virus, he hopes to find a cure and reach other people by making broadcasts every day hoping to meet other survivors. From 2009 till 2012, he does not hear from anyone until one day a woman named Anna and her son Ethan appear. While their arrival saves Neville from being taken by the infected, it later serves as an inspiration for Neville to find a cure in the end.

Humanity's change of faith is achieved thanks to the arrival of Ethan, who reminds Neville of his lost daughter Marley. As the only surviving child in New York City, Ethan fulfills many places. He is the only child in New York City and his presence at home makes Robert remember his daughter. Though Robert sometimes loses his belief to find a cure, he starts to feel more determined thanks to Ethan and continues his studies in the laboratory until he has finally and successfully achieved a result in the end. His daughter Marley contributes a lot to his achievement. The butterfly figure she does with her hands both in the car and on the helicopter turned out to be a message from Marley to her father. Remembering and hearing her saying "Look, father, it's a butterfly," led to his reaching the cure for Anna and Ethan even though it meant sacrificing his own self. Without Marley's former repetitions of the butterfly figure with her hands, Robert may not have remembered the symbol that appeared on the plexy glass at the end of the film.

Therefore, the end of the film reveals the child's importance when Robert sees the butterfly figure both on the glass and on Anna's neck as a tattoo. At the end of the film, when the mutants want to infect Robert, Anna, and Ethan, Robert realizes the great fear the innocent boy Ethan suffers and it is understood that he decides it will be Ethan to carry out the hope for the future. Helping Ethan to survive, Robert fulfills his lost desire of hope (he felt for his daughter) in Ethan. Therefore, combining several meanings, duties, and erasing Robert's fear of the future, Ethan becomes Robert's heterotopia.

Anna and Ethan are the two figures of the film who do not belong to a place in the life after post-apocalypse. However, this situation seems to have changed when they encounter Robert and start to share his house for a while and within a short time, Robert senses closeness to Ethan. When he takes the little boy to his daughter's empty room and tucks him in bed, he bitterly remembers the loss of his daughter but at the same time tries to find relief in the newly arrived boy. The scene when Ethan watches *Shrek* forms the other instance when the two start to establish a bond. This scene is significant within the spatial terms. The boy does not have a proper place before arriving at this home, he seems to adopt this new shelter as his own place because he sleeps in a proper bed and later he watches cartoons on television. When Robert sees one day that Ethan is watching *Shrek,* he initially feels strange and sad as he stays put without saying anything initially but later as he starts to say the film's lines, the boy looks surprised and weird and then finally feels relieved. As Robert later tells him that he likes *Shrek,* the cartoon becomes the moment when the boy and Robert share something in common in the house and hence set a connection between them.

Another scene when the feeling of sense of place and belonging becomes dominant in this film happens when Robert refuses Anna's advice to join them at the camp in Vermont where the remaining uninfected people are. Yet, by strongly rejecting this offer and saying "This is Ground Zero. This is my site," Robert shows his tight connectedness and responsibility to Manhattan city as his place where he was once a military officer. And referring to the place as "Ground Zero" instead of Manhattan, he apparently makes a reference to the September 11 attacks.

Tuan contends that "[t]o the local people sense of place is promoted not only by their settlement's physical circumscription in space; and awareness of other settlements and rivalry with them significantly enhance the feeling of uniqueness and of identity."[37] Robert may not have any rivalry here yet the factors exist that threaten human survival and thus Robert stays in the city as the last person trying to find a cure. During Robert's driving around in the new post-apocalyptic territory of an empty Manhattan, the once teeming-with-life streets become a symbol of non-place as nothing around is familiar to him now because these post-apocalyptic places now do not contain either a sense of attachment or memories. As the once pre-apocalyptic places no longer define anything, Freud's notion of *unheimlich*, which is *uncanny*, *unfamiliar* also fits this situation.[38] As a resident of the world before apocalypse, Robert has now become a foreigner in this newly shaped area.

In *I Am Legend*, which depicts scenes of the deserted landscape of the post-apocalypse, it is not possible to talk about space as a "frequented place," "an intersection of moving bodies,"[39] that Auge mentions about space for De Certau. From all these given examples, the non-places of the post-apocalyptic world are indeed references to the areas that humanity occupied in the world of supermodernity. Within all the situations of non-place environments, Robert's daughter Marley reminds her father that there is still a chance to continue and thus the hint she gives in the beginning of the film provides the most hopeful essence for the rest of humankind in the post-apocalypse. Since Marley is lost, the other child figure Ethan accomplishes and carries the hope needed. So, *I Am Legend*'s emphasis on the child is revealed with the little girl Marley and later the boy Ethan when encouraged to try the remedy for a contagious disease in order to save the future of the world.

"WHAT IS THIS PLACE, PAPA?"

The Road, a novel by Cormac McCarthy, was adapted to film in 2009, by director John Hillcoat and screenwriter Joe Penhall. In the film, Vigo Mortensen stars as the father, Kodi Smitt-McPhee as the boy, and Charlize Theron as the mother.[40] In its relation to 9/11, the novel and thus the film adaptation, "seems to be a response to an immediate and visceral fear of cataclysmic in the United States after the terrorist attacks on 9/11."[41] There are some critics who positioned the novel in the context of the political atmosphere post-9/11 in the criticisms of the novel, which is also suitable for the film adaptation. John Cant expresses how the novel fits into the context of post-9/11 considering it both in a local and universal context stating that "the apocalyptic tone of the novel reflects the mood of America following the destruction of the World Trade Center," and he also observes that "*The Road* seems to reflect the mood of fear that has permeated the Western mind in the first decade of the twenty-first century."[42] English novelist Ian McEwan's comment highlights the apocalyptic sense as he says: "Yesterday's apocalyptic scenes far outstripped anything Hollywood has ever imagined. Amid the confusion, only one thing seemed certain," says Ian McEwan "the world would never be the same again."[43] Among the writers and critics who commented on the attacks, Cormac McCarthy's feelings, which resulted in his writing of the novel, probably stand as the most valid link between the event and the novel. In his very first interview on television, when Oprah Winfrey tells him "If we had read this book twenty-five or twenty years ago, it would have seemed futuristic, but something about it feels ominous and real," McCarthy answers, "You know, I think it is maybe since 9/11 people's emotions are more concerned about apocalyptic issues. We are not used to that,"[44] he says. And when Winfrey asked him "had you not had this son at this time, this book wouldn't have been written?" McCarthy replied "No. Absolutely not. Never would have occurred to me to write, try to write a book about a father and a son."[45] Obviously, McCarthy has also felt the anxiety after a disastrous happening and like most people; the concern for his son's future formed the biggest part of his fright.

The main characters of the film are a father and son who try to keep being "good guys" in a decimated landscape where the reason for the nearly total destruction is unknown.

Though there are various scenes of despair in the film's screening of the end of humankind, there are also strong implications of hope throughout the film. The boy in the film is the one who most of the time provides a powerful frame for the feeling of hope and the father figure "convinces himself for the sake of his son that humanity will abide even in the face of appalling conditions."[46] Though the father protects his son against all the earthly hazards, he at the same time wants his boy to keep dreaming that good things will happen by keeping "the fire inside." The little boy's dreaming is crucial for the father as he says, "When I have nothing else, I try to dream the dreams of a child's imaginings." Generally, a child's dream has no limits and the desired things do not seem far and impossible. In the world of a child, there are no stereotypes and badness toward the other is generally an unknown thing. Due to the normally insistent behavior of a child, giving up is mostly refused in his/her world. However, adults' dreams are quite the contrary having experienced both feelings of happiness yet also anxiety and fear. Thus, having lived both in the pre- and post-apocalyptic world, the father has little or nothing to dream other than that of a child.

The flashbacks in the film tell us that the man and boy were not alone in the beginning of their journey through their search for hope in the film. There was also a woman, who is both a wife and a mother, carrying very little crumbs of desire, not enough to continue to struggle in that rotten land, and she, from time to time, suddenly occupies the father's memories in his longing for their life before the apocalypse. Unlike his father, the boy has little memory of the good old days the family once lived. In that sense, he differs from his father in regards to space and place. The memoirs of the boy cannot go any further from some objects, such as his mother's comb and some toys he gathered. However, the father can make comparisons between the old life

Figure 7.2. *The Road*, 2009, Dimension Films.

and the *new* one and therefore knows very well the sense of loss that over-shadows his tentative feelings of hope. In a scene where the boy and the man stroll in the streets, they pass by a home that has many connotations for the man, but not for the boy. After the man tells the boy that it was the place where the man grew up, they enter the house. There, the father touches and shows the boy the lines on the jamb where they used to mark height, prob-ably with his sisters or brothers.

He also tells his son the Christmas rituals and that they used to have a Christmas tree and stockings for hanging the presents when he was a boy. He then finds a cushion on the floor and places it slowly and neatly on the sofa and sits on it without taking off his backpack, putting his right hand on his forehead in a deeply thoughtful mood. With a long shot inside the room he is shown together with his reflection in the dusty mirror where he seems not interested his own reflection. Though seemingly interested, the boy is not very attracted to this place as much as his father. This is mostly because he does not feel strong attachments with the place even if it is the house where his father grew up. The reason for that can be explained by Tuan's words as he says:

> Place can acquire deep meaning for the adult through the steady accretion of sentiment over the years. Every piece of heirloom furniture, or even a stain on the wall, tells a story. The child not only has a short past, but his eyes more than the adult's are on the present and the immediate future. [47]

As the scene may suggest, the father and the boy show differences with regard to spatial terms. While the father enters his childhood house, all good memories come back in his head because where he enters is not an ordinary space but a space that has become a place, the house where he grew up. The father gets sad when he sees that the things he tells the boy do not make much sense for him, he still seems to believe that he will be the one to recover the good times his father and other survivors lost and long for. However, the son has not had a childhood full of memories to be remem-bered later on due to the post-apocalyptic world in which he has grown up. Though the child has some small souvenirs taken from his home, these are limited in comparison with the man's world. The things he remembers of the past are quite limited. His "stuff," which consists of her mother's hair comb, two keys, a crown cap, a small piece of stone, and a few more little things, show that the child barely has things to remember the past. But still in this condition, though the man sometimes seems to sink into despair, the boy always keeps his love, being good-hearted and just, although justice has become out of use in that bleak world. The boy's insistence and determina-tion in being the good guy and showing no contradiction in his behaviors, proves to be a powerful example that he is the carrier of hope.

When the boy and the father find a bunker full of tinned food, they stay there for a few days. This bunker becomes the most proper place they have encountered during their post-apocalyptic journey, providing them with the opportunity to bathe, sleep, and eat relatively comfortably. For the father, this bunker represents the loss of the familiar places that the visit to his childhood home signified. During their stay in the bunker, the boy experiences the different tastes of that loss in the variety of canned foods available. Upon finding the treasure of tinned food, the father explains to him what is in each can as such type of food is quite new to the boy. When they prepare dinner for themselves for the second time, they are clean and elegant; the father wears a jacket and enjoys whisky with a cigar. He sits smiling and enjoying himself. Although suffering from a bad cough, he smiles at the boy, probably silently thinking that we had such a life before the apocalypse. Feeling very little relieved for having shown his son a very short glimpse of their dinner rituals formerly, his looks do not seem pessimistic but they are pensive. It could be hardly said that the father becomes more hopeful after finding the bunker but there, he again understands that his boy will always be honest. The boy's thanking and praying to the "people" who have left all these and constantly asking if they have done something good proves his honesty once again. And the boy's reaction to the good things of the past does not go any further than showing a little surprise. He does not expose desires to insist on possessing everything or regretting the things that he does not have after having seen a very little part of the pre-apocalypse life in the bunker. And as a father, the man does not openly tell or advise the boy that he should be determined to create a world similar to the pre-apocalypse yet he just presents him with the small instances or places from his former life with the aim of leaving some things that the boy can remember. Anne Coyle comments that "they treat this bunker as their property, taking their time and acting in ways they had not in any other place . . . the bunker represents the closest they have been to actually possessing a territory, inhabiting a place."[48] There, the boy for the first time meets and experiences some of the felicities of pre-apocalyptic life whereas the father gets the very last treat of his life and an opportunity to feed and take care of his son in a place left untouched since the apocalypse. Despite the fact that the father experienced the world before the apocalypse, the boy's chance to obtain such a life is weak and he functions in this decimated space as if the ruined landscape were not a place to be feared. He has certain fears, he knows what theft, hunger, and cannibalism are; yet he does not lose his faith in encountering good people. The child is also promising since his space "expands and becomes better articulated as he recognizes and reaches out to more permanent objects and places. That way space is transformed into place as it acquires definition and meaning."[49] Although he cannot name what and how, he reveals his intention to belong to a place.

The boy's future lies in the continuation of his life in a world after a disaster for which he has no memory. For the father and the other adults in the grey land, this devastated space is totally new and different. However, for the child and the other children, this post-apocalyptic landscape is not that unfamiliar since they cannot make a comparison with another life. In most cases, as it was in the father's visit to his childhood house, it is always the father to call back the memories. Another example of such a case that visualizes the inequality of their experiences is in the scene when the father drops possibly the last tin of Coca-Cola from the broken and dirty vending machine. When he offers it to his son, the boy asks what it is. It is apparent that the man used to like Coca-Cola but this time he does not intend to narrate to his son anything about it, possibly already knowing that his memory would sound irrelevant to the boy, showing once again the scarcity of the experiences the two can share.

Although the father and the boy encounter many tinned products in the bunker, this makes a more intense and happier impression for the father. So, using Coca-Cola becomes crucial in this scene because one may naturally wonder whether there are any other products symbolizing civilization. As it initially appeared in the novel, McCarthy replies his purpose of applying Coca-Cola as follows:

> Well, it just struck me. It's the iconic American product. The one thing that everybody knows about America, the one thing above cowboys and Indians, above everything else that you can think of, is Coca-Cola. You can't go to a village of eighteen people in the remotest part of Africa that they don't know about Coca-Cola. [50]

Thus, when the father offers the drink to his son, he both wants him to show the pre-apocalyptic world's tastes and also, as he believes in hope that there might be a future for his son, the father might want to leave his son a memory that the two have shared one real, uncorrupted thing of the pre-apocalypse. Despite all the real things of the past, a can of Coke becomes one of the most important essences as regards to experience and memory for the father and the boy. Whereas the father remembers civilization, the boy will think of his father if he happens to come across it again. Already knowing and experiencing Coca-Cola, the father becomes the representative of the lost place.

The notion of hope in this scene can be linked to the slogan of Coca-Cola in 2009 which is *Open Happiness*. By not taking a sip from the "bubbly" thing and offering the whole can to the boy, the father may feel content thinking that he has improved the seeds of hope and happiness in his child.

Another and the last spatial concern in this film is the notion of heterotopia. In Foucault's explanation of the term, there are some principles that correspond to Americans' actions post-9/11 as well as to the plots discussed in the above-chosen post-apocalyptic films. Foucault defines heterotopia as having the following principles:

- The heterotopia has the power to juxtapose in a single real place several places, several emplacements that are in themselves incompatible.
- The heterotopias begin to function fully when people find themselves in a sort of absolute break with their traditional time.
- They have, in relation to the rest of space, a function.[51]

Both the previously given web pages and websites as well as these post-apocalyptic films orient to the idea of the child as the center of expectations and beginnings where they could join several occurrences and ideas. In this sense, hope carries heterotopic features in itself because

> as a category created but not occupied, the child could be a repository of cultural needs or fears not adequately disposed of elsewhere. . . . The child carries for us things we somehow cannot carry for ourselves, sometimes anxieties we want to be divorced from and sometimes pleasures so great we would not, without the child, know how to contain them.[52]

The boy in *The Road* is like the father's heterotopia as he is the father's only real place in that unfamiliar ruined landscape. Although this new land is full of unknown spaces, the boy, with his innocence and true character, is carrying the father's feelings of hope and fear. Though the father is aware that he will not be able to survive, he still has expectations that the boy will continue his way with good intentions as he says: "All I know is the child is my warrant." By warrant, he once again shows that for him the boy is the one symbolizing all the righteousness and expectation in this world.

CONCLUSION

Individuals turn to the notion of hope especially when they are at the edge of great suffering, shock, or loss. This can be seen either in the flow of daily life or after disastrous happenings such as the 9/11 attacks that left immense effects on individuals. Soon after the attacks, feelings of patriotism boomed in America as people hung large flags outside their houses or on their cars.[53] And regarding its visual part, it has left apocalyptic effects on many individuals who experienced that day. Expression of fear, anxiety, and shock resulted in many people's need to set a strong bond with the idea of the child. Soon, there appeared several websites, newspaper headlines, communities, and books such as *Faces of Hope* with the messages of unity in order to share the pain of the nation. All these actions proved that the idea of a child is seen as one of the most powerful things to maintain this hope.

This attitude has gradually shown that Americans started to reevaluate the sense of American space and place after the 9/11 *apocalypse*. It is on this dimension that the attacks on 9/11 and the post-apocalyptic films and post-9/11 films coincide. Related to the fear and anxiety of the event, several films have been made since 2001. Encountering the ones that center on the child as the symbol of hope makes one consider again the relationship between 9/11, post-apocalyptic films after that.

In the selected films, *Children of Men*, *I Am Legend*, and *The Road*, the dominant themes of survival, the future, and a better life, revolve around the child. In *The Road*, it is the boy's existence, dreams, determination to be a good person, and his belief in finding good people that gives the father the power to struggle and teach his son the basics of survival. In *I Am Legend*, Robert's daughter Marley initiates the possibility of a cure, yet her loss and the appearance of Ethan gave him the courage and hope to succeed in finding the remedy for the survival of mankind.

And in *Children of Men*, it is Kee's heterotopic baby girl that gives hope that humanity may not become extinct. It is also in this film that politics makes use of the child with its implication for a hopeful future, much like the post-9/11 coverage that used the child as a symbol of survival and hope.

All these films and the happenings in the public after September 11 reveal the human desire for a hopeful future so that the children can continue experiencing and learning how it feels to belong to a place. It is the children's never-ending dreams, play, and noise that gives hope to the adults in times of despair that life must go on. Thus, regarding these and the ideas discussed all throughout the article, the child becomes a mighty and an indispensable figure for the adults at times of great despair and hopelessness.

NOTES

1. Joseph J. Godfrey, *A Philosophy of Human Hope* (Dordrecht: Martinus Nijhoff Publishers, 1987), 7.

2. Maria Manuel Lisboa, *The End of The World: Apocalypse and Its Aftermath in Western Culture* (Cambridge: Open Book Publishers, 2011), 14.

3. Oxford Dictionaries Online, s.v. "Child," accessed June 6, 2014, www.oxforddictionaries.com/definition/english/child.

4. Philip Ariès, *Centuries of Childhood* (Harmondsworth: Penguin Books, 1960), 125.

5. Cited in Krysten A. Keches, "The Invention of Childhood Innocence," *Harvard Gazette*, April 29, 2010, news.harvard.edu/gazette/story/2010/04/the-invention-of-childhood-innocence.

6. These following newspaper headlines are important sources to understand the relationship between hope and salvation: Maria Croce, "New baby gives family hope after devastating cancer diagnosis," *Daily Record*, May 13, 2012, www.dailyrecord.co.uk/news/real-life/new-baby-gives-family-hope-877816; "Trapped Chile Miner's Wife gives birth to daughter," BBC News, September 14, 2010, www.bbc.co.uk/news/world-latin-america-11306900; and "Hope among the devastation: Woman gives birth to baby girl amidst chaos caused by Typhoon Haiyan," *Mirror*, November 11, 2013. www.mirror.co.uk/news/world-news/typhoon-haiyan-woman-gives-birth-2719325.

7. Peter B. Pufall and Richard P. Unsworth, "The Imperative and the Process for Rethinking Childhood," in *Rethinking Childhood*, ed. Peter B. Pufall and Richard P. Unsworth (New Brunswick: Rutgers University Press, 2004), 3.

8. Dale Hurd, "My 9/11: The End of a World," *Hurd on the Web* (blog), September 11, 2011 (12:20 p.m.), blogs.cbn.com/hurdontheweb/archive/2011/09/11/my-911-the-end-of-a-world-again.aspx.

9. Philip Sherwell, "September 11 Fireman: 'It felt like the end of the world,'" *The Telegraph*, September 10, 2011, www.telegraph.co.uk/news/worldnews/september-11-attacks/8754605/September-11-fireman-It-felt-like-the-end-of-the-world.html.

10. Andreas Huyssen, "Twin Memories: After Images of Nine/Eleven," *Grey Room* 7 (2002): 9.

11. Elizabeth Grosz, *Space, Time and Perversion: Essays on the Politics of Bodies* (New York: Routledge, 1995), 105.

12. Yi-Fu Tuan, *Space and Place: The Perspective of Experience* (Minneapolis: University of Minnesota Press, 1996), 12.

13. Setha M. Low and Denise Lawrence-Zúñiga, "Locating Culture," in *The Anthropology of Space and Place: Locating Culture*, ed. Setha M. Low and Denise Lawrence-Zúñiga (Oxford: Blackwell Publishing, 2003), 37.

14. John A. Agnew and Jonathan M. Smith, preface to *American Space, American Place: Geographies of the Contemporary United States*, ed. John A. Agnew and Jonathan M. Smith (Edinburgh: Edinburgh University Press, 2002), ix.

15. Caroline A. Bartel, "I Love New York More Than Ever: Changes in People's Identities as New Yorkers Following the World Trade Center Terrorist Attacks," *Journal of Management Inquiry* 11, no. 3 (2002): 247.

16. The Associated Press, "American Musician turns 9/11 Grief into Musical Hope," *All Alabama* (blog), September 2, 2013 (2:07 am), blog.al.com/wire/2013/09/american_musician_turns_911_gr.html.

17. Christine Naman, *Faces of Hope: Babies Born on 9/11* (Florida: Health Communications Inc., 2002).

18. *Reclaiming Hope in a Changed World*, directed by Robert Parish (2002, American Psychological Association, 2002), VHS.

19. "Living with Loss," *New York Times*, September 6, 2011. www.nytimes.com/2011/09/11/us/sept-11-reckoning/11portraits.html.

20. Regina Brett, "Boy born on 9/11 dreams of rebuilding the Towers," September 6, 2011, www.cleveland.com/brett/blog/index.ssf/2011/09/boy_born_on_911_dreams_of_rebu.html.

21. Janice Eidus, "Baby Lust," in *110 Stories: New York Writes after September 11*, ed. Ulrich Baer (New York: New York University Press, 2002), 88.

22. A co-founder of *Meetup*, Scott Heiferman, widely explains there's a son of his founding this website and he stresses that its rise is directly interlinked with the 9/11 happenings. Scott Heiferman, interview by Danielle Horry, The Meetup Organizer Boot Camp, June 10, 2009, www.meetup.com/organize/pages/Interview_with_Scott_Heiferman_-_Our_First_Event%21.

23. Similar to the emerging idea of this organization that later spread worldwide, there are some other communities under this name.

24. Connecting in Real Life, September 30, 2011. seattledesigner.blogspot.co.uk/2011_09_01_archive.html.

25. Morgen Bailey, "Meetup.com is a 9/11 Baby," *Morgen Bailey's Writing Blog* (blog), September 11, 2011, morgenbailey.wordpress.com/2011/09/11/meetup-com-is-a-911-baby/.

26. James Berger, *After the End: Representations of Post-Apocalypse* (Minneapolis: University of Minnesota Press, 1999), 6–7.

27. Lecturer Sue Weaver Schopf explains that "there have been fifty post-apocalyptic films produced in the last three years alone." Harvard Extension School Lectures, "The Post-Apocalyptic Novel and Film," September 7, 2013. cm.dce.harvard.edu/2014/01/14194/L01/index_H264SingleAudioOnly.shtml.

28. Karen Springen, "Children's Books: Apocalypse Now: Teens Turn to Dystopian Novels," *Publishers Weekly*, February 15, 2010, www.publishersweekly.com/pw/print/20100215/42087-children-s-books-apocalypse-now.html.

29. Charles Strozier, *Until the Fires Stopped Burning* (New York: Columbia University Press, 2011), 102.

30. Matt Brennan, "Now and Then: In 'Contagion' and 'Children of Men,' Disaster Runs Cold and Hot," January 9, 2012.

31. Lee Edelman, *No Future: Queer Theory and the Death Drive* (Durham: Duke University Press, 2004), 21.

32. Ibid., 12.

33. Ibid., 21.

34. Michel Foucault, "Of Other Spaces," in *Heterotopia and the City: Public Space in a Postcivil Society*, ed. Michiel Dehaene and Lieven De Cauter (New York: Routledge, 2008), 5.

35. Ibid., 7.

36. *September 11 in Popular Culture: A Guide*, ed. Sara E. Quay and Amy M. Damico (California: Greenwood, 2011), 180.

37. Tuan, 166.

38. Sigmund Freud, "The Uncanny," *Professor Laurel Amtower's Page on San Diego State University Website*, www-rohan.sdsu.edu/~amtower/uncanny.html.

39. Marc Augé, *Non-Places: Introduction to an Anthropology of Supermodernity*, trans. John Howe (London: Verso, 1995), 79.

40. *The Road*, directed by John Hillcoat (Icon Home Entertainment, 2010), DVD.

41. Lydia R. Cooper, "Cormac McCarthy's *The Road* as Apocalyptic Grail Narrative," *Studies in the Novel* 43, no. 2 (2011): 221.

42. John Cant, *Cormac McCarthy and the Myth of American Exceptionalism* (New York: Routledge), 266.

43. Ian McEwan, "Beyond Belief," September 12, 2001, www.theguardian.com/world/2001/sep/12/september11.politicsphilosophyandsociety.

44. Cormac McCarthy, interview by Oprah Winfrey, *The Oprah Winfrey Show*, www.dailymotion.com/video/xb74sg_cormac-mccarthy-bombs-on-the-oprah_creation.

45. Ibid.

46. Daniel King, "Faithful adaptation that still offers something new," *Reviews and Ratings for the Road*, last modified October 19, 2009, http://www.imdb.com/title/tt0898367/reviews.

47. Tuan, 33.

48. Anne Coyle, "Morels and Morals: Hope in the Postapocalyptic *The Road*," in *Critical Insights: Cormac McCarthy*, ed. David N. Cremean (Massachusetts: Salem Press, 2013), 283.

49. Tuan, 136.

50. "Cormac McCarthy on How Coca-Cola Ended Up in *The Road*, and Other Musings," November 12, 2009, blogs.wsj.com/speakeasy/2009/11/12/cormac-mccarthy-on-how-coca-cola-ended-up-on-the-road-and-other-musings/.

51. Foucault, 19–20.

52. Henry Jenkins, "Introduction: Childhood Innocence and Other Modern Myths," in *The Children's Culture Reader*, ed. Henry Jenkins (New York: New York University Press, 1998), 4.

53. Mikhail Lyubansky, "On 9/11, Patriotism, and U.S. Flag," *Psychology Today*, September 10, 2010, www.psychologytoday.com/blog/between-the-lines/201009/9-11-patriotism-and-the-us-flag.

BIBLIOGRAPHY

Agnew, John A., and Jonathan M. Smith. Preface to *American Space, American Place: Geographies of the Contemporary United States*. Edited by John A. Agnew and Jonathan M. Smith. Edinburgh: Edinburgh University Press, 2002.

Augé, Marc. *Non-Places: Introduction to an Anthropology of Supermodernity*. Translated by John Howe. London: Verso, 1995.

Ariès, Philip. *Centuries of Childhood*. Harmondsworth: Penguin Books, 1960.

Baer, Ulrich. *110 Stories: New York Writes after September 11*. New York: New York University Press, 2002.

Bartel, Caroline A. "I Love New York More Than Ever: Changes in People's Identities as New Yorkers Following the World Trade Center Terrorist Attacks." *Journal of Management Inquiry* 11, no. 3 (2002): 240–248.

Berger, James. *After the End: Representations of Post-Apocalypse.* Minneapolis: University of Minnesota Press, 1999.

Cant, John. *Cormac McCarthy and the Myth of American Exceptionalism.* New York: Routledge.

Children of Men. Directed by Alfonso Cuarón. 2006; London, UK: Universal Pictures, 2006. DVD.

Cooper, Lydia R. "Cormac McCarthy's *The Road* as Apocalyptic Grail Narrative." *Studies in the Novel* 43, no. 2 (2011): 218–236.

Coyle, Anne. "Morels and Morals: Hope in the Post-Apocalyptic *The Road.*" In *Critical Insights: Cormac McCarthy,* edited by David N. Cremean, 271–287. Massachusetts: Salem Press, 2013.

Edelman, Lee. *No Future: Queer Theory and the Death Drive.* Durham: Duke University Press, 2004.

Eidus, Janice. "Baby Lust." In *110 Stories: New York Writes after September 11,* edited by Ulrich Baer, 86–88. New York: New York University Press, 2002.

Foucault, Michel. "Of Other Spaces." In *Heterotopia and the City: Public Space in a Postcivil Society,* edited by Michiel Dehaene and Lieven De Cauter, 13–30. New York: Routledge, 2008.

Godfrey, Joseph J. *A Philosophy of Human Hope.* Dordrecht: Martinus Nijhoff Publishers, 1987.

Grosz, Elizabeth. *Space, Time and Perversion: Essays on the Politics of Bodies.* New York: Routledge, 1995.

Heiferman, Scott. *The Meetup Organizer Boot Camp.* By Danielle Horry. June 10, 2009. meetup.com/organize/pages/Interview_with_Scott_Heiferman_-_Our_First_Event%21.

Huyssen, Andreas. "Twin Memories: After Images of Nine/Eleven." *Grey Room* 7 (2002): 8–13.

I Am Legend. Directed by Francis Lawrence. 2007. New York, USA: Warner Brothers, 2007. DVD.

Jenkins, Henry. "Introduction: Childhood Innocence and Other Modern Myths." In *The Children's Culture Reader,* edited by Henry Jenkins, 1–37. New York: New York University Press, 1998.

Keches, Krysten A. "The Invention of Childhood Innocence." *Harvard Gazette.* April 29, 2010, news.harvard.edu/gazette/story/2010/04/the-invention-of-childhood-innocence/.

Lisboa, Maria Manuel. *The End of the World: Apocalypse and Its Aftermath in Western Culture.* Cambridge: Open Book Publishers, 2011.

Low, Setha M., and Denise Lawrence-Zúñiga. "Locating Culture." In *The Anthropology of Space and Place: Locating Culture,* edited by Setha M. Low and Denise Lawrence-Zúñiga, 1–48. Oxford: Blackwell Publishing, 2003.

Naman, Christine. *Faces of Hope: Babies Born on 9/11.* Florida: Health Communications Inc., 2002.

Pufall, Peter B., and Richard P. Unsworth. "The Imperative and the Process for Rethinking Childhood." In *Rethinking Childhood,* edited by Peter D. Pufall and Richard P. Unsworth, 1–24. New Brunswick: Rutgers University Press, 2004.

Quay, Sara E., and Amy M. Damico, eds. *September 11 in Popular Culture: A Guide.* California: Greenwood, 2011.

The Road. Directed by John Hillcoat. 2009. Pennsylvania, USA: Dimension Films, 2009. DVD.

Sherwell, Philip. "September 11 Fireman: 'It felt like the end of the world.'" *The Telegraph.* September 10, 2011. www.telegraph.co.uk/news/worldnews/september-11-attacks/8754605/September-11-fireman-It-felt-like-the-end-of-the-world.html.

Springen, Karen. "Children's Books: Apocalypse Now: Teens Turn to Dystopian Novels." *Publishers Weekly* 257, no. 7 (2010). Accessed December 10, 2013. publishersweekly.com/pw/print/20100215/42087-children-s-books-apocalypse-now.html.

Strozier, Charles. *Until the Fires Stopped Burning*. New York: Columbia University Press, 2011.

Tuan, Yi-Fu. *Space and Place: The Perspective of Experience*. Minneapolis: University of Minnesota Press, 1996.

Chapter Eight

"Until the World Deserves Them"

Representations of Apocalyptic Childhoods in The Day After, Testament, *and* Threads

Tarah Brookfield

INTRODUCTION

Since the earliest days of the Cold War, children's health and safety dominated discourse about the possibility of surviving a nuclear war. From family fallout shelters to school duck and cover drills, state civil defense officials promised solutions that would ensure their nation's youngest citizens survived to rebuild and repopulate. Meanwhile members of the peace movement, particularly women activists, refuted these notions and insisted the only way to ensure children had a future was to promote nuclear disarmament. This rhetoric represented real concerns about the risks posed to children during wartime. It also demonstrates the political symbolism of children and how understandings of their childhoods and futures could become imbued with national importance. [1]

During the renewed Cold War arms race of the early 1980s, three nuclear war films, *The Day After* (1983 USA), *Testament* (1983 USA), and *Threads* (1984 UK), typified this child-centric discourse by presenting the outcome of nuclear warfare as being one that leads directly to the mass annihilation of children and the symbolic destruction of childhood. To underline the horrific cost of nuclear war, the filmmakers present perverse versions of different stages of childhood. Babies, normally viewed as beacons of hope, are shown being born into postwar worlds in which only misery, deformation, or early death wait. Meanwhile school-age children, whose prewar childhood is portrayed as playful and innocent, are thrown into lives full of loss. For adolescents, often depicted as fertile young lovers, the nuclear holocaust derails their coming of age and chance to begin new families. For the handful of young characters who survive the war, they are positioned as heirs to a contaminated world where their own and humanity's survival remains uncertain.

The three films' choice to frame their depiction of nuclear war as an allegory of childhood is a recognition of the symbolic power of children and the product of the debate and anxiety surrounding the likelihood of a nuclear war in the early 1980s. As Susan Ferguson argues "childhood has long been a handy and effective device for filmmakers to awaken in their audiences a sense of social anxiety and/or, more usefully social critique."[2] Unlike most nuclear war films, *The Day After*, *Testament*, and *Threads* eschew overt discussion of international relations and military strategy in favor of relatable, emotionally domestic dramas focused on how families experience nuclear war. By presenting the fictional youth as dead or having no future, the viewers of *The Day After*, *Testament*, and *Threads* are expected to be saddened and angered at this sacrifice. They know they cannot protect these children; however, the films are only *predicting* a future. In their roles as active citizens and voters, viewers have a chance to prevent such tragedy from happening in reality. While it is impossible to quantify the impact these three films had, studies performed on American viewers in the early 1980s and more recent testimonies from North America, Britain, and Australia suggest the movies were successful in generating apprehension, anger, or curiosity about nuclear war, particularly among many young viewers who watched their fictional counterparts die and suffer. As a result, this trio of films serve as touchstones for understanding the cinematic uses of children as powerful conduits for apocalyptic prophecies and how real children and youth understood their fears and futures in the last decade of the Cold War.

REPRESENTING THE PAST, PRESENT, AND FUTURE: NUCLEAR WAR ON FILM

Throughout the Cold War dozens of films ranging from monster movies to spy thrillers to black comedies delved into the consequences of living on the brink of nuclear war.[3] As with other disaster films that imagine the end of civilization, nuclear war films share what Despina Kakoudaki calls the "desire for realism and cultural relevance, and the desire for fantasy and spectacle."[4] The nuclear war films made in the first three decades of the Cold War captured and interpreted the global cultural anxiety and paranoia spawned from the post–World War II disintegration of American–Soviet relations, the surge in atomic testing, an escalating arms race, the identification and persecution of suspected spies, civil defense planning, and warfare of a more conventional kind in Korea and Vietnam. At the same time, the destructive nature of nuclear warfare, often shown in great detail through special effects or real atomic test footage of mushroom clouds and firestorms, provided audiences with a cathartic adventure. Much like cinematic recreations of natural disasters, pandemics, or terrorist threats, the nuclear dangers lurking onscreen felt entirely possible, particularly during moments where the Cold War grew hot.[5] Yet the celluloid plots which show the nuclear clock ticking toward midnight present these tensions from a safe distance, within what Susan Sontag called in 1966 "the imagination of disaster," an inadequate response, in her opinion, "to the unassailable terrors that infect their consciousness."[6]

Within the plethora of nuclear war films, only a minority have sought to interpret the reality of atomic history by dramatizing historic disasters, such as *The Beginning or the End* (1947), which explores the origins and ethics of the Manhattan Project, or *The Bells of Nagasaki* (1950), which follows a Japanese survivor in the days after the Nagasaki bombing. Given that the history of nuclear weapons since 1945 has been one of deterrence, the vast majority of nuclear war films deal not in history, but in speculation, and present answers to queries about what would prompt governments to use such deadly weapons again and what the world would look like afterwards. Several films contemplate the causes and prevention of an accidental or deliberate nuclear explosion, with the usual emphasis seen in *Dr. Strangelove: Or How I Learned to Stop Worrying and Love the Bomb* (1964) or *Failsafe* (1964) being the military and political chain of command and their rationale for starting or avoiding a war. Meanwhile science fiction classics *Godzilla* (1954) and *Them!* (1954) explore the fantastical environmental consequences and mutation caused by nuclear testing and atomic energy. There were also a number of films, most notably *On the Beach* (1959) and *Ladybug, Ladybug* (1964) focusing on the subtle and gross shifts in human behavior and social norms caused by fear of the bomb or radioactive fallout. From this era of films, *Ladybug, Ladybug* is the only one to focus specifically on children's experiences with nuclear war. It examines how teachers and students at a rural school react when they are led to believe a nuclear attack is imminent. Here the shattered nativity and innocence of the children, some oblivious and others frightened, act as a metaphor for humanity's helplessness in the face of such inhumane weapons. Through its representation of bullying, risk-taking, and sheer terror, *Ladybug, Ladybug* portrays how psychologically damaging living under the shadow of the bomb could be for everyone, not only the very young. Meanwhile films such as the *Planet of the Apes* series (1968), *The Boy and His Dog* (1975), and the *Mad Max* series (1979) are set in post-apocalyptic dystopian futures, decades after a nuclear war has decimated the most recognizable features of contemporary culture.

Before the 1980s, few films contemplated how civilians, living on a home front turned battlefield, would realistically experience a nuclear war; rather that was a subject typically left for civil defense training films.[7] One exception is *The War Game* (1965), a short film made as a mock documentary by Peter Watkins who wanted to "break the silence in the media on the nuclear arms race."[8] In a series of black and white news broadcasts, *The War Game* depicts an atomic attack on the city of Rochester, England, and the subsequent misery caused by fire, injury, refugee crisis, radiation sickness, food shortages, and post-traumatic stress. *The War Game* shows a postwar civilization in ruins, the failure of civil defense, and a world unable to recover its previous standards of living or social values. It features several shots of cowering families, shirking children, and tear-stained mothers. Funded by the BBC, *The War Game* was banned from television broadcast after completion due to its disturbing imagery and the stylistic blurring of fact and fiction. The film had a brief cinematic release and despite its fictional plot won an Academy Award for Best Documentary.[9] The themes and images presented in *The War Game* would not be explored again until 1983–1984, when under a renewed threat of nuclear war *The Day After*, *Testament*, and *Threads* attempted to present a realistic look at how everyday life could turn apocalyptic.

After a decade of détente, the 1979 Soviet invasion of Afghanistan ended any pretense at arms control between the Soviet Union and United States. This triggered massive investments in missile development, missile defense, and troop deployment, followed by both sides attempting to influence the outcomes of revolutions across the Middle East and Latin America. It was amid these tensions that Ronald Reagan would characterize the Soviet Union as an "evil empire," an attempt to alert Americans to the moral necessity of crushing their enemy and approve the Pentagon budget doubling between 1980 and 1985.[10] In the United States and among its NATO allies, the preparations for war led governments to reemphasize the need for families to build fallout shelters and positioned nuclear warfare as survivable and winnable. This mindset was infamously promoted by Thomas K. Jones, Deputy Under Secretary of Defense for Research and Engineering under Reagan, who proclaimed in 1981 that the United States could fully recover from an all-out nuclear war with the Soviet Union in just two to four years, "If there are enough shovels to go around, everybody's going to make it."[11] His comment referred to the civil defense advice to cover basement windows with three feet of dirt to prevent fallout seepage. These intensifying preparations for war resulted in ambiguous public support for nuclear weapons. The majority of American voters supported Reagan's military buildup in the name of national security, but opinion polls suggest that the most Americans agreed nuclear weapons were dangerous and "the nuclear arms race [needed to be] brought under control."[12] One 1981 poll claimed three-fourths of Americans expected a nuclear war within a few years. [13] A Gallup poll conducted in the United Kingdom in 1982 had 38 percent of Britons claim a nuclear war was inevitable. [14] Concurrently, there was escalating concerns about the dangers of nuclear energy marked by the 1979 reactor accident at Three Mile Island, Pennsylvania. [15]

As a result of the increased nuclear proliferation, an international disarmament campaign known as the Nuclear Freeze was organized, asking all nuclear powers to agree to a verifiable and bilateral ban on weapons development. In 1981 there were large antiwar demonstrations in Western European capitals and American cities, culminating in a 1982 rally at the United Nations' New York headquarters which drew over a million protesters. [16] The year before in Britain, women formed a peace camp outside Greenham Common Royal Air Force Base in England to protest the American nuclear cruise missiles on site and the dangers they posed to children's health and safety. In 1983 the Greenham women formed a human chain fourteen miles long which gathered an estimated fifty thousand supporters. [17] Much like the ban-the-bomb groups in the late 1950s and early 1960s, the early 1980s Nuclear Freeze movement represented civic mobilization around what was positioned as a life or death cause, and a grassroots critique of deterrence as a dependable strategy for peace. This sense of unease produced dozens of films, once again in a number of genres, centered around the probability and outcomes of nuclear war, including the screwball comedy *Die Laughing* (1980), the documentary *The Atomic Cafe* (1982), and the action-adventure thriller *The Terminator* (1984). Meanwhile *The Day After*, *Testament*, and *Threads* were answers to a much-discussed question from the period, "What would happen if a nuclear war occurred today?" While their films do not overtly suggest disarmament is the answer, they blatantly suggest that a nuclear war is not worth surviving.

The biggest and most well-known of the three films is ABC's "major event" TV movie, *The Day After*, directed by Nicholas Meyers, which was seen by over 100 million viewers when it first premiered in November 1983. [18] The movie is set in present-day Lawrence, Kansas, and the surrounding rural region along the Kansas-Missouri border. Before the blast we meet dozens of characters, including a pregnant woman near delivery, four families with young children, and several college students, including a young couple soon to be wed. As the characters go about their lives, attending school, work, leisure activities, and church, radio and TV news reports amplify the conflict between America and the Soviets. Then seemingly without warning one morning, missiles strike across the sky and a mushroom cloud erupts from Kansas City. This is followed by a two-minute segment depicting a firestorm enveloping and vaporizing the majority of the characters introduced in the first hour of the film. A handful of people survive the bomb, including three Dahlberg children: Denise, the young bride-to-be who retreats to the family's cellar with her parents, her younger sister Jolene, and her brother Danny who has been blinded by the blast. Their family is joined in their cellar shelter by Stephen, a young college student unable to make it home. In the last half of the film Stephen, Denise, and Danny either succumb to wounds from the initial blast or are greatly stricken by radiation sickness. Jolene remains fairly healthy, as she was the only one not exposed to radiation in the weeks following the bomb, but her fate is left in peril after a gang of men squatting on her farm shoot her father. Although their final fates are left unseen, the youths' individual frailty and vulnerability suggests death is imminent for all. The film concludes with a title card indicating that "the catastrophic events you have just witnessed are in all likelihood, less severe than the destruction that would actually occur in the event of a full nuclear strike against the United States. It is hoped that the images of this film will inspire the nations of this earth, their people and leaders, to find the means to avert the fateful day."

Positioned as more than the network's usual thrilling movie-of-the-week, *The Day After* was promoted widely across North America before its premiere as a "giant public-service announcement" to show "ordinary people who haven't dealt with this problem what life is like after a nuclear attack."[19] To validate the film's educational value, the network emphasized that an enormous amount of research had gone into ensuring the accuracy of the science and representation of warfare in the film. The Cultural Information Service, a non-profit educational organization worked with ABC to produce a viewer's guide distributed prior to the broadcast to schools and other educational associations. It offered a history of the atomic bomb, a bibliography, and pre- and post-viewing activities.[20] To further add to the public's education, the original broadcast was followed by a live debate about the merits of disarmament versus deterrence between scientist Carl Sagan, writer and Holocaust survivor Elie Wiesel, conservative author William F. Buckley, and past and current State Department officials, Henry Kissinger, Robert McNamara, and George Schultz. By not blaming any one government for causing the onscreen war, the filmmakers insisted the film was politically neutral, though as film scholar Deron Overpeck notes, most of the research used by *The Day After*'s screenwriter was anything but apolitical, since he drew almost exclusively on the work of scientists and other scholars promoting disarmament. Furthermore, Meyers grew openly anti-Reagan during his publicity circuit for the film.[21] The film's politics and subject made it difficult for ABC to secure sponsors who did not want their products associated with the film's graphic violence or a critique of nuclear weapons. This led the network to not show any commercials during the second half of the film, after the bombs detonated, a business decision that also had artistic merit since it kept the audience focused on the terror before them.[22] Some of the commercials were paid spots made by disarmament groups, including one ad produced by Women's Action for Nuclear Disarmament which featured actress Meryl Streep (who was not associated with the film) making a plea to mothers to help prevent nuclear war, which she called "one of the last major childhood diseases."[23] After viewing the decaying Dahlberg children, it was hoped that viewers would advocate for disarmament to be the necessary "vaccine" to eradicate the risk of childhood turning apocalyptic.

Produced a year later for the BBC, *Threads*, directed by Mick Jackson, follows a similar narrative, though one with a far grittier and gloomier depiction of a post-nuclear war—fewer survivors, further environmental destruction, and a much more violent breakdown of law and order.[24] The film is set in the industrial city of Sheffield, England, and divides its time between the families of middle-class Ruth and working-class Jimmy, a young couple, who find themselves accidently pregnant on the eve of nuclear war. Jimmy and his little sister are shown to be outside during the attack on Sheffield and are never seen again, presumed to have died in the bombing, while his parents, younger brother, and Ruth's parents die from radiation sickness and blast wounds. Ruth survives to give birth to her baby alone in a famine-stricken nuclear winter. The film's epilogue jumps thirteen years later to the life of Ruth's daughter Jane, who spends her days alternating between manual labor on a commune and scavenging ruined cities for old technology and canned food. Like the other youth in her era Ruth speaks in a drastically diminished form of English. Just after watching her mother die from an unspecified illness, Jane is raped by a boy and becomes pregnant. The film concludes with Jane giving birth to her baby. Screenwriter Barry Hines explained *Threads* was made "to step aside from the politics and—I hope convincingly—show the actual effects on either side should our best endeavors to prevent nuclear war fail."[25] The film was first broadcast in September 1984 when it was watched by 6.9 million people. On the following night, the BBC aired *On the Eighth Day*, a documentary exploring the concept of nuclear winter portrayed in the film and hosted a discussion about issues related to nuclear war on *Newsnight*. The strong critical appreciation and high ratings for *Threads* caused the BBC to finally air *The War Game* in 1985 on the anniversary of the bombing of Hiroshima.[26] *Threads* was repeated the following year in Britain and also aired in the United States, Australia, and Canada.

Testament, directed by Lynne Littman, was originally made for PBS Playhouse, but was switched to a theatrical release when producers were impressed with the film's quality.[27] It follows an American housewife Carol Wetherly and her three children living in a suburb outside San Francisco after a nuclear attack on the United States. Even though their town of Hamelin has no blast damage, the community is contaminated with fallout and the children's father never returns from his workday in San Francisco. Carol watches helplessly as the children die around her, first her youngest son

Scottie, then Larry, the neighbor boy she took in, and finally her eldest child, Mary Liz. Throughout the film, twelve-year-old Brad is seen taking over his father's role as he guards the family home from looters and helps an elderly neighbor contact other communities on the radio. The film ends with Carol contemplating suicide alongside Brad and Hiroshi, another orphaned child she is caring for, before deciding to carry on. Compared to its counterparts, *Testament* is a much quieter film, with minimal special effects and a more limited look at nuclear war. It grossed just over $1.5 million during its theatrical release and found a secondary audience on home video and repeated television broadcasts, though not to the same level as *Threads* and *The Day After*.[28] Littman characterizes the film's "entire purpose" as being to "avert nuclear war," adding that *Testament*, like all her films is about "life on the edge of death which makes life so precious."[29]

Since all three films were pitched at a mass television audience, it is not surprising their stories captured the spectacle of nuclear war as a domestic drama, which focused on the experiences of ordinary people, presumably much like the audiences themselves. Film historian Toni Perrine theorizes that films depicting a realistic nuclear war and its aftermath tend to focus on the "The disruption of domestic life" which is "most terrifying to watch, but not in the manner of horror films. Here the individual threat to hearth and home must be generalized, as the audience is forced to acknowledge the larger societal implications of individual loss, separation and despair."[30] In an interview with the *New York Times*, Meyers explained he would not have made *The Day After* as a feature film since he "did not want to preach to the converted. I wanted it to reach the guy who's waiting for *The Flying Nun* to come on."[31] With this goal in mind the filmmakers strove for creating relatable characters to help the audience connect and feel more shocked when disaster struck. As Patrick Stoddart, a reviewer of *Threads* commented, it was as if Hines plucked character types that would have been at home on the popular soap opera *Coronation Street* and showed how "family life, human dignity and community spirit would simply evaporate at the moment of nuclear impact, and that the ragged remnants of mankind would be reduced to uncaring animalism by the need to survive."[32] This was a change of pace from the nuclear war films of the 1950s and 1960s which were dominated by the actions and imagery of childless adult protagonists, usually male, and set in nondomestic spaces, such as war rooms or military bases. Rather than focus on generals or scientists, this trio of films show the events leading up to and after a nuclear war from the perspective of ordinary people identified as parents and children, whose suffering, separations, and deaths are meant to parallel the mass annihilation and broader societal collapse. It is also notable that children's lives and deaths take center stage in all three films, making the apocalyptic representation of childhood, the clearest transmission of the films' antinuclear war message.

REPRESENTATIONS OF APOCALYPTIC CHILDHOODS

Since the early twentieth century, film and photographs, both staged and candid, have memorably documented the grief and pain of children's suffering in wars and other crises. Prime examples of this has been Dorothea Lange's Great Depression era photo of the "Migrant Mother," featuring two small hungry children looking away from the camera as they embrace their forlorn mother, the United Nations's film, *Seeds of Destiny*, showcasing the horrific existence of postwar Europe's homeless war orphans, or Nick Ut's image of burned nine-year-old Kim Phuc's flight from the napalm attack captured during the Vietnam War. These images simultaneously signify the specific vulnerabilities the violence of war can have on the young, and how the suffering of children can act as an effective symbol for something larger than the children themselves. As a result, injured, orphaned, or feral child can become emotionally driven representations used to characterize entire wars, condemn or praise government action, spawn fundraising, fuel activism, or serve as evidence in calls for justice. These photos and films are provocative because they translate into what Patricia Holland calls "the defining characteristics of childhood—dependence and powerlessness."[33] According to Holland "suffering children appear as archetypal victims, since childhood itself is defined by weakness and incapacity . . . as they reveal their vulnerability, viewers long to protect them."[34] Images of children's wounded, crippled, or starving bodies, complete with tear-stained, panic-stricken faces, tend to draw a predictable set of emotions from those who view them: sympathy, charity, and compassion for the children in question, and guilt, fear, or anger over the circumstances that forced the young subjects so far from the innocence of childhood. Furthermore Holland argues that the association of innocence, held so dear in the Western conceit of childhood, means that "a child can be the bearer of suffering with no responsibility for its causes."[35] In *The Day After*, *Threads*, and *Testament*, the children have not caused the war or built the bombs; they are shown to be the victims of adults' misuse of power or their apathy. The cinematic evidence of adults failing children is in the surrender of innocence, depicted differently depending on the particular stages of childhood.

In all three films, there is at least one baby shown soon after their first appearance as a tiny corpse. In *The Day After*, the wife of Airman Billy McCoy is vaporized in the firestorm sequence while clutching her newborn son. As pregnant Ruth stumbles through the rubbles of postwar Sheffield in *Threads*, she comes across an unnamed dirty, bloody woman, presumably the mother of the charred infant still swaddled in her arms. *Threads*'s perversion of the mother/child figure is juxtaposed against a relatively unscathed billboard placed in the same scene, advertising Standard Life insurance. It features an illustration of a large, smiling baby under the deliberately ironic

catchphrase "Standard Life for all of your life." In the case of *Testament,* we
do not see the body of the dead baby, only the borrowed dresser drawer
carried by the grieving father to be used as the coffin. "We didn't have a
bureau the right size. She'll fit in. She'll fit in here," the father explains to
Carol, his way of announcing his newborn daughter's death from radiation
sickness. He continues by saying, "We thought we were so lucky. We didn't
think there would be more bombs. Then she had to get sick." Seeing her
neighbor's baby die so quickly after the attack prompts Carol to pose the
question in her journal, "What if the baby is the lucky one?" This is in
reference to the quick death and her anxiety about what is still to come for
herself and her own children.

Not only are these shocking images meant to drive home the films' antiwar message, they were used to depict the reality that the babies' physical
smallness and dependence on adult caretakers make them the first casualties
in any war. Since the 1960s scientists and physicians had predicted that due
to infants' undeveloped immune systems and smaller bodies, they would be
the first population group to succumb from radiation sickness, followed by
older children, the elderly, and the sick. [36] In fact the images in these fictional
dramas parallel descriptions of those seen in the days after the bombings of
Japan. Journalist John Hersey's *Hiroshima* contains two particularly harrowing accounts of mothers found alive in the rubble holding their dead infants,
including one mother who refused to let go of the four-day-old corpse of her
baby. [37] Similar images are presented in the anime drama *Barefoot Gen,* also
released in 1983, which is based on the manga written by Keiji Nakazawa, a
child survivor of the Hiroshima bombing. In the film, there is a memorable
sequence of preteen Gen scouring the city's ruins to find milk for his newborn sister when he encounters a different baby trying to nurse from its dead
mother's breasts. This scene is soon followed by the appearance of a woman,
driven mad from her own child's death, who attempts to kill Gen's baby
sister out of grief for her own lost child. Unable to find enough milk, Gen
returns home one day to find his baby sister, cradled in his mother's arms,
dead from malnutrition. Forty years later, the real-life traumas of Hiroshima
parallel the imagined fates of infants in a new war.

Both *The Day After* and *Threads* include births of babies born into uncertain worlds after the bomb explodes to greatly ambivalent mothers where
medical care, food, water, shelter, law, and order are practically nonexistent,
suggesting a high probability of infant mortality. *Threads* also features the
birth of a child conceived and born more than a decade after the nuclear war.
The film's final shot is a freeze-frame of the mother Jane with her mouth
open wide to scream when she sees her baby for the first time. The audience
does not see what she sees, a stillbirth or mutation perhaps, or at best her own
panic at not knowing how to mother. But the audience knows the baby is no
way a harbinger of a better world. This plot choice parallels real-life con-

cerns over radiation's impact on fertility and fetal development which had existed since the first atomic explosions. Although American surveillance of pregnancies from Hiroshima and Nagasaki in the six years after the bombing claimed not to show any long-term genetic difficulties or higher than normal rates of birth defects, miscarriages, and cancer, this evidence did not erase the fears of adults or youth. Studies of high school students in the months before the Cuban Missile Crisis reported teenage girls being afraid of having deformed babies and boys being cynical about their futures because they believed them to be nonexistent. [38]

Therefore it is not surprising that babies in the film are irreconcilably linked to the older youth. Each of the films contain lead characters in their late teens or young adults in their early twenties who are sexually active and thinking about starting their own families. *Threads* opens with Ruth and Jimmy chatting casually about their futures in his car before they begin to kiss. In the next scene, set several weeks later, Ruth tells Jimmy that she suspects she is pregnant, pointedly stating, "What if I am? It's not the end of the world is it?" Of course the end of the world as Ruth knows it is actually in progress. Each of the following scenes contain background media reports of the Soviet invasion of Iran and other escalating conflicts, yet everyone is preoccupied with the pregnancy news. Only Jimmy's father links the children's futures to wider current events, but even then it is only a reference to the state of the British economy, commenting, "It's a hell of a time to start a family in the middle of a recession." Only after her personal crisis is calmed with a promise of marriage from Jimmy, does Ruth become aware of the explosive current affairs that could literally end everything. After witnessing a disarmament protest and hearing civil defense advisories, Ruth recognizes she is no longer in control of her own or her baby's destiny and breaks down in tears at the thought of war.

The young couple in *The Day After* are also similarly oblivious about the state of the world until it is too late. In the days leading up to her wedding, Denise exudes frustration at having to live under her father's curfew and her younger sister's teasing. The night before the nuclear attack, and two days before her scheduled wedding, she ducks back into the house to retrieve her diaphragm so she can have sex with her fiancé. Denise's next significant scene shows her retreat to the family's fallout shelter where she clutches her wedding dress and teddy bear, symbols of her shattered innocence and thwarted future. In the shelter she openly laments using birth control, "Why did I use that thing? Wait to get married? I could have been pregnant!" Like *Thread*'s Ruth, Denise frets about her shattered dreams, particularly about the chance of not being a mother. In an attempt to grasp the last shreds of their dissipating futures, both Denise and Ruth flee their family's shelters prematurely, deaf to their fathers' demands to stay put, risking exposure to heavy radiation in hopes of reuniting with their fiancés. With both men dead, this dream is dashed. Denise is dragged back to the shelter where she grows weak with radiation sickness, though unlike Ruth, whose parents and grandmother die soon after she leaves, Denise finds comfort in the company of her family. Rather than these plots play out as critiques of youth's rebellion or the dangers of engaging in premarital sex, the larger threat of nuclear war is what ruins these young women's futures and any chance they have for marriage and motherhood.

In *Testament* the eldest child, Mary Liz, is in her midteens and not yet sexually active. After the bomb, she appears to understand that she will never get the chance. In a poignant scene with her mother not long after their neighbor's baby has died, but before any of her own family has passed, Mary Liz sits in a rocking chair flipping through a family photo album, reminiscing about family vacations while her mother makes a bed nearby. The photos trigger nostalgia for the past and recognition she will never have an album like this of her own. This leads her to ask, at first coyly, and then curtly, about sex:

> Mary Liz: What's it like?
> Carol: What's what like?
> Mary Liz: Making love. Don't play mother with me.
> Carol: That's what I am. What's it like? I was so ignorant as a girl. Worried about it. So full of fantasy. I thought some man would come along and sweep me off my feet. And your father . . . he wasn't at all what I was looking for. Not the size or shape, or what he did exactly, I still don't know. When you love someone, you want to be as close to them as you can get. You make love and you feel almost like the same body. Like it was intended. You have a space, and that person fills it up. We would fight. We wouldn't listen to each other. We'd miss thoughts. We'd miss goodbyes. But sometimes, most times, there was this feeling, and I couldn't wait for him to be here with me. Everyone's always alone. And yet there can be this gift. This making of miracles. You.
> Mary Liz: Not for me.

Although younger and less experienced than Denise and Ruth, the war has placed Mary Liz in a threshold that will permanently keep her stuck between childhood and adulthood. She yearns for a future she will never have, though she wants in this exchange with her mother to get a glimpse of it. By doing so she reveals her own childish innocence about love, sex, and marriage, coupled with a maturity beyond her years in being pragmatic about what her own future holds. Several scenes later, Carol is shown sewing a shroud made of bed sheets around her dead daughter.

For the school-age children in the movies, their prewar childhood is depicted as playful and innocent. Before the war, the children appear immersed in their own universes, listening to music on their headphones, glued to the television, practicing the piano, playing with pets and action figures, and doing minimal chores. They are seen arguing with their parents and fighting with siblings, such as when *The Day After*'s Jolene steals Denise's diaphragm as a prank, not knowing its purpose, only that it would annoy her sister. It is not a coincidence that the bomb goes off in *Testament* while the children are watching *Sesame Street*. Of course after the bombs detonate, familiar childhood props vanish as pets die, electricity is nonexistent, and batteries are needed for more important things than video games. In *Testament*, young Scottie is seen burying his favorite toys in the graveyard, an act he explains to the priest by saying there is not enough food for them. Later, when Scottie dies of radiation sickness, Carol turns the house upside down as she frantically searches and fails to find the missing teddy bear she wants to bury with him.

The teddy bear is a recurring totem in all films, standing out as a remaining, but fleeting token of the comfort and softness associated with childhood. In *Threads*, a teddy bear makes a brief appearance in the post-apocalyptic landscape of ruined Sheffield thirteen years later. Soiled, missing one leg, with a rag tied around its middle, Jane is shown to tenderly hold this relic, most likely found during one of her scavenging trips. Like Jane herself, the bear is an unlikely survivor, and her proximity to this relic only serves to emphasize the horrific nature of every other aspect of her childhood.

Meanwhile the children in midchildhood often appear to play a role distinct from their teenage or infant siblings, that of an oracle. Even their rosy prewar scenes carry a sense of doom as the children slowly become aware about the lurking threat of the bomb. For these children born in the mid- to late 1970s, this is most likely their first nuclear scare, unlike their parents and grandparents who lived through the Cuban Missile Crisis or the nuclear tests

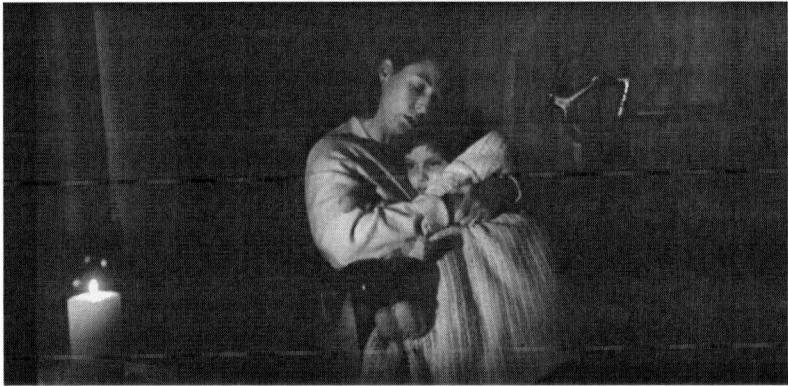

Figure 8.1. Carol Wetherly (Jane Alexander) cradles her son Scottie (Lukas Haas) before he dies of radiation sickness. *Testament*, 1983, Paramount.

of the 1950s and 1960s, hence they are shown to be hyperaware, often the only ones paying attention to the news, even if they do not understand it. "There's not going to be a war, is there?" asks *The Day After*'s Jolene, perplexed after hearing an announcement about the war on the radio, minutes from the attack. At other points, the children's innocent comments reflect their own and humanity's doomed fate. A poignant scene in *Testament* has the postattack community deciding to go on with a scheduled school play. The choice of the play *The Pied Piper* is not subtle as it features a title character for whom literary scholars suggest is a symbol of a catastrophe which destroyed the real town of Hamlin in the sixteenth century. The scene featuring the play opens with the director announcing that the child playing the narrator is sick, suggesting radiation sickness is beginning to affect the children. The next scene jumps to the end of the play, just after the piper has lured the children away to punish the town for not compensating him for eradicating the rats. Scottie plays the crippled boy who is not fast enough to join the other children wooed away by the piper. When the child playing the mayor cries over his lost son, Scottie replies, "Your children are not dead. They will return. They are just waiting until the world deserves them." The shell-shocked audience watching the play cannot hold back their tears as they undoubtedly draw parallels to a similarly doomed fate for their own children. This last attempt at normality is the final moment of innocence in *Testament*, as the children's deaths begin in the next scene. Soon young Scottie is weakened, and seen hemorrhaging as he suffers from the side effects of radiation sickness.

Figure 8.2.   Ruth (Karen Meagher) barters a dead rat for food in front of the Standard Life Insurance billboard in post-nuclear war Sheffield. *Threads*, 1984, BBC.

The film's last lines harken back to Scottie's dialogue from the play when Carol tells her oldest son, "That we [should] remember it all. The good and the awful . . . that we were the last to be here . . . to deserve the children."

ABSORBING APOCALYPTIC CHILDHOODS

So what effects did apocalyptic childhoods in *The Day After*, *Testament*, and *Threads* have on the youth who first watched them in the 1980s? Toni Perrine argues that there are multiple lenses in which to interpret the particular affects nuclear war films have on audiences' psyche, and more broadly on their support for defense strategies and foreign policy. Unless there is an immediate cut to black after the bomb explodes like in *Dr. Strangelove*, "Some critics believe the history of nuclear images has tended to minimize, even undermine the nuclear threat, since the imagery of the end of the world most often acts as a denial of extinction or an allegory of survival."[39] Alternatively, Perrine suggests that "representations of the end of the world have forced the possibility into our collective consciousness and actually served as a powerful deterrent to such an event."[40] For children, it was suspected that exposure to these films would be traumatic, and many psychologists discouraged children from viewing them. Media Studies scholars Joanne Cantor, Barbara J. Wilson, and Cynthia Hoffner predicted older youth would be more troubled by the films like *The Day After*, since unlike their younger peers, teens could cognitively understand fears related to world conditions, and therefore understand the real risks posed by nuclear weapons. They would be more sensitive to presentations of abstract violence—slow death by radiation sickness or fear of contaminated food—conveyed by dialogue or the character's emotional reactions.[41] The Physicians for Social Responsibility issued parental guidance warnings for *The Day After*, asserting it was unsuitable for preteens and ages twelve to fifteen "should be closely monitored."[42] Despite these recommendations, youth of all ages watched all or parts of these films, alone in secret, with their parents, or later in school as part of a science, religion, or social studies class. Although much of how children experienced the films remains a private experience, there are two sets of evidence that give some clues to how young people actually responded in the immediate aftermath of the films, and again decades later.

One is the quantitative data gathered from at least four separate academic studies performed on American youth, from preschoolers to college students, in the days and weeks following the premiere of *The Day After*. The primary goal was to measure the effects of media on children's emotional development and learning. A number of conclusions were drawn from parent phone surveys and student questionnaires, notably that young peoples' knowledge about nuclear weapons, their delivery methods and effects on human life increased after seeing the films, particularly among younger students for whom the films may have been their first exposure to the subject.[43] The majority of students in all age categories believed that "a real war would be a whole lot worse than the movie."[44] As predicted, older students were more troubled by the film, results that still stand even when considering that older

Figure 8.3.   Jim Dahlberg (John Cullum) assists his daughter Denise Dahlberg (Lori Lethin), who is preparing to enter the family's fallout shelter. *The Day After*, **1983, ABC Circle Films.**

youth were more likely to have seen the film in the first place and that "children who tend to be emotionally responsive to mass media offerings" may have been directed away from the film by their parents or by their own choice.[45] Despite teens being more affected by the film, youth of all ages in the Lawrence, Kansas study, notable for being the setting of the film, denied being unduly frightened or upset by *The Day After* and many students answered that they had seen movies on TV that were more frightening.[46] Given that there was only four minutes of graphic violence in *The Day After*, much less than what is featured in horror films popular among youth in the early 1980s (*Poltergeist, Gremlins,* and *Ghoulies*), researchers in a similar Wisconsin study were unsurprised that children were not more upset by *The Day After*.[47]

In two of the studies focusing on teens and college students, there was also keen interest in seeing if the results could be used to predict how the this generation would view nuclear weapons and warfare. Zwiegenhaft's North Carolina study had comparable data taken from a similar cohort of youth in 1982, where he found that opinions about nuclear war grew more pessimistic in 1984. When asked if they wished to survive a nuclear war in 1982, 63 percent of high school students and 70 percent of college students said yes. By 1984, those numbers had dramatically shrunk to 41 percent and 19 percent respectively. Zwiegenhaft attributes the change in opinion to youth's receptivity to the emotional nature of movies like *The Day After*, rather than news media or textbooks containing data about nuclear war. Since students in both years of his study remained quite unknowledgeable about their government's foreign policy and international relations, Zwiegenhaft argues that popular culture was a more accessible source of knowledge about nuclear war.[48] None of the studies consider variables such as race, gender, or class, though French and Van Hoorn's study of youth in Northern California note that students from the high school in the affluent neighborhood felt more empowered than other students that youth could do something to avoid nuclear war.[49] French and Van Hoorn argue that despite these results, films like *The Day After* were unlikely to inspire youth to formally support disarmament. Without any understanding of the political decision-making or geopolitics, *The Day After*, as well as *Testament* and *Threads*, presents the destructive nature of nuclear weapons too much like a natural disaster, something unpreventable. Overall, the studies suggest that *The Day After* acted as a source of knowledge for youth in the 1980s and generated minimal to moderate fear about nuclear war.

Another set of data are the recollections by adults who grew up during the 1980s in North America, Britain, and Australia, who have written about their experiences watching *The Day After*, *Testament,* and *Threads* as children. "That there is no hope. That mankind is doomed to failure. This is the message that so many of us took to our second-grade classes the next morning," recalls blogger Dustin Rowles in relation to watching *The Day After* as a child. Sources such as Rowles provide more details than the academic studies about individual children's specific viewing experiences, interpretations of nuclear war, and suggest a lingering public memory of the films for the generation who came of age during the renewed nuclear scare. These contemporary reflections, found in movie message boards, blogs, and one memoir, come from adults who describe themselves as being traumatized by the films in their youth, which explain the movies sticking with them three decades later. For instance, the Internet Movie Database contains over one hundred posts, either structured as a review or message board discussion thread about *The Day After*, *Threads*, and *Testament* from people who watched the films between twenty and thirty years ago and want to publically share their viewing experiences. These posts are made under a screen name and rarely contain any other identifiers such as gender, level of education, or cultural background. The reflections have a common style, often describing in great detail where, when, and how they first encountered one or all the films in their youth, what parts stood out to them the most, and how it affected their childhood view of the Cold War. One American poster recalled that when *The Day After* "first aired in 1983, I was only seven and my folks wouldn't let me watch it; I had to sit in my brother's room and listen to kiddie records."[50] A year or two later he recalls watching an American broadcast of *Threads* with his older brother when his parents were out. Others watched the movies alongside their parents, such as one poster who wrote that "No, the [*The Day After*] was not for kids, but my parents wanted me to watch it. I remember going back to school the next day, and everyone in school that had actually seen it all looked like they'de [*sic*] seen a ghost."[51] Another poster discusses how seeing *The Day After* at school was even worst: "I actually saw it for the first time when a teacher made us watch it in class. It was so much harder to deal with because I didn't want to freak out in front of the other students. I had nightmares then, and it still haunts me when I see or hear anything about nuclear weapons or war."[52] After viewing the films, several posters found themselves more sensitive to aircraft sounds, thunder, or out of the ordinary occurrences, believing them to be the first signs of an attack. One more extreme reaction was related by one poster who said:

> [I] Was 14 in November 1983, and was scared/scarred by it [*The Day After*]. We lived 20 miles from a major metropolitan area, and after that, when a simple power outage [*sic*] occurred, I'd grab onto the edge of a counter, curl up in a ball on the floor, or tell my nearest sibling or friend, "I've always loved you" (or "I'm sorry I've only been pretending to be your friend," to allay Final Judgment later), but then the lights would come back on, and people would find me in the crash position.[53]

As found in the academic studies from the early 1980s, older youth and teens appear to have connected the fictional depictions to the present-day threat of nuclear war. A British poster recalls first watching *Threads* in 1985 at age nine: "Unlike most horror films I'd seen as a child up until that time, the horror and terror in this film seemed a very real and scary possibility, even to my young self."[54] One poster recalls how when they first saw *Testament* on HBO in the 1980s it reminded them of a "realistic" *ABC Afterschool Special*, a series of television movies made between 1972 and 1997 that focused on challenges confronting youth, such as teen pregnancy, eating disorders, child abuse, or divorce. This poster recalls specific scenes in the film, including the deaths of Scottie and Mary Liz and ends the post by declaring, "[It] totally disturbed me for weeks!"[55]

Based on the available information about the identity of those sharing their reflections, there does not seem to be a particular set of criteria that would make a young person likely feel particularly traumatized. Sometimes those writing about their memory of the films describe themselves as having an overactive imagination or being particularly sensitive when they were young. Other posters specifically mention their fear stemmed from having a parent in the armed forces. Bryan Hargrave who "happened upon a presentation of *Threads* when I was about eleven years old" explained that "As a Navy family, we were stationed in Washington, D.C. After viewing it, I was frightened to the point of vomiting. I had nightmares for weeks."[56] For some, living in a target city could make the terror feel all the more real, such as the young man who saw *Threads* on PBS in 1985 or 1986 when he was fifteen or sixteen years old. He recalls how "It came near the end of my childhood obsession with World War III, in which I terrified myself to sleep many nights worrying about it. . . . Having grown up in the strategic target city of Chicago, I thought: Okay, this is what I could expect if it does happen."[57] For the youth who addressed what they did to calm their anxiety, only a few report joining a disarmament organization, while others recall planning their own emergency shelter or civil defense plans.[58] These memories include one from a poster who participated in peace marches in Australia from 1984 through to 1989 after viewing *The Day After* when they were thirteen or fourteen, a film they refer to as "the one piece of media that had the greatest influence on my life."[59] Another poster claimed "From about 6th grade to probably freshman year of high school, I had plans for what I would do in the case of an attack. Just in the back of my head, nothing crazy. Unless you call purposefully knowing where my math teachers [*sic*] truck keys were crazy."[60] Several posters recall finding solace in *Red Dawn* or *War Games*, two other films from 1983 and 1984 which portrayed young characters actively and successfully fighting to prevent a nuclear war or save their families and communities from Cold War conflicts.[61]

The most in-depth personal contemplation of nuclear war films and apocalyptic childhoods comes from Steven Church's haunting memoir *The Day After The Day After: My Atomic Angst*, which explores the post-traumatic stress he felt from watching *The Day After* be filmed in his hometown and his subsequent viewing of the film when he was ten years old. Church situates his atomic angst within the context of the Lawrence, Kansas's apocalyptic past as violent frontier town and prime property in the Midwestern tornado alley, as well as more domestic strife, such as his parent's separation occurring in the weeks before *The Day After* premiered. Surprisingly, *The Day After The Day After* it is one of the few recollections to make a specific reference to the films' horrific representations of childhood. Church, now a Professor of English, recalls, "the film spoke to a generation of kids" and it was notable to him because the movies featured "kids like me. Just like me."[62] Church describes a particular kinship with Danny Dahlberg, the son from *The Day After* blinded by the explosion. In his memoir, Church goes so far as to rewrite scenes showing the movie from Danny's perspective and inventing different, often happier, endings for him. Ultimately Church's impressions are that his and his peer's reactions to the:

> manufactured trauma were unique and varied, as the kids who shared them. Some kids like me *were* scared out of their minds. Some kids felt helpless and despair. Some were worked up with anxiety. Other kids thought it was boring

or melodramatic. Still others found it momentarily compelling and transiently traumatic as a car wreck on the side of the highway. Some of them just thought it was cool to see Kansas City get totally wasted by bombs. [63]

Church's statement reflects the range of possible reactions from young viewers, including those like him who interpreted the films' representations of apocalyptic childhoods as foreshadowing their futures.

Of course in these accounts like Church's or the Internet Movies Database posts, the children are now grown adults and their memories of the films are filtered through their exposure to other factual and fictional depictions of nuclear war, as well as their having lived (and survived) the end of the Cold War and subsequent wars. Additionally, many of the people sharing their memories are now parents themselves whose memories may be influenced by thinking not only of themselves as a child, but of their own children's future survival. The films also appear to resonate with a new generation of viewers who have come of age during the War on Terror. A special 2004 screening of *Testament* for students at the Renaissance Arts School in Los Angeles was done in conjunction with the film's twentieth anniversary. In a postviewing discussion, students at this charter school made comparisons between the films, the fear of a terrorist attack on the United States, and their own and adults' responsibility to change the world. [64] All of these layers of interpretation coalesce and inform what could be considered, to borrow from Sontag, the reimagination of disaster. As a result, there are multiple layers of apocalyptic childhoods, one within the films themselves and secondly in the young viewers' impressions of the films gathered when they first premiered and thirty years later. Both of these layers capture the symbolic power of children and childhood, particularly when it comes to crafting antiwar ideologies. These intertwined legacies harken back to the last words spoken in *Testament*, "That we [should] remember it all. The good and the awful . . . that we were the last to be here . . . to deserve the children."

NOTES

1. Karen Dubinsky, *Babies without Borders: Adoption and Migration across the Americas* (Toronto: University of Toronto Press, 2010).

2. Susan Ferguson, "Capitalist Childhood in Film: Modes of Critique," *Jump Cut: A Review of Contemporary Media* No. 55, Fall 2013. www.ejumpcut.org/currentissue/Ferguson-Childhood/index.html. Accessed: 23 December 2013.

3. For a detailed examining of nuclear war films, see Toni Perrine, *Film and the Nuclear Age: Representing Cultural Anxiety* (New York: Garland Publishing, 1998).

4. Despina Kakoudaki, "Representing Politics in Disaster Films," *International Journal of Media & Cultural Politics* 7(3): 2011, 349.

5. For a succinct history of the Cold War, see John Lewis Gaddis, *The Cold War: A New History* (New York: Penguin Press, 2005).

6. Susan Sontag, "The Imagination of Disaster," *Against Interpretation: And Other Essays* (New York: Farrar, 1966): 225.

7. For an evocative look at the performance aspect of civil defense education, see Tracy C. Davis, *Stages of Emergency: Cold War Nuclear Civil Defense* (Durham and London: Duke University Press, 2007).

8. Peter Watkins, "The War Game," pwatkins.mnsi.net/warGame.htm, accessed 7 January 2014.

9. Perrine, 157–158.

10. Gaddis, 224–225.

11. Quoted in Robert Scheer, *With Enough Shovels: Reagan, Bush and Nuclear War* (New York: Vintage Books, 1983): 18.

12. Douglas C. Walker, *Congress and the Nuclear Freeze: An Inside Look at the Politics of a Mass Movement* (Boston: University of Massachusetts Press, 1987): 35.

13. Deron Overpeck, "'Remember! It's Only a Movie!' Expectations and Receptions of *The Day After* (1983)," *Historical Journal of Film, Radio, and Television* 32, 2 (June 2012): 271.

14. Jack Kibble-White, "Let's All Hide in the Linen Cupboard," http://www.offthetelly.co.uk/oldott/www.offthetelly.co.uk/index126a.html?page_id=1835, accessed 3 January 2014.

15. Walker, 26.

16. See David S. Meyer, *A Winter of Discontent: The Nuclear Freeze and American Politics* (New York: Praeger, 1990).

17. Elaine Titcombe, "Women Activists: Rewriting Greenham's History," *Women's History Review* 22(2): 2013, 310–311.

18. *The Day After*, directed by Nicholas Meyer (1983: Hollywood, CA: MGM Home Entertainment, 2004). DVD.

19. Steve Farber, "How a Nuclear Holocaust Was Staged," *New York Times*, 23 November 1983, 34.

20. Cultural Information Service, "*The Day After* Viewer's Guide," 1983, conelrad. blogspot.ca/2010/08/day-after-viewers-guide.html, accessed 17 January 2014.

21. Overpeck, 273.

22. Farber, 34.

23. Sally Bedell Smith, "Film on a Nuclear War Already Causing Wide Fallout of Partisan Activity," *New York Times*, 17 November 1983, 20.

24. *Threads*, directed by Mick Jackson (1984: London: 2Entertain, 2005). DVD.

25. Quoted in Kibble-White.

26. Kibble-White, www.offthetelly.co.uk/oldott/www.offthetelly.co.uk/index126a.html?page_id=1835, accessed 3 January 2014.

27. *Testament*, directed by Lynn Littman (1983: Hollywood, CA: Paramount, 2004). DVD.

28. "Testament Box Office," Internet Movie Database, www.imdb.com/title/tt0086429/business?ref_=tt_dt_bus, accessed 17 January 2014.

29. Bill Greenhart, "Interview with TESTAMENT Director Lynne Littman," January 31, 2010, conelrad.blogspot.ca/2010/08/interview-with-testament-director-lynne.html, accessed 3 January 2014.

30. Perrine, 34.

31. Farber, 34.

32. Quoted in Kibbler-White.

33. Patricia Holland, *Picturing Childhood. The Myth of the Child in Popular Imagery* (New York: I.B. Taurus, 2004): 143.

34. Holland, 143.

35. Ibid., 156.

36. Tarah Brookfield, *Cold War Comforts: Canadian Women, Child Safety and Global Insecurity* (Waterloo: Wilfrid Laurier University Press, 2012), 28.

37. John Hersey, *Hiroshima* (New York: Vintage Books, 1946): 54, 76.

38. Brookfield, 60, 44.

39. Perrine, 4.

40. Ibid.

41. Joanne Cantor, Barbara J. Wilson, and Cynthia Hoffner, "Emotional Responses to a Televised Nuclear Holocaust Film," *Communication Research* 13, 2: 259–261.

42. Overpeck, 278.

43. See results in Richard Zwiegenhaft, "Students Surveyed about Nuclear War," Bulletin of the Atomic Scientists," 41, 2 1986: 26; Margaret Sadler et al., "Young Persons View the Day After," Paper Presented at the Annual Meeting of the American Psychological Association, Toronto, August 1984, 5.

44. Sadler et al., 4.

45. Cantor et al., 271.

46. Sadler et al., 6.

47. Cantor et al., 272.

48. Zwiegenhaft, 27.

49. Perrin L. French and Judith Van Hoorn, "Half a Nation Saw a Nuclear War and No one Blinked? Reassessing the Impact of The Day After in Terms of a Theoretical Chain of Causality," *International Journal of Mental Health* 15, 1–3 1986: 293.

50. Internet Movie Database (IMDB), "When did you first see *Threads*?" response by funngy, March 13, 2011, www.imdb.com/title/tt0090163/board/nest/179627717?ref_=tt_bd_2, accessed 5 November 2013.

51. IMDB, "This movie traumatized me as a child," response by gf_bran, April 15, 2009. www.imdb.com/title/tt0085404/board/thread/112245647?p=2, accessed November 5 2013.

52. Ibid., response by heyjude98, February 7, 2009, accessed November 5 2013.

53. Ibid., response by FormsInFlux, January 24, 2009, accessed November 5 2013.

54. "When did you first see *Threads*?" response by Faralotte, July 26, 2011, accessed 5 November 2013.

55. IMDB, "This movie terrified me as a child of the 1980s," response by sansatexas, November 27, 2013, www.imdb.com/title/tt0086429/board/thread/22003327, accessed 16 January 2014.

56. IMDB, "Simply the most devastating film I've ever seen," review of *Threads* by Bryan Hargrave, November 7, 2005, www.imdb.com/title/tt0090163/reviews, accessed 16 January 2014.

57. IMDB, "Never far from my Thoughts," review of *Threads* by Chriss2006, July 6, 2006, www.imdb.com/title/tt0090163/reviews, accessed 16 January 2014.

58. "When did you first see *Threads*?" response by stellaceagle-1, March 22, 2011, accessed 5 November 2013.

59. "This movie traumatized me as a child," response by Emerald72, May 28, 2013, www.imdb.com/title/tt0085, 404/board/thread/112245647?p=2, accessed November 5 2013.

60. Ibid., response by rxfoster, March 25, 2010, accessed November 5 2013.

61. Zwiegenhaft, 27; Steven Church, *The Day After The Day After: My Atomic Angst* (New York: Soft Skull Press, 2010), 123.

62. Church, 24, 41.

63. Church, 149–150.

64. "Nuclear Thoughts," Special Feature, *Testament*, DVD.

BIBLIOGRAPHY

Brookfield, Tarah. *Cold War Comforts: Canadian Women, Child Safety and Global Insecurity.* Waterloo: Wilfrid Laurier University Press, 2012.

Cantor, Joanne, Barbara J. Wilson, and Cynthia Hoffner. "Emotional Responses to a Televised Nuclear Holocaust Film." *Communication Research* 13.2 (1986): 259–261.

Church, Steven. *The Day After The Day After: My Atomic Angst.* New York: Soft Skull Press, 2010.

Cultural Information Service. "*The Day After* Viewer's Guide," 1983. conelrad.blogspot.ca/2010/08/day-after-viewers-guide.html (accessed 17 January 2014).

Davis, Tracey C. *Stages of Emergency: Cold War Nuclear Civil Defense.* Durham and London: Duke University Press, 2007.

The Day After. Directed by Nicholas Meyer, 1983. Hollywood, CA: MGM Home Entertainment, 2044. DVD.

Dubinsky, Karen. *Babies without Borders: Adoption and Migration across the Americas*. Toronto: University of Toronto Press, 2010.

Farber, Steve. "How a Nuclear Holocaust was Staged." *New York Times*, 23 November 1983, 34.

Ferguson, Susan. "Capitalist Childhood in Film: Modes of Critique." *Jump Cut: A Review of Contemporary Media* 55 (2013). http://www.ejumpcut.org/currentissue/FergusonChildhood/text.html (accessed 23 November 2013).

French, Perrin L., and Judith Van Hoorn. "Half a Nation Saw a Nuclear War and No One Blinked? Reassessing the Impact of *The Day After* in Terms of a Theoretical Chain of Causality." *International Journal of Mental Health* 15.1–3 (1986): 276–297.

Gaddis, John Lewis. *The Cold War: A New History*. New York: Penguin Press, 2005.

Greenhart, Bill. "Interview with TESTAMENT Director Lynne Littman," January 31, 2010. conelrad.blogspot.ca/2010/08/interview-with-testament-director-lynne.html (accessed 3 January 2014).

Hersey, John. *Hiroshima*. New York: Vintage Books, 1946.

Holland, Patricia. *Picturing Childhood: The Myth of the Child in Popular Imagery*. New York: I. B. Taurus, 2004.

Internet Movie Database. "Never far from my Thoughts," review of *Threads* by Chriss2006, July 6, 2006. www.imdb.com/title/tt0090163/reviews (accessed 16 January 2014).

———. "Simply the most devastating film I've ever seen," review of *Threads* by Bryan Hargrave, November 7, 2005. www.imdb.com/title/tt0090163/reviews (accessed 16 January 2014).

———. "Testament Box Office." www.imdb.com/title/tt0086429/business?ref_=tt_dt_bus (accessed 17 January 2014).

———. "This movie traumatized me as a child." www.imdb.com/title/tt0085,404/board/thread/112245647?p=2 (accessed 5 November 2013).

———. "This movie terrified me as a child of the 1980s." http://imdb.com/title/tt0086429/board/thread/22003327 (accessed 16 January 2014).

———. "When did you first see *Threads*?" www.imdb.com/title/tt0090163/board/nest/179627717?ref_=tt_bd_2 (accessed 5 November 2013).

Kakoudaki, Despina. "Representing Politics in Disaster Films." *International Journal of Media & Cultural Politics* 7.3 (2011): 349–356.

Kibble-White, Jack. "Let's All Hide in the Linen Cupboard." www.offthetelly.co.uk/oldott/www.offthetelly.co.uk/index126a.html?page_id=1835 (accessed 3 January 2014).

Meyer, David S. *A Winter of Discontent: The Nuclear Freeze and American Politics*. New York: Praeger, 1990.

"Nuclear Thoughts," Special Feature. *Testament*. DVD.

Overpeck, Deron. "'Remember! It's Only A Movie!': Expectations and Receptions of *The Day After* (1983)." *Historical Journal of Film, Radio, and Television* 32.2 (2012): 267–292.

Perrine, Toni. *Film and the Nuclear Age: Representing Cultural Anxiety*. New York: Garland Publishing, 1998.

Sadler, Margaret, et al. "Young Persons View *The Day After*." Paper presented at the Annual Meeting of the American Psychological Association, Toronto, August 1984, 5.

Scheer, Robert. *With Enough Shovels: Reagan, Bush, and Nuclear War*. New York: Vintage Books, 1983.

Smith, Sally Bedell. "Film on a Nuclear War Already Causing Wide Fallout of Partisan Activity." *New York Times*, 17 November 1983, 20.

Sontag, Susan. "The Imagination of Disaster." *Against Interpretation: And Other Essays*. New York: Farrar, 1966. 209–225.

Testament. Directed by Lynne Littman, 1983. Hollywood, CA: Paramount, 2004. DVD.

Threads. Directed by Mick Jackson, 1984. London: 2Entertain, 2005. DVD.

Titcombe, Elaine. "Women Activists: Rewriting Greenham's History." *Women's History Review* 22.2 (2013): 310–11.

Walker, Douglas C. *Congress and the Nuclear Freeze: An Inside Look at the Politics of a Mass Movement*. Boston: University of Massachusetts Press, 1987.

Watkins, Peter. "*The War Game.*" Peter Watkins Films. pwatkins.mnsi.net/warGame.htm (accessed 7 January 2014).

Zwiegenhaft, Richard. "Students Surveyed about Nuclear War." *Bulletin of the Atomic Scientists* 41.2 (1986): 26.

Chapter Nine

Emperor Tomato Ketchup

The Child as the Dictator of Mankind

Frank Jacob

INTRODUCTION

Terayama Shûji (1935–1983) has been called a lot of things. "Artiste-provoc-ateur,"[1] a "controversial cultural presence in Japan today,"[2] and "a man of extremes"[3] are some of the positive terms ascribed to him. Terayama was one of the most well-known directors of avant-garde theater in the 1960s and 1970s, but he was more than just a director, he produced poetry, lyrics, songs, essays, journal articles, critiques, film scripts, and many other things as well. His influence on the international avant-garde scene was important and he became famous not only in Japan, but also in European countries and their avant-garde scenes.[4]

Terayama was described as "Japan's most venturous theatrical profes-sional"[5] and a German yellow press paper named him and his troop the "pestilence from Japan"[6] in 1972. The Japanese press was not as negative as the European press following his tour through several countries, where the shocking nature of his plays was too much for some spectators. The *Asahi Shimbun* merely depicted him as a man who was willing to destroy existing habits and boredom.[7] Terayama tried to overcome reality because to him it was just a lie, so he produced a great deal of artistic work in different areas of the performing arts. As a result, his own life became "an allegory of Japan's ambivalence toward modernity and the world at large."[8] The director founded his own theater, Tenjô Sajiki, in 1967, which has "pervaded the Japanese consciousness with revolutionary ideas and colorful visual effects since the 1960s."[9] Despite the fact that he was so productive, his work was not fully recognized while he was alive. After his death, Terayama's work was reconsidered and he finally received the recognition he deserved. In 1997, the Terayama Shûji Memorial Museum was opened in Misawa City and many of his works remain classics of avant-garde theater to this day.

Terayama shot films as well, and they reveal a very ambivalent image. While *Show o suteyo, machi ni deyô* (*Throw Away Books, Rally in the Streets*) (1971) is still seen as a classic of Japanese experimental drama performed by actors and ordinary people,[10] his second avant-garde movie, *Emperor Tomato Ketchup* (*Tomato Kechappu Kōtei*) (1971), is a film "which most people outside of Japan have never seen."[11] In the United States, the film was not shown, because it is illegal to show explicit sexual acts between adults and children. Due to its content *Emperor Tomato Ketchup* is "a film that Japan has tried hard to forget"[12] and it was simply "dismissed as kiddie porn."[13] For many spectators the film was just an absurd caricature and a nightmare.[14] That *Emperor Tomato Ketchup* is mostly unknown is a consequence of the long-lasting censorship,[15] and scientific research that acknowledged the film but did not analyze it in a sufficient way[16]—the sole extensive discussion of the movie was the one by Terayama himself.[17]

The following chapter will change this. After a survey of Terayama's life and the film, the developments that led to *Emperor Tomato Ketchup* and its shooting will be described. The history of the different versions—there is a long and short version—will be analyzed as well, which will reveal the effect the director himself hoped to achieve with this work. Finally, I will question why Terayama used children to depict his utopian version of an evil past. Was it just a desire to shock the audience, or was there no other option than to use children to show exactly what Terayama wanted to express? Why was he so eager about the idea of a childish dictatorship depicting an apocalyptic utopia of mankind? The term apocalyptic cinema could be used in an ambiguous sense with regard to *Emperor Tomato Ketchup*, because not only does the movie describe a post-apocalyptic situation, but it was shot just two and a half decades after Japan's own apocalyptic nightmare, the bombing of Hiroshima and Nagasaki. Consequently, this chapter will also try to analyze the driving aim of Terayama during the creation of this child-centered postapocalypse. The biography of the director will show that there could be more than one motive for his final choice and its creation, many of the scenes can be interpreted in an autobiographical way and work as a personal criticism of a Japanese society that was not willing to accept the duty of coming to terms with the past.

TERAYAMA—THE *ENFANT TERRIBLE* OF JAPANESE AVANT-GARDE

Anyone wanting to understand *Emperor Tomato Ketchup* has to try to understand Terayama and his theatrical work, because even if the movie was just another medium for the artist, the message as well as his motives is evident in his other projects as well. One of the most important avant-garde experimentalists would not just shoot an ordinary film, but would create something that was part of the Japanese avant-garde. [18] With regard to his whole oeuvre, Terayama "explored a variety of means to grasp a special kind of reality more real than the generally accepted reality in his own way," [19] but all of these were influenced by his personal experiences. Thereby he wanted to create an exaggeration that forced people to think about their actual reality, meaning that an extreme caricature of reality would be used as a kind of artistic tool.

In 1945 Terayama's father died on an Indonesian island, and after Japan's defeat his mother had to move to serve at a U.S. military base in Kyûshû. As a consequence, the young boy was sent to live with his uncle who owned a movie theater. It was here that the young Terayama had his first contact with movies. [20] Next to his artistic awakening, this period of his life was important for his image of the female sex. Deserted by his mother, the lonely Terayama developed a rather negative evaluation of women and he believed "that a girl and a prostitute are basically the same creature," [21] a thought that could have led to the depiction of sexually charged performances in his artworks. Another motif that is visible in his plays is a dominant mother whose rule is broken by the son through an act of incest. [22] After an unstable and mainly emotionally lonely life, [23] Terayama tried to come to terms with his own past by expressing through theater plays and other forms of artwork, and that is why he founded the Engeki jikkenshitsu Tenjô sajiki (Theater laboratory—Places of Olympus) in 1967. [24] The name of the theater already specified, that Terayama's theater works would be avant-garde in style, but the main topics Terayama tried to stage were related to his own childhood, the postwar and post-apocalyptic situation of Japan and its society, where individualism and a critical consideration of the recent past were unusual things. Terayama's theater would create an artistic space, where such topics could become part of the spectator's perception.

However, this would not be his first artistic success, as Terayama had been highly productive in previous years. In 1954 he won the newcomer prize of the journal *Tanka Kenkyû* (*Tanka Research*) for his *tanka* poetry. [25] Despite his success this was not a happy time, as he was being accused of plagiarism. Some colleagues called Terayam's works "a cheat" because he had taken *haiku* poetry and simply changed it to *tanka*. [26] Irrespective of this discussion, his lyrical works remain popular today. [27] Terayama had already used this form of artistic expression to come to terms with his childhood, which is why he often depicts taboo subjects like incest and matricide.[28] In 1957 his first book of poems was published,[29] and he would be highly productive until his death, publishing lyrics which achieved a great degree of popularity.[30] Three years later he started his theater career by writing and staging his first play.[31] The fact that Terayama had developed a highly critical stance against Japanese society in general and the family system in particular, might have been due to the fact that he had been abandoned by his mother and had no chance to experience a stable social or family environment himself. He was left by his mother, his father had died in the war and for a young boy in the post-apocalyptic environment of Japan's post war society, this situation must have had a tremendous effect on his own emotions, beliefs, and values. His rather critical view with regard to adults was already visible in his work before the shooting of *Emperor Tomato Ketchup*.

In 1960, Terayama created a radio play, *Otona gari (Adult Hunting)*, in which "children revolt against the authority of their parents and begin to kill and enslave them."[32] Due to the subject matter this radio play could be seen as a "precursor"[33] to *Emperor Tomato Ketchup*. The radio play caused a scandal; many listeners believed it to be a true story, mainly as a consequence of its journalistic style, so it had the same effect as Orson Welles's *War of the Worlds* in the United States. Terayama was blamed for the fact that some people believed the radio play to be a report of true events and he became angry with the officials who could not understand the merit of his play. Some years later his book *Ie de no susume (Encouragement to Run Away)* (1963) was published. This book led to him being called the "runaway guru,"[34] because many Japanese youths left home and visited Terayama, who was later said to have given them jobs in his theater ensemble.[35] The book, like his radio play, described an alternative childhood. In contrast to the existing hierarchical order, in which the children were meant to be subordinated to the will of their parents—as if Terayama was a young boy, too—they were inspired to break with this order and to leave their homes. By producing *Emperor Tomato Ketchup*, he went even further and depicted a revolution by the children which he combined with a caricature of the adult failures of the past. In one way this film was meant to break with the social order that existed in Japan, on the other hand it was also intended to criticize the lack of sufficient discussion about the recent past.

His theater troop Tenjô Sajiki, founded in 1967, was one of the most famous groups of the 1960s and 1970s, both inside and outside Japan. The troop was known not only for its plays, but also for the program posters[36] and the theater building[37] itself. The plays of the Tenjô Sajiki were legendary, but also highly experimental and avant-gardesque. Terayama and his actors tried to create a situation during the staging in which actors, participants, and spectators would become the same, because the director wanted to change society through his plays. The amalgamation of the different levels during a theater play seemed the most suitable option for doing so.[38]

There were three phases of Terayama's staging styles. During the early phase he produced provoking and surreal plays, in the second he mixed documentary and drama, creating *dokyurama*, where the spectator's room and the stage were interconnected, and finally, in the third phase, Terayama developed street theater, by which real life became his stage.[39] In the first phase, like in his poetry, the director used motives like rape or matricide and had a great interest in physical deformations, which he tried to depict as well.[40] Many of these early motives, already assembled by Sorgenfrei, are shown in *Emperor Tomato Ketchup* as well:

> *Women*: seen simultaneously as demon whores and as sacrificing mothers.
> *Traditional social outcasts*: seen simultaneously as tainted sideshow freaks and as martyred saints.
> *Japan's past*: seen simultaneously as a corrupt, superstitious, militaristic society and as a lost, idyllic paradise.
> *American culture*: seen simultaneously as a grotesque bully and as a cultural icon.[41]

However, this explicit violence against the mother figure was not just a consequence of his childhood experiences. Terayama "often attacked the notion of traditional Japanese family systems"[42] by criticizing parental habits. Despite the political interpretations, Terayama did not long for a political revolution. What he wanted was a sexual revolution, the natural consequences of which would be the freedom of language and writing. Above all else he longed for a sinful, criminal, and definitely more offensive form of theater.[43] By staging such theater works he also attempted to criticize the existing order in Japan, which wanted the highest level of conformity. What was seen as spectacular avant-garde in Europe had a more shocking effect on Japanese spectators.

At first, his theater was famous and European festivals extended special invitations to the *enfant terrible* of Japanese performing arts,[44] but even in Europe his plays regularly put the cat among the pigeons. He imprisoned his audience or gave them sleeping pills without informing them, just two of the occurrences that happened on one European tour.[45] For Terayama the theater was meant to confront the spectators with the dark sides of their own existence, an aim he especially wanted to achieve with *Emperor Tomato Ketchup*. History in this case should have served as a guide for the staging of it, but the horrific methods and brutal violence acted out by the children was what made the movie particularly repulsive for the people who watched it.[46]

THE FILM: DICTATORSHIP, SEXUAL ABUSE, AND UNLEASHED CHILDREN

Due to the fact that the film is not very well-known to U.S. spectators, I will give a survey of the short version to illustrate what kind of images Terayama used to construct *Emperor Tomato Ketchup*.[47] The first scene shows a girl, being beaten by two adults with a stick, while other children in military uniform are watching the scene from outside. In the following sequence, several pictures (including portraits of Marx and Mao) are scratched with a black X. A scene of adult violence against a child is scratched many times and the spectators can hear the screams of children from offstage.

After that introduction there is a love scene with a naked man and woman that is interrupted by one of the child soldiers, who kills the adults with a rifle. The next scene shows two of these soldiers posing with a corpse in front of a memorial. A flash of words appears: "A butcher likes mathematics." Accordingly, one sees children in uniforms; they mark every door and all the posters with a black X, the sign of their revolution, which is also visible on their uniforms. In the next scene, naked adults are gathered and forced to march in a circle around two soldiers while a flash of words is telling the spectator that the adults are punished for several things, especially because they forced the children to be obedient—"the adult who monopolizes enjoyment will be severely punished."

Afterwards the young Emperor Tomato Ketchup is shown while he views himself in a mirror. In his throne room, he is accompanied by a naked man who has to polish his shoes and a woman that plays violin for him. The emperor himself is sitting on his throne below a big X flag. In the following scene, the boy-emperor is sitting in a bathtub while a nude girl with a blonde wig is lying on the bed and is calling someone on the phone. The nude emperor enters the sleeping room, watches the blonde girl, and opens a closet, where two nude adults are bound.

The subsequent scene shows a boy in a military uniform doing exercises while a nude bound woman and a dog are watching him. Again, a flash of words is shown that demands freedom for all children. After that some children are playing ping pong while using a nude woman lying on the table as their net. Adults are rounded up by the children and a boy in uniform is smoking and laughing while he stands in front of a naked woman. The next scene shows the children, dressed like members of the Ku Klux Klan, who are hunting an old man down the street. After that two soldier children pull the corpse of an old man through a devastated environment. The subsequent images show a nude child with a wig playing with puppets and a crucified adult surrounded by smoke. Next to this three nude people are shown while performing aesthetic sexual acts, as well as a pregnant nun and a running spectator, who seems to be hunted by someone. The runner flees from the child soldiers, asks several boys to help him and the last one he asks is willing to protect the adult by hiding him in his closet on which a naked adult is posing. As soon as the danger of the soldiers was gone, the adult comes out of the closet where a nude woman with a blonde wig was sitting next to him. In the moment that the man recognizes that he was saved, he starts to choke the boy.

In the subsequent scene the emperor dances with an old lady, dressed like a schoolgirl. After that image a stunted man dressed in a uniform hunts down a white chicken and chops off its head while a girl, dressed like a nun is watching. The next shot depicts a woman on a sofa playing with a gramophone record. A child soldier enters the room and forces her to have sex with him while flashing words appear stating: "I seduce my mother and become my father." After that a child, in a room with puppets and two bound and naked adults, is shown reading a book. Three boys try to dress like women and use cosmetics.

The next scene shows four prostitutes—three with blonde wigs and one with a black wig, who is smoking—and the boy-emperor entering the room. The three blondes undress the boy and get naked as well, but finally the young emperor has sex with the black-haired prostitute. When the sex scene ends, the Tomato Emperor is shown sitting on a corpse and playing a ball game. The short version finally ends with a scene where the emperor and two child soldiers paste on artificial beards. It is a strange film work, which definitely has its meanings, even if some explanations still remain unknown, or are still open for further discussion. I will at least try to give some more detailed insight into Terayama's motifs and his criticism of the Japanese society and thereby try to explain some of the rather weird images that are confronting the spectator when they watch the film for the first time.

EMPEROR TOMATO KETCHUP AND ITS MEANINGS

The movie is a violent, sexually explicit, and shocking depiction of children who seize power and establish an empire, ruled by a little boy who loves ketchup and makes it the national symbol. By depicting such an image, Teryama is destroying the Japanese social order, which is based on clearly defined hierarchies and the factor of conformity. By the use of a child as a dictator he is on the one hand caricaturing the period of the Second World War and on the other he is describing a child that is able to break all existing rules of a society to create his own value system, which is directed against the adults. Terayama mixes his own autobiographic experiences with criticism against the Japanese postwar society as a whole. Instead of confessing its own guilt, the Japanese tended not to speak about the past and tried to hide behind the dropping of the atomic bombs on Hiroshima and Nagasaki. It seemed to be a better alternative to be a victim instead of taking responsibility for the recent past and its cruel aspects.

The catalyst for the rebellion is the beating of a child, the depiction of which later became one of the opening scenes of the shorter version of the film.[48] As a consequence of this violent act, the children stage a revolt, and the adults are enslaved and forced to work for their child masters. For example, the father of the boy emperor has to lick the imperial shoes clean and his mother has to entertain him.

Most of the children in the film are dressed like soldiers, and the so-called *gewalt babies* hunt the adults in the name of the new empire. They wave flags that are marked with a black X and the whole movie resembles a totalitarian system in which adults are public enemy number one. They are caught, made to undress and are sent to concentration camps, where they have to work for the children. To sum up, in McDermott's words, "[t]he revolution of Ketchup is based on non-sexual erotic purity, Nazi brutality, and the grass roots organizational power of the communist party, all for the purposes of overthrowing the myth of civilization."[49] What in the first instance seems to be a confused collection of images of violence and incestuous sex is actually a collage of motives that resemble the problems and thoughts about postwar Japanese society. Children, like Terayama were born into a society that suppressed individualism, because it valued conformity and unity. A child had to function to make the family function as well. Terayama disliked this, especially as a consequence of his own experiences of loneliness when his mother decided to make him live with his relatives.

One of the first scenes of the film shows *gewalt babies* dressed like soldiers running down a street with the X flag, which would remind spectators not only of the wartime parades of soldiers or the loyalty of the Japanese fighters to their rulers but also of the student revolts of the 1960s.[50] Thereby Teryama is criticizing not only Japan's war society but also the postwar radicalism of the later decades. While the leftwing forces had attacked the pro-American policy of the Japanese government in the late 1950s and early 1960s the radical right was able to attract people again in the 1970s. Mishima Yukio (1925–1970) tried to seize power by a coup d'état in 1970. However, he failed and committed suicide to protest against Japan's politics, which seemed to be far too nontraditional for him. By describing a fascist state,[51] *Emperor Tomato Ketchup* consequently also scandalizes the reactionary forces of Japan and its figurehead Mishima.[52] As a satire of the recent Japanese past and present it votes against the glorification of former times and old traditions, and by producing a "travesty of revolution,"[53] it is targeted against the political left as well.

The film has a dominant political dimension, but it does not stint on explicit sexual content, which like in the above-mentioned Terayama plays also provides a vote against existing traditional family ties, which seems to be in some way ironic, because it was exactly these ties that he must have missed as a young boy. Consequently, *Emperor Tomato Ketchup* offers several models of interpretation and is a "simultaneous satire of political action, advocacy of disturbing sexual revolutions and rejection of paternalistic traditions and family ties."[54]

The shooting of the movie itself resembles a news broadcast or documentary, because there is just one camera and the cuts move from image to image without multiple shots of the same scene.[55] One example is the opening scene showing the boy-emperor for the first time. Terayama uses a long camera angle to use the full abstractness of such a scene. As a result, one is reminded of the mentioned radio play *Adult Hunting*, which was produced in the same style, similar to a news broadcast, which means that the director wanted to provide a high grade of reality when he shot his movie. For the audio effects Terayama used a "burlesque theatrical tableaux and a collage of voiceover and found audio documents,"[56] for example, a Hitler speech, and with regard to the depiction of the actors, he shows scurrilous figures and "deranged faces."[57]

The film originally had a length of eighty-five minutes, which was shortened to seventy-six minutes for the premiere, and was finally cut to twenty-eight minutes because the "guerilla shooting techniques"[58] were not able to hold the audiences' attention for a long time, the perpetual shocking images were not able to create a climax and thereby forced most people to leave the cinema before the movie had ended, because they were either too shocked or just bored after the first few scenes.[59] The premiere at Sogetsu Hall in Tôkyô on June 19, 1970, made it obvious that the movie was too long, even for an audience interested in avant-garde.[60] Terayama later claimed that the movie's shortening was a consequence of this impression.[61] An especially long scene (twelve minutes) in which two boy-generals fight an endless rock-paper-scissors war was taken out and shown as a single movie with the title *Paper-Scissors-Rock War*. The two boy-generals resemble the trauma of Japanese militarists in 1945, but it is not clear if that was Terayama's intention, because he never spoke about that scene in later years. What was clear in contrast was the fact that the movie was a financial flop. With production costs of 1.3 million yen the movie became a commercial disaster, because the audience was bored by its length and sometimes exaggerated satire.[62]

Despite its economic failure—possibly due to the fact that it could not even be shown in most countries at that time—the movie was important for Terayama, because it was a project that combined "his ideas of image and time with a utopian revolution of myth and history based upon a myriad of sources ranging from his hometown ghost stories to Hegel, from Auschwitz to a schoolyard bully."[63] He created a Terayama-version of truth and believed that theater could work as a metaphor for history.[64] By this, *Emperor Tomato Ketchup* could be interpreted "as a genealogical work in the Foucauldian sense"[65] as well, because it was a kind of "travesty of all the values and causes that illuminated the postwar epoch."[66] Terayama fought against the anomie of modern Japan "by invoking cataclysmic historical forces through theater."[67] It was not only a utopian depiction of a revolution of the child, but far more a depiction of the ongoing Japanese right-wing reversal of Japanese war history, due to which some people claimed it would be better to return to the traditional values of the Japanese society which seemed to have been destroyed by Western influence in Japan.[68] The highly critical movie was and remains hard to understand without knowledge of the Japanese postwar years from 1945 to 1970. Terayama created a form of social critique, sometimes unfortunately highly exaggerated by using extremely violent and sexually explicit images, shocking not just the audience, but also invoking censorship, in particular because he used children to create an alarming form of social group identity which resembled postwar Japanese society.[69]

CHILDREN AND THE DICTATORSHIP OF SEX AND VIOLENCE

Even if Terayama wanted to overcaricature the existing society, the "shocking, perverse, and even obscene content"[70] was not just a "vicious satire of militant leftist student radicals," an "indictment of rightist militarism," and a "reminder of shameful, wartime Japanese atrocities," but also a "warning about the dangers of American cultural hegemony,"[71] symbolized in the film by ketchup, cigars, the Bible, and the American Constitution. Ketchup was a symbol of the American way of life, because the Japanese youth were not only confronted with Jazz music during the occupation years, but also with American food, like burgers and ketchup. For Terayama, the Bible seemed to resemble the religious foundation of the American nation-state and if one considers that general Douglas MacArthur (1880–1964) tried to convert the Japanese population to Christianity it also could be a critique of the U.S. occupation itself. That the American Constitution is criticized could be a consequence of the occupation as well, because for many Japanese the measures of the Supreme Command of the Allied Powers in Japan resembled an attempt to "Americanize" Japan by implementing Western values and structures into the daily life of the Japanese. While the children use different measures against the adults "including fascistic bullying, rampant and indiscriminate sexual perversions, drunkenness, rape, murder, and atrocities committed in the name of political or ethnic purity,"[72] for example, when they use a nude woman as a net on their table tennis table, they show the dark side of humanity, which exists even inside the innocent mind of a child.

To show that existence, Terayama used seventy common and nameless children, whom he sometimes recruited immediately before a shooting,[73] along with the actors of his theater ensemble, Tenjô Sajiki, to create "an odyssey of innocence, revolution, and an erotic utopia built on horror. It is political, ideological, artistic, and disgusting. It is banal and vulgar, and if you take a mouthful of it, it might make you puke."[74] Like William Golding in his famous work *Lord of the Flies* (1954), Terayama purposefully uses children to underline the weakness of human civilization, even if the power should be assembled or taken by the innocent ones, when the children in the film start to force the adults to leave their homes and concentrate them in some kind of labor camps. By their use, Terayama wants to "cr[y] out the doom of revolution, the futility of power, and the innocence of fascism"[75] and depicts the ambivalence of innocence, beauty, destruction, and brutality.[76] The post-apocalyptic empire of the children is built on enslavement of the adults—the apocalypse from an *adult* point of view—who became victims of rape and murder. While the children want to recreate their existing world according to their own likes or dislikes, they "represent perversion of the civil symbolic state."[77] Sex, like death, is rather an element of control and destruction of existing family ties.

Furthermore, children are used to caricature the emperor worship of the Japanese right-wing, which still deified the emperor and wanted to see him strong and leading the state again, especially the emperor warship by Mishima Yukio (1925–1970) and his Tate no Kai[78] when "[t]he coup d'état depicted in *Emperor Tomato Ketchup* replaces the 'humanized' former emperor Hirohito with an amoral, role-play child, who proclaims the vulgar North-American condiment of the film's title as the national symbol."[79] The children become willing subordinates of this boy-emperor who starts the adult diaspora. The children become the Nazi members of a type of Third Reich as well as the Japanese secret police officers, and finally "they are the rapists and sadists; they are all the things that haunt our past and present."[80] While the audience did not want to see the dark side of human nature, Terayama tried to show human cruelty by using children for his post-apocalyptic scenario.[81]

At first instance, the use of children was a parody of the Western view of Japanese smallness, meaning that all Japanese are small, by infantilization of this image.[82] That the children were shown in explicit sexual acts was not problematic for Terayama, because at the same time he was shooting *Emperor Tomato Ketchup*, formerly big studios like Shochiku and Tôei were being forced to shoot soft porn movies to combat decreasing sales. Explicit sexual content was common in Japanese films at this time, but the use of children was too much, even for a scandal-accustomed Japanese audience. The repressed public memory of the Pacific War was revived, and when the children discuss the use of adult trousers, it becomes obvious that they will become adults in the future. This usage of adult clothing on a child implies that adult Japanese spectators of the film could have been one of these children during the prewar years.[83] For this reason Terayama "intertextually incorporates the idea of the other within, that is, the adult latent in every child, into his film to refute the idea of a self-evident subject filled with light, as in the positive fascist ideal, precisely because he recognized the risk that his film ran of being seen as a utopian vision."[84] The brothel scene in which a *gewalt baby* has fun with four prostitutes just resembles another dark point in Japanese memory—the story of forced prostitution of the so-called comfort women (*ianfu*), who were forced to "pleasure" soldiers during the war.[85]

Despite showing young children engaged in sexual content and hoping for a sexual revolution in Japan, a thought that might have been influenced by European radical thinkers, the depiction of explicit material should not consequently lead to a transformation of the state power itself, meaning that Terayama did not want to provoke a revolution by showing children having sex with adults, because he thought such beliefs would lead to an American-style hippie lifestyle.[86] All in all, *Emperor Tomato Ketchup* is "neither un-critical nor permissive" and the children themselves are not idealized as innocent humans, who are not responsible for the things they are doing. Terayama is demanding dissolution of traditional family bonds instead of a return to innocence, suggesting the innocence of the Japanese nation as a junior partner of the United States. Furthermore Terayama underlines the postwar criticism of the emperor, who also depicted postdefeat Japan as a family. While demanding the dissolution of family bonds, Terayama there-fore also criticizes the incumbent Emperor Hirohito who had asked for these family ties during his official surrender message in 1945: "Let the entire nation continue as one family from generation to generation, ever firm in its faith in the imperishableness of its divine land, and mindful of its heavy burden of responsibilities, and the long road before it."[87]

Due to all these aspects one has to state that the children of *Emperor Tomato Ketchup* were used as a metaphorical approach for criticism against the existing Japanese society and its values, which seemed to be the same in 1970 as they were during the war period, at least from Terayama's point of view. Despite the fact that Terayama was accused of pornography, incestu-ous sex scenes, violent and brutal depictions of children, for example, play-ing ping pong using a naked woman as a net, and making a caricature of the emperor using a boy-dictator, I believe his goal was to remind the audience of its own past in a time when new fascist thoughts were being expressed by men like Mishima.

CONCLUSION

There are different levels of explanation to conclude this analysis of *Emperor Tomato Ketchup* and to answer the question of why Terayama used children to present his idea of criticism against the existing Japanese society. For him, the use of children to depict the post-apocalyptic society of postwar Japan fulfilled several functions. He not only criticized the actual political situation, but also Japanese infantilization by foreigners. Furthermore, the "brutal satire of political activism and ideologues"[88] was developed by Terayama to question existing "institutions, such as the body, family, sexuality, and war, which tended to be taken as natural truths in his time."[89]

The movie fulfilled not just politically motivated aspirations, but it was also an expression of Terayama's own feelings and autobiographical experiences:

> He had no need for nations, for it was the nation that had killed his father, taken his mother, and destroyed his youth. He had no need for family, for it was family that had left him all but an orphan in a closet in the back of a theater. This, combined with his own terminal illness, gave him a darkness few could touch, and a freedom that few could comprehend.[90]

Despite his aims, audiences were shocked by the movie, as they mainly focused on the sexual content showing copulation between children and adults. Consequently *Emperor Tomato Ketchup* was censored or not even shown in most countries outside Japan, and while Japanese society itself did everything to forget this outrageous movie, the outside world did not even recognize it. The short version was shown at avant-garde film festivals, but for most people who recognized the title it remained child pornography. But as I have shown, Terayama had a specific reason for using children in his post-apocalyptic movie that was not recognized by the general public. In order to fully appreciate and understand *Emperor Tomato Ketchup*'s meaning it is necessary to have an understanding of Japanese postwar history. Consequently the film is an example of the interrelation between art and history and Terayama's post-apocalyptic vision of Japanese society after 1945.

NOTES

1. Carol Fisher Sorgenfrei, *Unspeakable Acts: The Avant-Garde Theatre of Terayama Shûji and Postwar Japan* (Honolulu. University of Hawai'i Press, 2005), 2.

2. Ibid.

3. Ibid., 3.

4. M. Cody Poulton, "Unspeakable Acts: The Avant-Garde Theatre of Terayama Shûji and Postwar Japan," Carol Fischer Sorgenfrei (Honolulu: University of Hawai'i Press, 2005)," *Performance Paradigm* 2 (2006): 139–144, 139.

5. "Hitler war besser," *Der Spiegel*, 44 (1972): 170–171, www.spiegel.de/spiegel/print/d-42787578.html, 170.

6. Ibid.

7. "Keikan no Engisha? Angura Tenjo Sajiki Rojô no Happening," *Asahi Shimbun*, October 31, 1970, 23.

8. Poulton, 140.

9. Rei Sadakari, "'Fatherless Girl' and 'Domineering Mother': Terayama Shuji's Portrayak of Women" (Master Thesis, University of Hawai'i, 2004), 1.

10. Morita Norimasa, "Avant-garde, Pastiche, and Media Crossing: Films of Terayama Shûji," *Waseda Global Forum* 3 (2006): 53–58, 55.

11. Taro E. F. Nettleton, "Throw Out the Books, Get Out in the Streets: Subjectivity and Space in Japanese Underground Art of the 1960s" (PhD diss., University of Rochester, 2011). hdl.handle.net/1802/14175, 63.

12. Joshua McDermott, "Terayama Shuji and *The Emperor Tomato Ketchup*: The Children's Revolution of 1970" (Master Thesis, Universiy of Hawai'i, 2005), 4.

13. Poulton, 141.

14. Moriyasu Toshihisa, "Terayama Shûji no eiga 'Tomato Kechappu Kôtei'—Giga to akumu," *Bulletin of the Faculty of Education, Utsunomiya University. Section 1* 47(1) (1997): 23–35.

15. Nyay Bhushan, "Japan's 'Asura' to Open India's 2012 Cinefan Festival," www.hollywoodreporter.com/news/japans-asura-open-indias-2012-348407.

16. Ben Crawford, "Emperor Tomato-Ketchup: Cartoon Properties from Japan," in *Hibakusha Cinema. Hiroshima, Nagasaki and the Nuclear Image in Japanese Film*, ed. Mick Broderick (London/New York: Kegan Paul International, 1996), 75–90.

17. Terayama Shûji, *Theater contra Ideologie* (Frankfurt am Main: Fischer, 1971), 66–80.

18. Endo Yukihide, "The Revisioning of the Real: Film Director Shinoda Masahiro's Empathic Use of Korogo in *Shinjû ten no Amijima*," *Hamamatsu Ika Daigaku-kyô (Ippan Kyôiku)* 20 (2006): 37–53, 38.

19. Ibid., 39.

20. Terayama Shûji, *Kanashiki Kuchibue: Jidenteki Essay* (Tôkyô: Rippu Shobo, 1993), 80–92.

21. Sadakari, 165.

22. Ibid., 5.

23. Sorgenfrei, 25–25.

24. Ibid., 35–37.

25. Stephan Köhn and Martina Schönbein, "Schausteller und Zur-Schau-Gestellte. Zur Renaissance der *misemono*-Tradition in Terayama Shûjis (1935–1983) dramatischem Werk," *NOAG* 171/172 (2002): 39–73, 39.

26. Haiku is a form of Japanese short poetry which usually juxtaposes two things or images and consists of seventeen single phonetic sounds, which are divided into three phrases of five, sevene, and five sounds. Tanka is an older form of poetry dating back to the eighth century AD and consists of five phrases of phonetic sounds (5–7–5–7–7).

27. Terayama Shûji, *Gogatsu no Shi: Poems of May*, trans. David A. Schmidt and Fusae Ekida (Lewiston, NY: Edwin Mellen Press, 1998).

28. Köhn, 40.

29. McDermott, 21.

30. Takatori Ei, "'Tanka shinjinshô' to sono yoha," in *Terayama Shûji ron*, ed. Takatori Ei (Tôkyô: Shichôsha, 1992), 57–70.

31. McDermott, 21.

32. Ibid., 22.

33. Ibid.

34. Miryam Sas, *Experimental Arts in Postwar Japan: Moments of Encounter, Engagement, and Imagined Return* (Cambridge, MA: Harvard University Press, 2010), 37.

35. Ibid.

36. "The Spectacular, Wild World of Tenjo Sajiki and ist Posters," pingmag.jp/2013/04/29/tenjo-sajiki-poster/.

37. For a photograph of the building see Stuart Munro, "Shuji Terayama's underground public stage," *Special to the Japan Times*, September 4, 2013, www.japantimes.co.jp/culture/2013/09/04/arts/shuji-terayamas-underground-public-stage/#.UupaU_15Mpo.

38. Sas, 3–11.

39. Köhn, 41–42.

40. Ibid.

41. Terayama Shûji, *Zôki kôkan josetsu* (Tôkyô: Pharao kikaku, 1992), 180; Terayama Shûji, Kikei no shimborizumu (Tôkyô: Hakusuisha, 1993), 136.

42. Sorgenfrei, 4.

43. Sadakari, 3.

44. McDermott, 30.

45. Sadakari, 3.

46. Köhn, 62.

47. The short version (twenty-seven minutes) of *Emperor Tomato Ketchup* could be watched at www.tofu-magazine.net/newVersion/pages/Terayama_ETK.html.

48. Ibid., 59–60; McDermott, 43.

49. Nettleton, 106.

50. McDermott, 25.

51. Nettleton, 68.

52. The author is in the know of the discussion about the use of the term "fascist" which is proper unsuitable for the Japanese case, but due to the fact, that the term is mainly used by Japanese historians as well, it is taken with regard to an easier understanding.

53. Thomas Dylan Eaton, "The Imaginary Theatre of the Emperor Tomato Ketchup," *Afterall Journal* 22 (2009), http://www.afterall.org/journal/issue.22/the.imaginary.martial.theatre.of. shuji.terayamas.emperor.tomato.ketchup, 2.

54. Ibid., 3.

55. Ibid., 5.

56. McDermott, 44.

57. Eaton, 1.

58. Joanna Barck, "Den Film aufs Gesicht projizieren. Terayamas Gesichter des Sekundären," *montage/av. Zeitschrift für Theorie & Geschichte audiovisueller Kommunikation* 13, 1 (2004): 90–111, 90.

59. Nettleton, 64.

60. McDermott, 6; Sorgenfrei, 123.

61. Nettleton, 65.

62. McDermott, 6.

63. Ibid., 25.

64. Ibid., 3.

65. Michel Foucault, "Hanzai to shiteno chishiki," *Jyokyo* (April 1976), 45–46.

66. Nettleton, 60.

67. Eaton, 5.

68. Ibid.

69. Ibid., 2.

70. Ibid., 4.

71. Sorgenfrei, 120.

72. Quotations from Ibid.

73. Sorgenfrei, 121.

74. Terayama Shûji, *Terayama Shûji Image Zukan* (Tôkyô: Film Art, 1993), 72.

75. McDermott, 40.

76. Ibid., 23.

77. Ibid., 5.

78. Ibid., 82.

79. On Mishima, his life, works, and influence, see Roy Starrs, *Deadly Dialectics: Sex, Violence, and Nihilism in the World of Yukio Mishima* (Honolulu: University Press of Hawai'i, 1994).

80. Eaton, 3.

81. One is tempted to compare this aim with William Golding's (1911–1993) novel *Lord of the Flies* (1954).

82. McDermott, 43.

83. Nettleton, 72–74.

84. Ibid., 90.

85. Ibid., 91.

86. Ibid., 96–97. For a survey of Japan's comfort women see: Frank Jacob, "Comfort Women—Japan's Forced Prostitution Policy during World War II," in *Prostitution—Eine Begleiterin der Menschheit/A Companion of Mankind*, ed. Frank Jacob (Frankfurt am Main et al.: Peter Lang, 2014).

87. Mishima Yukio and Terayama Shûji, "Taidan: Erosu wa teikô no kyoten ni narieruka," *Ushi* (July 1970), 144.

88. Quoted in Nettleton, 110.

89. Ibid., 60.

90. MacDermott, 15–16.

BIBLIOGRAPHY

Japanese names are left in the traditional way, meaning that the family name is mentioned first.

Barck, Joanna. "Den Film aufs Gesicht projizieren. Terayamas Gesichter des Sekundären, *montage/av*. Zeitschrift für Theorie & Geschichte audiovisueller Kommunikation 13, 1 (2004): 90–111.

Bhushan, Nyay. "Japan's 'Asura' to Open India's 2012 Cinefan Festival," www.hollywoodreporter.com/news/japans-asura-open-indias-2012-348407.

Crawford, Ben. "Emperor Tomato-Ketchup: Cartoon Properties from Japan," in *Hibakusha Cinema: Hiroshima, Nagasaki and the Nuclear Image in Japanese Film*, ed. Mick Broderick (London/New York: Kegan Paul International, 1996), 75–90.

Eaton, Thomas Dylan. "The Imaginary Theatre of the Emperor Tomato Ketchup," *Afterall Journal* 22 (2009), www.afterall.org/journal/issue.22/the.imaginary.martial.theatre.of.shuji.terayamas.emperor.tomato.ketchup.

Endo Yukihide. "The Revisioning of the Real: Film Director Shinoda Masahiro's Empathic Use of Korogo in *Shinjû ten no Amijima*," *Hamamatsu Ika Daigaku-kyô (Ippan Kyôiku)* 20 (2006): 37–53.

Fisher Sorgenfrei, Carol. *Unspeakable Acts: The Avant-Garde Theatre of Terayama Shûji and Postwar Japan* (Honolulu: University of Hawai'i Press, 2005).

Foucault, Michel. "Hanzai to shiteno chishiki," *Jyokyo* (April 1976), 45–46.

"Hitler war besser," *Der Spiegel*, 44 (1972): 170–171, www.spiegel.de/spiegel/print/d-42787578.html.

"Keikan no Engisha? Angura Tenjo Sajiki Rojô no Happening," *Asahi Shimbun*, October 31, 1970, 23.

Köhn, Stephan, and Schönbein, Martina. "Schausteller und Zur-Schau-Gestellte. Zur Renaissance der *misemono*-Tradition in Terayama Shûjis (1935–1983) dramatischem Werk," *NOAG* 171/172 (2002): 39–73.

McDermott, Joshua. "Terayama Shuji and *The Emperor Tomato Ketchup*: The Children's Revolution of 1970" (Master Thesis, University of Hawai'i, 2005).

Mishima Yukio, and Terayama Shûji, "Taidan: Erosu wa teikô no kyoten ni narieruka," *Ushi* (July 1970), 144.

Munro, Stuart. "Shuji Terayama's Underground Public Stage," *Special to the Japan Times*, September 4, 2013, www.japantimes.co.jp/culture/2013/09/04/arts/shuji-terayamas-underground-public-stage/#.UupaU_15Mpo.

Morita Norimasa. "Avant-garde, Pastiche, and Media Crossing: Films of Terayama Shûji," *Waseda Global Forum* 3 (2006): 53–58.

Moriyasu Toshihisa, "Terayama Shûji no eiga 'Tomato Kechappu Kôtei'—Giga to akumu," *Bulletin of the Faculty of Education, Utsunomiya University. Section 1* 47, 1 (1997): 23–35.

Nettleton, Taro E. F. "Throw Out the Books, Get Out in the Streets: Subjectivity and Space in Japanese Underground Art of the 1960s" (PhD diss., University of Rochester, 2011). hdl.handle.net/1802/14175.

Poulton, M. Cody. "Unspeakable Acts: The Avant-Garde Theatre of Terayama Shûji and Postwar Japan," Carol Fischer Sorgenfrei (Honolulu: University of Hawai'i Press, 2005)," *Performance Paradigm* 2 (2006): 139–144.

Rei Sadakari, "'Fatherless Girl' and 'Domineering Mother': Terayama Shuji's Portrayak of Women" (Master Thesis, University of Hawai'i, 2004).

Sas, Miryam. *Experimental Arts in Postwar Japan: Moments of Encounter, Engagement, and Imagined Return* (Cambridge, MA: Harvard University Press, 2010).

Takatori Ei, "'Tanka shinjinshô' to sono yoha," in *Terayama Shûji ron*, ed. Takatori Ei (Tôkyô: Shichôsha, 1992), 57–70.

Terayama Shûji, *Gogatsu no Shi: Poems of May*, trans. David A. Schmidt and Fusae Ekida (Lewiston, NY: Edwin Mellen Press, 1998).

Terayama Shûji, *Kanashiki Kuchibue: Jidenteki Essay* (Tôkyô: Rippu Shobo, 1993).

Terayama Shûji, *Kikei no shimborizumu* (Tôkyô: Hakusuisha, 1993).

Terayama Shûji, *Terayama Shûji Image Zukan* (Tôkyô: Film Art, 1993).

Terayama Shûji, *Theater contra Ideologie* (Frankfurt am Main: Fischer, 1971).

Terayama Shûji, *Zôki kôkan josetsu* (Tôkyô: Pharao kikaku, 1992).

"The Spectacular, Wild World od Tenjo Sajiki and ist Posters," pingmag.jp/2013/04/29/tenjo-sajiki-poster/.

"The Spectacular, Wild World od Tenjo Sajiki and ist Posters," pingmag.jp/2013/04/29/tenjo-sajiki-poster/.

Chapter Ten

The Specter of the Postcolonial Child and Faux Long Takes in Cuarón's *Children of Men*

James M. Hodapp

In his seminal 1963 postcolonial work, *The Wretched of the Earth*, Franz Fanon defines the postcolonial project as "a whole society being changed from the bottom up" which "seeks to change the order of the world."[1] Recently the prominent scholar Robert Young echoed Fanon's sentiment as a wide-ranging political project that seeks to "reconstruct Western knowledge formations, reorientate ethical norms, turn power structures upside down [and] refashion the world from below."[2] As two of the most important postcolonial scholars of their eras, Fanon and Young define postcolonial studies in strikingly similar ways despite different time periods and contexts. Fanon is discussing colonialism itself, in particular in regards to Algeria, and Young gestures to the context of globalization. Their similar understandings are useful because they overcome narrow understandings of the field, but more importantly here they inadvertently crystallize the role of children in much of post-apocalyptic cinema. More than simply a naïve hope for a utopian future, children in these films symbolize the potential for a differently orientated society, especially when they come "from below," from the subaltern refugee class, as is the case with Alfonso Cuarón's 2007 film, *Children of Men*. Just as postcolonialism does not offer simple solutions to the complexities of colonialism and globalization but rather a new ethically charged way of seeing and being in the world, children offer new complex opportunities to see and be differently in the ruined worlds of post-apocalyptic films.

Alfonso Cuarón's 2007 *Children of Men* presents a unique case in this context because the child in question in the film is a subject-in-process as unborn for most of the film and the ultimate fate of the child is ambiguous.[3]

Slavoj Žižek has argued that Clive Owen's character of Theo is the prism through which the film's social tensions become visible but it is through the subject-in-process baby that the film projects myriad postcolonial futures. [4] This child, born of a refugee in a detainment camp, is more than just the embodiment of hope but a politically charged resource that can potentially legitimize the organization that controls it and represents it in the world's media. In this way, the child as a projection of the future is highly fragmented as a subject. If the child does survive it will represent a postcolonial moment in which "the world from below" of the refugee "change[s] the order of the world." The specter of a potentially postcolonial child dominates the futurity that *Children of Men* takes as its subject.

In seeming contrast to the fragmented nature of the baby's present and future subjectivity, the most unavoidable formal characteristic of the film is its usage of numerous long takes. Several of these measure multiple minutes and provide seemingly fluid movement through the hectic world of the film. However, these long takes have been revealed to be composed of multiple takes, shot over weeks in numerous locations and stitched together via clever digital editing despite Cuarón's claim "not to use editing or montage . . . to create a moment of truthfulness, in which the camera just happens to be there to just register that moment. So that leads into the long shots." [5] Long takes traditionally gesture toward the documentarian but these faux long takes complicate this sense, and the digital stitching of different takes via a complex transition system belie a more fragmented filmic grammar at work. The longest and perhaps most celebrated is a seven-minute-long take of a mother carrying the first child born in eighteen years. This chapter explores the slippery position of the child subject in relation to the use of these equally slippery faux long takes to argue that just as the long take is actually a difficultly tracked patchwork of a multitude of takes used to create a postcolonial film that has now become a subject of contention, the child in *Children of Men* is a postcolonial, fragmented, and contested subject.

CHILDREN OF MEN

In *Children of Men* there is a distinct lack of children yet the entire film is haunted by the questions of what children mean, what a world without children would be like and if the interjection of one into a childless world can reconfigure dystopia. Set in 2027, the film begins with the murder of the youngest person on earth, baby Diego, who we are told is "18 years, 4 months, 2 days, 16 hours and 8 minutes old." We learn that eighteen years ago women mysteriously stopped getting pregnant and that humans are inexplicably infertile. Much of the world has fallen into anarchy and unrest as disease, poverty, and terrorism abound. England, the setting of the film, has been largely inoculated from these forces but in doing so has created a totalitarian state that restricts movement, encourages xenophobia, and practices extreme violence to enforce its laws. Resistance remains though largely via a shadowy organization calling itself the Human Project and various related smaller organizations such as the Fishes, a violent faction.

Much of the film lays the groundwork for this dynamic via the main character Theo Faron, played by Clive Owen. As a former activist, Theo has many connections in the resistance movement and as the cousin of a powerful minister he has access to transportation documents needed to travel in England. Because he can seemingly be trusted by both the government and the resistance he is chosen by the resistance to secure documentation for the only pregnant woman on earth, Kee, by the radical Fishes organization who hope to deliver her to the Human Project. As a condition of the documents though Theo must accompany Kee and it becomes clear that the Fishes and the government both want the baby for their own self-serving ends. The government wants the baby to legitimize its brutality as saving the nation and the Fishes want the baby to challenge the authority of the government. Theo comes to realize that Kee will not make it to the Human Project without his protection and that he is extraneous to both sides' plans. Navigating several violent encounters, including a full-scale war between the government and the Fishes, Theo delivers Kee and the baby to the Human Project ship off the coast only to die from a wound he sustained in helping her escape. The film ends off the foggy coast of England with an opaque finale in which the viewer is left to wonder whether Kee's baby signals the rejuvenation of humanity and what designs the Human Project has on her child.

Postcolonialism

To get a sense of how postcolonial studies broaden perspectives on *Children of Men* and the child in it, it is helpful to understand the central project of the field. Postcolonial studies has been extensively debated in numerous ways but one fundamentally agreed-upon principle of the field is that there is not an ossified postcolonial aesthetic or form because the postcolonial seeks to achieve real-world political change. It is in fact the measurement of a work's ability to do so that makes a work postcolonial or not. Unlike other contemporary movements such as postmodernism in which form dominates discussion, postcolonial studies are based on an ideology of political resistance. Postcolonialism is a way of understanding the world and a way of analyzing rather than a form. Thus, in arguing that *Children of Men* is a postcolonial work, I am contending that one can apply the postcolonial lens to it in such a way that exposes how its sympathies and modes of representation align with those of postcolonial studies. Certain works lend themselves to postcolonial readings more so than others, and these are the works that we can tentatively term postcolonial, but one could touch on the topics Cuarón does without being postcolonial. What makes a work postcolonial then is whether or not it adheres to the ethics of postcolonial studies, not whether it comes from a particular place at a certain time and discusses specific topics.

A primary concern of postcolonial studies is resistance. Postcolonial cinema argues *against* something, namely asymmetrical power relationships, underrepresentation, and misrepresentation. One of the founders of postcolonial studies, Edward Said argues in his seminal *Culture and Imperialism*, that postcolonial studies has created a discourse in which "For the first time Westerners have been required to confront themselves . . . as representatives of a culture and even a race accused of crimes—crimes of violence, crimes of suppression, crimes of conscience."[6] This characterization by Said works particularly well in thinking about classic postcolonial films like *The Battle of Algiers* (1966) wherein the occupying and totalitarian regime that tortures and terrorizes is squarely Western. Cuarón, his cinematographer and his visual effects supervisor have stated that they tried to emulate the shooting style of *Battle of Algiers* to give the film a "documentary feel."[7] *Children of Men* via its homage to *Battle* and taking the metropole of the largest colonial power as the principle oppressor positions itself squarely in a postcolonial filmic genealogy. Postcolonial films present confrontations that take place in the world of filmic representation as well as in the world outside the text to resist the long pervasive historical hegemony of the West over the non-West. Postcolonialism might even be better termed, especially in its earliest forms, as anticolonialism or antihegemony. This focus on the ability of representations to resist as a quintessential quality of the postcolonial has allowed the field to disavow an association with any particular form or style and to incorporate various texts whether they are novels, memoirs, comics, drama, poetry, or film.[8] As postcolonial films, both *The Battle of Algiers* and *Children of Men* feature a palatable resistance to an oppressive state and sympathies toward those who resist it.

The postcolonial raison d'être to intervene in the world, not simply describe it or map it for literary or filmic conventions, aesthetics or reportage is an interesting challenge for *Children of Men* because it takes place in a near-future England. As Žižek has pointed out though, the filmmakers do not "point towards an alternate reality, they simply make reality more what it already is . . . [and] makes us see better. The nightmare we are expecting is here." For Žižek the film is not a projection of a possible future but a comment on the present. Rather than a crystal ball presenting a possible "alternate reality," the film is grounded in complicating contemporary issues of immigration, refugees, and human rights in the context of nation-states and their attempts to delimit these phenomena. We see this in the issues of assisted suicide, immigration, torture, and government surveillance, but if there is any doubt one need only notice in a scene near the end of the film, a man in a black hood standing on a box with electric wires attached to him recreating the infamous photo of a hooded man being tortured in Abu Ghraib. Cuarón also names the government body in charge of this torture and the general abuse of refugees "Homeland Security" in another clear gesture that the film sees the dystopic in the present world, not only in its fictional future. The questions, then, that the film raises are not what *will* our attitudes toward the arbitrary transnational movement of people and our acceptance of free speech being compromised in the name of national security cost us later, but what are they costing us now. The detention centers in the film already exist in Europe and the United States and the wrath of Western governments against those who speak freely without permission has been felt from Wiki-Leaks to Edward Snowden to Pussy Riot and beyond. We do not have to project ourselves into a possible future to understand what it means to live in the violently paranoid state in *Children of Men*, because Abu Ghraib, Guantanamo, and other totalitarian tools of oppression already exist. For Cuarón, the future is not the nightmare, rather "the nightmare we are expecting *is* here." The film then aligns with early postcolonial pioneers such as Fanon in *The Wretched of the Earth* and Aimé Césaire in *Discourse on Colonialism* who articulated the hypocrisy of colonialism as well as with later fiction like *Things Fall Apart* that confronted Western readers with their own complicity in the abuses of colonialism to fuel colonizers distaste for maintaining colonies.[9] *Children of Men* then extends the trends evident in indefinite detentions in Guantanamo, mass deportations, and the brutality of the states that enact these policies. The film may couch itself in a future world to deflect and defer a direct comment on issues salient around the world, a result of its studio production, but its value lies in its ability to tackle the real world.

Žižek usefully describes *Children of Men* as an anamorphosis featuring a necessarily distracting banal foregrounding story of an apathetic antihero who slowly reengages the world with a more complex background of social commentary. For Žižek, confronting gross social inequality, torture, and censorship is too troubling to confront directly. In postcolonial terms, the contemporary moviegoer cannot take up Said's call to be "required to confront themselves" as members of a society than perpetrates injustice. Žižek says in an interview that "the true focus of the film is there in the background" because if one "looks at the thing too directly, the oppressive social dimension, you don't see it." The film splits its focus between Theo finding something worth caring about by hesitantly participating in a scheme to avoid detection of Kee and a more substantive comment on the unethical manner in which the accident of nationality predetermines one's value.

The anamorphosis model for the film can be extended to consider the baby and its postcoloniality in a slightly different sense. The baby can be seen directly for what it is in the world of the film and yet its true importance can only be viewed indirectly. It can itself be seen and realized as extraordinary but the nature of that extraordinariness is unclear. The baby is simply born under perilous conditions and one can hope and fear for its delivery but its true importance as the only child in the world cannot be looked at directly because it lies in an inaccessible future. In the film these two senses of anamorphosis come into the foreground briefly when the Fishes and government soldiers stop fighting once they see the baby. The viewer is shown the power of the baby to dramatically alter the world and the way that those living in it see themselves in relation to each other. Time seems to stop as distinctions of refugee, soldier, revolutionary, and civilian fade away when the baby intervenes. Kee carries her down several flights of stairs to the wonder of all and a new way of being in the world opens up for all who see it. Theo, Kee, and the baby make their way outside and once they pass a group of government soldiers the fighting suddenly continues as vigorously as before. The moment has passed, the baby's ability to reorientate the world has faded and focus shifts to whether or not a different kind of deployment of that power, seen so fleetingly in a powerful seven-minute-long take, can permanently reorder the world. We cannot directly see postcolonialism at work but we are granted a sideways glance in this scene.

The question then is not if the child is postcolonial, but what *kind* of postcolonial child it will be. Is this the problematic postcolonialism of abusive kleptocracies that has followed many independence movements in many formerly colonized countries that simply replicated the violence and oppression of their colonial predecessors? Or is this the postcolonialism of self-determination in which struggles abound, but the yoke of hegemony has been removed and is largely a memory? The potential turn to a new relationship with the world is fraught in the film because if either the government or the Fishes can use the child then the only change on the horizon is a different flavor of oppression that may or may not focus so intently on fertility. The way out is for the child to transcend these two groups via the altruistic Human Project. However, the world of *Children of Men* precludes a simple savior in favor of an opaque futurity as dense as the fog in the last scene. [10] This difficult way forward for the child parallels the difficult futures faced by postcolonial societies.

One of the ultimate criteria for postcolonial cinema is an appeal to ethics. Cuarón, as Žižek suggests, does not make a straightforward film about oppression, refugees, and human rights but rather takes an oblique, yet ultimately substantive, position on these issue by foregrounding elements of the film that implicate the Western reader in contrast to a more conventional story of Theo as a broken white man trying to recover his dignity and get a clear sense of the government's wrongdoing from his earlier activist days. An individualistic recovery of selfhood by Theo directly confronts the reader while an oblique background enables the film to handle more substantive and uncomfortable material.

The foregrounding of a palatable and marketable reluctant hero story eliding complicated material is the same approach used in delineating the role of the child in the film. Postcolonial studies are founded on the notion that its ethical imperative is not only to be against colonialism but *for* an equitable ethics of representation and *Children of Men* via the child proposes just such a new postcolonialism.[11] Just as postcolonial studies takes the lived experiences of individuals caught inside large historical events as its primary subjects, Cuarón purposefully chooses disempowered groups such as refugees and allows viewers to reflect on their situation while imagining another reality in which they possess the agency to assert their humanity, all within the confines of a rather mundane story with a marquee movie star. Although the film's parallels to *Battle of Algiers* are somewhat stretched, especially in terms of filming style, Cuarón does stay loyal to *Battle*'s core commitment to represent a subaltern group as a leading force in the future development of postcolonial societies in world cinema. Cuarón makes this point himself explicitly: "The fact that this child will be the child of an African woman has to do with the fact that humanity started in Africa. We're putting the future of humanity in the hands of the dispossessed and creating a new humanity to spring out of that." Africans as a subaltern group in reality and in the world of the film are the "bottom" that Fanon and Young identify as the groups that must be empowered in postcolonialism and Cuarón takes up their call in the film. Both *Children of Men* and *Battle* confront viewers with an imperative to empathize with traditionally marginalized groups and eschew the privileged subject position that many of their Western viewers inhabit.

Unsurprisingly, postcolonial studies antagonizes the societies that produced it (the United States and Europe) and Cuarón embodies this further by bringing into frame subjects that his society have maligned or ignored and moreover making those maligned and marginalized peoples (namely nonwhite refugees) the potential saviors of the human race. Postcolonial studies assumes that although colonialism proper has ended, its traces, sometimes explicit in neo-colonialism, continue to influence the world and Cuarón embraces this attitude that things are not as simple or prosperous as they may seem in the era of globalization. His extreme version of global inequality though is not just an accusation pointed at the powers that be, but a proclamation of the centrality of the refugee child as the true globalized citizen who, when the world is turned upside down, become central.

Cuarón and the Faux Long Take

Having established that *Children of Men* is certainly a postcolonial film and that the child as a subject-in-process and constant specter is postcolonial, the crucial question becomes: what are the formal filmic techniques used to enact this effect? Stylistically *Children of Men* is unique for a large budget Hollywood film due to its use of long takes. The average shot length in most Hollywood films is about three to four seconds. With such short shot lengths editing becomes the mechanism by which continuity in a scene and between scenes is achieved. *Children of Men* though has an average shot length of sixteen seconds with sixteen shots that are over forty-five seconds or longer and shots that are 3:19, 4:07, and 7:34 in length.[12] Using such long takes is a risk both economically because they challenge audiences used to a status quo of quick cuts in contemporary cinema, and artistically because they are notoriously difficult to pull off. Although critically acclaimed, *Children of Men*'s performance was mediocre at best at the box office, taking in just under $70 million with a budget of approximately $76 million, though it sold an additional $25 million in American DVDs and has been licensed for various broadcasts.[13] More importantly for this discussion is the fact that the long takes are not nearly as straightforward as they appear to the film's viewer.

There are three principle long takes in *Children of Men*. The first begins inside the car driving through the countryside. Kee, Theo, Julian, Luke, and Miriam are joking around and are attacked on the road when a car set alight blocks their path and a mob chases them. Julian is killed and Luke murders two police officers who stop the survivors for questioning but they narrowly escape the attack. In what appears to be one long brilliant take, the shot begins inside the car where five people are having a discussion as the camera floats between, continues during the attack that is shown through the car's various windows, and ends ultimately outside the car as Theo exits to see the dead policemen. The scene is a brilliant execution of a unique long take involving camera movement in closed space, a fantastic attack involving stuntmen shooting the vehicle and being thrown off their motorcycle and an exterior shot that puts the whole car in frame as if to say that it was just a camera in a car all along.

This version of the scene is the one viewers walk away with and the one Cuarón himself pursues. He has on several occasions discussed his filming style of *Children of Men* as a "documentary approach" because he wanted the near future to appear gritty and real rather than distant and computer enhanced. However, the visual effects supervisor, Frazer Churchill, has revealed that in fact this amazing long take in the car is too good to be true. He explains: "we did the shot in six sections, and sometimes the actors weren't in the car. As the camera swung around, we used pans to do digital transitions to the next day's photography . . . the scene was really made possible by digital transitions."[14] Churchill reveals that Cuarón "asked us [the crew] not to talk about the technical aspects" which involved digitally fusing different takes to appear as one long take. Other elements affected by the use of digital editing abound, such as how the car, which actually held thirteen crew members in all including a large camera rig on top it, could be seen as simply a car at the end of the take. Digital editing is common in contemporary cinema (though not in long takes) so it is the filmic consequences of purporting on screen and in interviews to a commitment to long takes and the documentarian that makes these faux long takes noteworthy.

The same digital transition technique used between takes to give the appearance of single long takes is also used in the other two long takes: the birth scene and the battle scene in the refugee camp. As James Udden notes "Cuarón did not want the artifice behind these 'long takes' to be readily known" as he told the crew not to mention them, but also in interviews on those very scenes on the DVD extras and elsewhere, he never fully acknowledged the use of digital editing to create the faux long takes. [15] Instead one is told of the great achievement these long takes represent. Even with digital editing these scenes *are* achievements and Cuarón trying to draw attention to the difficulty of achieving them and the thematic ends to which they serve is understandable. Rather than calling Cuarón out on a half-secret, we should instead consider the importance of the film as not being as fluid as Cuarón contends but rather highly fragmented and how understanding the nature of the editing process impacts its subject. Cuarón best explains his philosophy in shooting long takes in *Children of Men* when he states:

> Because then you just register the moments as they go. So what becomes important, then, is not the camera, but the moment. If you are going through life and something happens, you don't have the luxury of going, "Stop, stop, guys, and let me get a close-up!" [16]

Cuarón incriminates himself because we know of course that complex editing was indeed used, somewhat clandestinely, so that he could in effect yell at his crew to get a close up whenever he wanted. Cuarón wants to be considered as an auteur who overcomes the challenges of traditional filmmaking rather than one of the first to use new digital technology to circumvent those challenges. Moreover, the idea of a camera just recording an event or moment in a fictional film is always going to be a tenuous conceit but the long take is a way for viewers to suspend their disbelief enough to imagine that some elements of the take are beyond the absolute control of the director. Cuarón of course does not have absolute control over the *mise-en-scène* in these long takes but he does exert an amount of control tantamount to being able to stop and get a close up when long takes can be constructed over weeks in different locations and be meticulously edited for as long as needed.

The most spectacular long take in the film is over seven minutes long when Theo tries to deliver Kee and her baby to the Human Project boat. Like the other long takes, the scene is stitched together from several shots to appear as a long take. More than simply multiple shoots at a single location, this faux long take was shot in two different locations two weeks apart and is composed of six shots. [17] In this scene we do get a sense of the documentary when a blood packet on the bus Clive Owen ducks into for cover went off prematurely spraying fake blood on the lens. Apparently, Cuarón yelled cut but "there were so many elements going on it was impossible to communicate the 'cut' to everyone."[18] This unplanned moment made it into the film in true documentary style, but the amount of blood was greatly decreased by digital editing and the blood drops were made to thin out and roll away when the camera moved around so that the remaining minutes of the shot were not compromised by a blood splattered camera lens.[19] We see here then that despite a moment of true documentary when the camera is rolling and something unexpected happens, Cuarón actually lessened the effect by digital editing. This is not to say that the shot could have been used with the camera covered in blood, but that the gestures Cuarón makes toward the documentarian should be abandoned for one that embraces the way technology can be used to achieve a documentary effect in different and new ways.

The phenomena of the long take and the postcolonial nature of the film and the child in the diegesis of that film are not merely coincidences. Rather the use of long takes amplifies the postcolonial nature of the child, especially when the true fragmented nature of the long takes are revealed. Both the child and the long takes appear to be naturalistic extensions of their environments yet both are contested sites of meaning. The child represents a reassertion of nature in an inhospitable environment. We do not know in the film why fertility ceased but the insinuation is clear that social and environmental decay has some role to play. The same ambiguity imbues the first pregnancy in eighteen years. Whatever the cause for human biology to reassert itself, the burgeoning of fertility is an assertion of nature, even if at odds with the world of the film. This switching on of human reproduction, which one would imagine to be a straightforward boon for all, is instead highly contested and politicized. Before the baby is even born various organizations have designs on it. The name of the baby is also an interesting field in that Kee originally wants to name the baby Froley which Theo responds to with "It's the first baby in eighteen years. You can't name it Froley." Later she tells Theo that Froley is a man's name and she wants to name the girl Bazooka. Finally, when approaching the Human Project boat, she tells Theo that she is going to name her daughter Dylan after the son that he lost. The name begins as an original expression that is etymologically unbound in the same way that Kee, her baby and the other refugees in the film are unattached to any national identity. They are "fugees" and that is all we are told about their backgrounds. Kee brings up the name Bazooka when she and Theo are on the run from the government and the Fishes. Beyond being a childish and silly name given by a young girl, the name demonstrates a desire for influence, as if Kee knows that her daughter will need explosive power to survive. Her final choice of Dylan is passed off in the film as a homage to Theo, but it is also a moment in which a refugee whose very existence has been made illegal by England gives her child a decidedly English/Welsh name. Again the child does not have the benefit of a straightforward identity but one in which she is named after a dead friend of her mother's in the tradition of the country that attempted to kill all of them. Even her name is not at home in the world but contested.

The long takes themselves also appear as naturalistic moments during which the camera simply captures what unfolds in front of it. Of course, we know that long takes are meticulously planned but we also know that because of the demanding nature of them directors only get a couple of chances to pull them off and quite often the unexpected *does* transpire. The nature of the long take lends a sense of the documentarian but the nature of the digital editing used to create the long takes appears to operate in clear opposition to that sense. Digital editing allows for things that never happened to happen. We must then, like with the contested nature and future of the child, decide what to make of these oppositional forces. Do we take up the perspective of the viewers who for the most part have no idea that they are not watching a long take, or do we cynically accuse the director of using the most invasive of editing techniques while bellowing about the artfulness of long takes to capture something real and true? Just as the child is torn between activists and government, these long takes present a problem for our analysis because the stated methods of the director are misleading, yet the finished product aligns with the ethics and style of the representation he asserts. As Udden notes: "In the end, perhaps being true to 'reality' or being 'documentary-like' are not of primary importance: being true to one's own status as an auteur in contemporary Hollywood offers as much motivation for the long take as anything."[20] In other words, just as the refugees and the child seek a kind of mediated freedom that they know cannot actually provide them with a pure form of freedom, the faux long take provides enough of a specter of the documentarian freedom, not frequently offered in many contemporary Hollywood films, to pass as a highly mediated yet powerful expression of a filmic style and postcolonial ethic.

NOTES

1. Fanon, Frantz. *The Wretched of the Earth* (New York: New Grove, 1963).

2. Young, Robert. "Postcolonial Remains." *New Literary History* no. 1 (2012): 19.

3. An interesting edit made from the book by P. D. James in which the story ends in the baptism of the first child born in decades, an ending that signals a rebirth of humanity much more than the film's ending.

4 Žižek, Slavoj. "Slavoj Žižek on Children of Men." www.youtube.com/watch?v=pbgrwNP_gYE (accessed February 2, 2014).

5. Panosian, Diane. "Alfonso Cuarón in His Own Words: From Film School to 'Gravity.'" www.studiosystemnews.com/alfonso-cuaron-in-his-own-words-from-film-school-to-gravity/ (accessed February 2, 2014).

6. Said, Edward. *Culture and Imperialism* (New York: Vintage Books, 1994).

7. The parallels drawn between these two films is interesting because *Children of Men* strives for a style that focuses on the dilapidated futuristic setting via long and medium shots and *Battle of Algiers* does the same for the Kasbah in strikingly different ways. *Battle* does not use long takes. In fact, its use of quick takes happens in some of the most iconic scenes, such as the women bombing civilian targets. Also, Cuarón on several occasions when discussing *Children of Men* has stated that he did not want to rely on cheap dramatic tricks like close-ups because he wanted the characters to inhabit the scenery rather than to transcend it. *Battle of Algiers* though features innumerable close-ups and extreme close-ups to bring sympathy to subjects too often dismissed simply as terrorists or just ignored. Arab protagonists resisting colonialism with honor required close-ups to express the humanity of a subjugated people but Theo, a white British man, requires no such move.

8. This freedom of form has not been easily achieved or always unanimously agreed upon. For example, many anticolonial literatures, especially in the mid-twentieth century, felt the need to practice realism to resist the modernist movements in the West but also to provide ethnographic corrections to long histories of ethnographic and realist misrepresentations of colonized peoples. However, forms such as magical realism also took root at this time and offered alternative forms of resistance literature.

9. Césaire, Aimé. *Discourse on Colonialism* (New York: Monthly Review Press, 1955). Achebe, Chinua. *Things Fall Apart* (London: Heinemann Press, 1958).

10. *Battle of Algiers* also ends in a fog, though the fog is smoke. The endings of the two films juxtapose interestingly in that the Algerians emerge from behind the fog and advance toward the camera while in *Children of Men* Kee heads into the fog to meet the Human Project. Whereas the Algerians boldly assert a subjectivity to the camera and the French military whose point of view the camera shares, Kee hides and her subjectivity and that of her baby are left in doubt.

11. Leela Ghandi has fielded accusations against postcolonial studies as interested in "postcolonial revenge" against the West. She argues that postcolonial studies does not seek to turn the tables on the West by now making it a marginalized and demonized entity. In fact, that would be the antithesis of postcolonial ethics as cultural equity is the goal of the field.

12. Cuarón continued this trajectory by opening his next film, *Gravity*, with a seventeen-minute-long take.

13. The Numbers. "Children of Men." www.the-numbers.com/movies/2006/CHLDM.php (accessed Feburary 2, 2014).

14. Fordham, Joe. "Children of Men: The Human Project." *Cinefex* (July 2007): 39.

15. Udden, James. "Child of the Long Take: Alfonso Cuarón's Film Aesthetics in the Shadow of Globalization." *Style* (Spring 2009): 32.

16. Moviefone. "Interview: *Children of Men* director Alfonso Cuarón." news.moviefone.com/2006/12/25/interview-children-ofmen-director-alfonso-cuaron/ (accessed February 2, 2014).

17. Udden, 31.

18. Fordham, 43.

19. A similar event occurred in the car scene and Cuarón again tried to cut but could not be heard. In the car scene blood splatter was going to be added in postproduction but a blood pack exploded and splattered blood on the camera instead.

20. Udden, 34.

BIBLIOGRAPHY

Achebe, Chinua. *Things Fall Apart*. London: Heinemann Press, 1958.

Césaire, Aimé. *Discourse on Colonialism*. New York: Monthly Review Press, 1955.

Fanon, Frantz. *The Wretched of the Earth*. New York: New Grove, 1963.

Fordham, Joe. "Children of Men: The Human Project." *Cinefex* (2007): 39.

Moviefone. "Interview: *Children of Men* director Alfonso Cuarón." news.moviefone.com/2006/12/25/interview-children-ofmen-director-alfonso-cuaron/ (accessed February 2, 2014).

Panosian, Diane. "Alfonso Cuarón in His Own Words: From Film School to 'Gravity.'" www.studiosystemnews.com/alfonso-cuaron-in-his-own-words-from-film-school-to-gravity/ (accessed February 2, 2014).

Said, Edward. *Culture and Imperialism*. New York: Vintage Books, 1994.

The Numbers. "Children of Men." www.the-numbers.com/movies/2006/CHLDM.php (accessed Feburary 2, 2014).

Udden, James. "Child of the Long Take: Alfonso Cuarón's Film Aesthetics in the Shadow of Globalization." *Style* (Spring 2009): 32.

Young , Robert. "Postcolonial Remains." *New Literary History* no. 1 (2012): 19.

Žižek, Slavoj. "Slavoj Žižek on Children of Men." www.youtube.com/watch?v=pbgrwNP_gYE (accessed February 2, 2014).

Chapter Eleven

Persistently Ambivalent

Children, Race, Sexuality, and a Post-Apocalyptic Hollywood Interracial Future

Glen Donnar

Images of destruction and apocalypse have persistently fascinated Hollywood, tied variously to its thrall to the spectacle of disaster, the (often underdeveloped) articulation of contemporary cultural anxieties and fears, and even long-held cultural ambivalence toward America's key urban centers.[1] Yet Hollywood apocalypses also invariably offer warnings of the spectacular annihilation of a world order deemed corrupt or broken, marking not only retribution and judgment, but a period of tribulation *after the end*. Roslyn Weaver rightly observes contemporary secular apocalypses diverge in important ways from their biblical antecedents.[2] Nonetheless, Hollywood post-apocalyptic fictions, which depict a world after catastrophe and a sustained period of devastation, also often proffer a subsequent revelation or unveiling and initiate, however tentatively or partially, some form of rebirth and renewal. That is, whether progressive or conservative, they persistently focus on (the need for) cultural renewal and societal reinvigoration.

"FINAL MEN," FATHERS, RACE, AND CHILDREN

The related post-apocalyptic mainstream American films explored in this chapter, *The World, The Flesh, and The Devil* (USA 1959, Ranald MacDougall), *The Omega Man* (USA 1971, Boris Sagal), and *I Am Legend* (USA 2007, Francis Lawrence), each seemingly revolve around the lonely, post-apocalyptic urban experience of their (apparently) "final man" protagonists.[3] They variously use post-apocalyptic scenarios to explore contemporary cultural and sociopolitical crises and uncertainties, from Cold War atomic fears to civil rights issues to post-9/11 threats, in periods of instability in American society (and cinema). Yet their apocalypses variously reveal persistent anxieties about race, sex and gender; isolation and invasion; community and its Others; and threats to (the persistence of) hegemony. [4]

Cinematic apocalypses routinely offer an opportunity to redress perceived social ills through the reinvigoration of dormant-though-desired human qualities, such as innocence (the child) and order (the father), and prohibitions on supposedly undesirable contemporary social realities. Mick Broderick finds that postnuclear cinematic apocalypses increasingly reinforce the symbolic order and conservative social regimes, typically through the restoration of patriarchal law. [5] Indeed, Broderick finds post-apocalyptic science fiction invariably promotes heteronormative "renewal" of the couple, family, and community. [6] Hence, Hollywood representations of catastrophe and apocalypse often become an opportunity to restore or reinvigorate authority (and the status quo) *and* recenter (white) masculinity through the mythic figure of the survivalist hero as "strong father."

Issues of race, and particularly blackness, and interracial relationships in post-apocalyptic narratives further reinforce the cultural need for the restoration of white "final men." Adilifu Nama, who persuasively critiques Hollywood's strict policing of racial difference in science fiction, contends that only an apocalyptic context allows the imagining of racial change, ambivalently cuing social change while associating black visibility and power with oncoming apocalypse. [7] For example, Nama asserts that *The World, The Flesh, and The Devil* (henceforth *TWTFTD*) and *Omega Man* similarly connect Cold War paranoia about radioactive contamination with racial contamination, associating "the implosion of racial boundaries with dystopian and apocalyptic visions of the future." Interracial relationships are both only viable after apocalypse or the collapse of Western civilization and implicitly associated with their onset.

The often central post-apocalyptic concern with (white) patriarchal and paternal restoration typically centers on child characters and their protection, and reinvigoration of the family or community. Yet as Debbie Olson and Andrew Scahill observe, children are rarely part of the "theoretical landscape of film analysis" despite being significant features of the film landscape. [8] This is particularly the case in post-apocalyptic cinema, where the conventional representation of children, as either convenient symbols of futurity and hope or marginal and silent, is reiterated in subsequent scholarly invisibility of childhood in film analysis—admittedly, my earlier writings on these films too repeats this invisibility. [9] Nonetheless, there is a growing body of scholarly work that finds that although constructions of the modern child in America as sacralized and vulnerable persist—and perhaps predominate in mainstream popular culture—images of childhood innocence are now questioned, even contested.[10] Olson and Giselle Rampaul further observe that children now *also* trouble romantic ideals of "the child" and "childhood" as passive and analogously associated with nature, with children equally represented "as knowing, adultified and sometimes menacing." Karen Lury nonetheless observes that although more complex than generally held, the child figure in film frequently remains overdetermined by the priorities of adults.[11] Such "overdetermined" qualities and metaphoric meanings associated with adult anxieties, fears, fantasies, desires, and nostalgia—and yoked onto "children" and childhood—are arguably amplified in a post-apocalyptic context.

However, the conventional function of children as signifiers both of the past and the future (or the lack thereof) is uniquely spotlighted in post-apocalyptic cinema. Post-apocalyptic fictions are ideally placed to explore the fluid, complex, and often contradictory meanings of the child and diverse, "messy" experiences of childhood. In post-apocalyptic contexts, innocence and youth are not only idealized, but threatened, fractured and corrupted; childhood horrific and the future particularly fraught. And childhood need not solely mark futurity and hope, but (also) becomes a site of knowing and death. Children are not only victims in need of protection, and representative of humanity as fragile, but evidence of its resilience and endurance. Children not only represent innocence and purity, but also spotlight adult guilt and responsibility, with their ultimate shepherding to a new world paradoxically restoring patriarchal order. These characteristics suggest a need to explore the significances of the child and children in all their troubling *and* troublesome complexity and ambivalence.

Thus, this chapter interrogates whether a neglected examination of the child and children in these "final man" post-apocalyptic films reveals children not only as bearers of key symbolic significance, but ones that expose rather than absolve, reflect rather than salve, American racial anxieties and preoccupations. Privileging child characters and notions of the child in the consideration of these post-apocalyptic films arguably demonstrates how children variously *make* the survival and sacrifices of the "final men" *meaningful*. More than timeless symbols of survival and hope, children persistently belie their relative invisibility or marginality, even their absence, to troublingly announce persistent *and* persisting American cultural ambivalence concerning issues of race and sexuality, interracial romance and miscegenation, and patriarchy and masculinity.

THE FRIGHTENING PROSPECTS OF MISCEGENATION AND (ABSENT) CHILDREN: THE PRESERVATION OF "CIVILIZATION" IN *THE WORLD, THE FLESH, AND THE DEVIL* (1959)

Reflecting much cinema scholarship, children are literally absent throughout *TWTFTD*, seemingly "present" only as a particularly feared type or idea of "child" in 1950s America: the mixed-race child. Starring Harry Belafonte, *TWTFTD* is a post-apocalypse/"social problem" film about a black miner, Ralph Burton, who frees himself from a Pennsylvania mine collapse to find a world suddenly emptied after atomic conflict and poisoning. [12] Despite believing himself now alone, racial and class prejudices haunt Burton from his arrival in a radically depopulated New York, even though "civilization"—represented by the dominant ideological notions held by contemporary society—has ostensibly ended. This haunting, however, is primarily articulated through Burton's own preservation of "old world" social roles and ideologies; ones that prohibit the possibility of black-white interracial romance and miscegenation. Class, race, and sex issues foreshadowed in Burton's early interactions with a white mannequin "couple" he collects for companionship are explicitly—if always indirectly—explored with a later white female survivor; a blond "final woman." For Burton, the mannequins symbolically (re)animate and preserve (white) "civilization"; one marked by racial prejudice, white privilege, and his exclusion and invisibility. The mannequins communicate how Burton's class and race identity is discursively circumscribed by society even post-apocalypse. [13] The late arrival of a white male sexual rival thereafter seemingly shatters the pair's fledgling hope of (interracial) romance. Yet the film's narrative is perhaps equally disruptive, and although *TWTFTD* was the first film produced by Belafonte's production company, he later criticized its timidity in depicting the interracial romance. As such, the film was inevitably associated with the black-white "miscegenation film" cycle of the late 1950s. [14]

However, *TWTFTD* arguably more successfully deploys Cold War atomic anxieties to examine pre-apocalypse (read: contemporary) class, race and gender relations, and especially the psychic effects of racial and sexual codes on black masculinity, than is generally critically recognized. This conclusion is solidified by explicit consideration of the significance of the mixed-race child, an idea or prospect rather than actual child; and a child *meaningfully* absent. Before Burton locates a New York apartment, an empty pram is blown past where he uncertainly huddles in the cold rain. The pram is a potent signifier of humanity's and the black final man's shared void future. Yet the conclusion of this sequence reveals Burton is not alone—a pair of female feet follows behind unbeknownst to him. The empty pram, sandwiched between shots of the two strangers and directly preceding her introduction, thus also prefigures Burton and the young blonde's, Sarah Crandall

Figure 11.1. *The World, The Flesh, and The Devil*, 1959, HarBel Productions.

(Inger Stevens), relationship. Nama rightly notes the clear sexual innuendo implied by the pram carriage. [15] However, its *emptiness* more ambivalently foreshadows the prospect, logic, *and* impossibility of their interracial coupling. The empty pram variously foreshadows the couple's mutual desires and suggests the post-apocalyptic "logic" of their union, but equally the contemporary societal (im)possibility, fears, and threat interracial romance and miscegenation represents—in a time interracial unions remained prohibited in over thirty states across America. [16]

Throughout the film, there is an abiding ambivalence about the idea of children, who, rather than symbols of survival and hope, represented both a fearful possibility for some contemporary audiences *and* a feared prospect for the black protagonist; that is, a persistent and heavy un-presence. When Sarah eventually reveals her presence to Burton, their awkward first meeting rapidly reinvokes race, class, and gender undertones of their relationship—foreshadowed in the mannequins. [17] These roles are reinforced over succeeding weeks, especially in their gendered clothing and behaviors (she shops while he labors), before predating race issues overwhelm the possibility of interracial romance, with Burton swiftly rejecting Sarah's suggestion she move into his building: "No, people might talk." Burton's words are visually emphasized, particularly in beautiful black and white photography by Harold J. Marzorati, with close-ups of Burton's hand against her white skin, white dress, and blond hair, as he—still in work clothes—clears up the lunch he prepared. Moreover, the haircut she hastily requests as a means to return to the "safe" performance of pre-apocalypse social roles ultimately encourages unusually loaded moments of touch and intimacy between the pair, with clear sexual implications. An extreme close-up of blond hair on his black hand follows as he gently blows it off, before he shocks her with a sudden, too-deep cut she playfully provoked. This scene has been variously characterized by Stéphanie Larrieux as first highlighting Burton's discomfort—as Burton reluctantly plays another race-identified "service role"—and Susan Courtney for signaling Burton's subsequent "butchering" as that of a "black beast."[18] Nonetheless, despite the shock of Burton's cutting, Sarah is emboldened: "This is the world we live in; we're alone in it. We have to go from there." However, while her sexual desire—and thereby the "idea" or prospect of mixed-race children—is persistently signaled, it is always only euphemistically so, and she does not look directly at Burton when she tentatively suggests their union. That is, although the post-apocalyptic persistence of white privilege allows her to "look forward," there remain limits on what she can imagine, or *speak*, post-apocalypse. Even this indirection is unavailable to Burton, for whom the past, represented by pre-apocalyptic societal norms, prevents the possibility of interracial romance, as he reminds Sarah, showing her his hand, and the *meanings* of color he cannot forget.

Indeed, the possibility of sex (and idea) of children can only be annunciated by an older white male survivor, Ben Thacker (Mel Ferrer), who Burton saves when he later arrives in New York gravely ill. Ben's arrival seemingly forever disturbs Burton's tenuous steps toward romance with Sarah. Moreover, his status as *white* romantic rival, is confirmed when Burton explicitly likens Ben to the white male mannequin Burton earlier "murders"—a futile attempt to extinguish the continuing feelings of black invisibility the black man preserves through his labor and behaviors—after declaring his sexual interest in Sarah.[19] However, Ben's inability to woo Sarah, with phrases that betray both his perceptions of her and claims over her, "Me man, you girl. How about it?" and implied threats of rape, eventually leads him to view Burton's presence as the prime impediment to his sexual success. Although Ben's growing hostility toward Burton is explicitly claimed to not relate to racism, as Williams observes, the white male's violent anxieties certainly center on the perceived threat to white patriarchy Burton and Sarah's union would represent.[20] Indeed, any mixed-race child threatens white hegemonic masculinity in numerous ways; after all, Burton is not only black, but working-class. The prospect of any interracial union and children threatens the "civilization" that Ben embodies and the traumatized black repeatedly invokes and preserves, one defined as white, male, and middle class. A prospective mixed-race child thus doubly falls outside idealized notions of the "perfect" 1950s child as white and middle class.

Ben provokes armed conflict with Burton, but Burton ultimately thwarts Ben's desires for violent resolution when he throws down his rifle. However, while scholars predominantly focus stakes and consequences of the conflict between the two men, the significance of Sarah's subsequent actions—and the manner of their depiction—is too readily overlooked. Following the dissipation of the armed showdown, Sarah extends her hand toward Burton,

Figure 11.2. *The World, The Flesh, and The Devil*, 1959, HarBel Productions.

who slowly reaches out to take hers, before she calls out to the defeated and departing Ben and takes his hand in her other. Sarah's symbolic reincorporation of each man on her terms implies a radically refigured notion of "civilization" and romantic love post-apocalypse—the men throw down their firearm-phalluses after all. She gets the fearful black man to finally accept her hand and only offers hers to the white man after he (however ambivalently) renounces violence *and* thereby his patriarchal (sexual) claims. However, Sarah takes Burton's hand in a highly sensual extreme close-up, a symbolic consummation tellingly withheld in her taking of Ben's hand, which thereby foreshadows the cautious prospect of an interracial child. Sarah's (and Burton's) actions tentatively signal a move toward a fledgling, fragile new world, as the three survivors walk off together ("The Beginning"). Nevertheless, the prospect of an interracial child can only be cinematically imagined post-apocalypse once "civilization" is thoroughly recast.

Both the persistent post-apocalyptic possibility and corollary contemporary American *im*possibility of an interracial child shadow *TWTFTD*'s narrative. While its undeniable logic is resisted by the haunting persistence of "civilization's" (read: contemporary American) norms for Burton, the unresolved (im)possibility of interracial romance (and children) not only paralyzes the protagonist, but confused contemporary audiences and critics. Indeed, protests against the film on its release were mirrored by criticisms of its unwillingness to show an interracial romantic liaison *even* "after the end."[21] The ambiguous ending disappoints *because* it does not afford the panacea of classical narrative resolution, progressive or otherwise. The film's unresolved "ending" offers only an unrepresented (and *unrepresentable* at the time) beginning, and thus exposes rather than relieves persistent cultural ambivalence over race, class, and sex issues. More radically, however, the ambiguous interracial coupling—either polygamous pansexuality or a platonic trio—that now begins America's post-apocalyptic future troubles conventional understandings of the child as a symbol of heteronormative futurity and hope. Far from the conventional offering of "sanitized themes" of race and miscegenation and "reassuring interpretations of contemporary social conditions" and attitudes that Olson and Rampaul observe, the child in *TWTFTD* may not be part of the future at all.[22]

SACRALIZING *AND* INDICTING THE WHITE INSTITUTIONAL "FATHER": CHILDREN SPEAK IN *THE OMEGA MAN* (1971)

While the child in *TWTFTD* is meaningfully absent, the children in *The Omega Man* seemingly conform to conventional adult constructions and understandings of childhood, of innocence, passivity, and futurity; a *meaningless* presence. More disconcertingly, children are mobilized in the symbolic restoration of threatened white patriarchy, cured by the blood of a redeeming white institutional "father," and the sacrificial death of a black "child" facilitates the survival of whiteness, thereby doubly equated with humanity's future. However, the black teenager likewise significantly disrupts the restoration of white patriarchy and compromises his province over America's post-apocalyptic future.

Omega Man stars Charlton Heston as military scientist and polymath bachelor, Robert Neville, three years after a global viral atomic plague wipes out much of the world's population.[23] Neville is a survivalist holdout in Los Angeles against the Family, a cult of albino-like infected survivors violently opposed to Neville's defiantly unchanged, even intensified, consumer lifestyle. Neville daily searches for the Family, to experiment on (to replicate his own immunity) but mostly exterminate them, and is nightly besieged by the group, led by newsreader cum zealot, Matthias (Anthony Zerbe). While *Omega Man* too explores Cold War atomic fears, the film's focus arguably centers more on perceived domestic threats to white male hegemony in late 1960s America; the film both foregrounding and effacing, embracing and mocking, the contemporary politics of race and sex. Indeed, Nama argues *Omega Man* exemplifies expressions of masculinity in 1960s Hollywood science fiction, with urban "racial paranoia" augmenting the perception that white masculinity and institutions were under constant threat.[24] For example, scholars uniformly associate the Family's rhetoric with late sixties civil rights unrest and black militancy.[25]

Such claims, however, ignore how the film is also about 1970s urban decay more generally, as well as its incoherent address of racial, gender, and sexual politics, and parallel reinforcement *and* unsettling of (white) male power.[26] Mark Gallagher identifies Neville's alignment with progressive,

Figure 11.3. *Omega Man*, **1971, Seltzer Productions.**

countercultural values, and the manner in which this threatens his hegemonic "command of narrative space," but ultimately argues the film represents the heroic adaptability of cinematically idealized American masculinity.[27] For example, after Neville is captured by the Family, he is surprisingly rescued by two countercultural archetypes, Dutch (Paul Koslo), a younger male awash in biker gear and hippie vernacular, and Lisa (Rosalind Cash), visually and rhetorically associated with black militancy. Yet Neville's immunity and capacity to cure thereafter recenters white institutional masculinity. Nevertheless, the film's gender and race incoherence, which ambivalently depicts the initial success of miscegenation but also requires the parodic disavowal of a racial politics of difference, highlights the value of a more nuanced consideration of the film's racial politics rooted in a focus on children and "childhood."

On the surface, children in *Omega Man* signify conventionally; near silent, innocent, and passive symbols of futurity and hope. When Dutch and Lisa rescue Neville they take him to their mountaintop compound on the city's outskirts, where he finds a band of child survivors. The children are conventionally linked with nature, symbolically surviving outside the city. They are, most tellingly, predominantly white and blond, both historically implicitly idealized in popular cultural images, as universally "innocent" or "perfect" (with nonwhite children stereotyped, caricatured, or excluded altogether).[28] The glaring exception is Lisa's younger brother, who is also at the most advanced stage of infection and thereby signified as the most susceptible to the plague. The children are largely mere *mise-en-scène* "dressing," adorned neatly across the back of the frame, and primarily talked *about* rather than *with*. Indeed, when a little blond girl, the perfect "innocent child," does speak, her words elevate the failed scientist as "father" of their future: "Are you God?"

Yet despite their innocent superficies, the orphaned children's postlapsarian militaristic reality is unsettlingly normalized. That is, the children are armed, and readily assume militarist behaviors, diligently manning a machine gun nest and willing to shoot Neville on first sight. The post-apocalyptic context has irrevocably changed children in *Omega Man*, and their capacity to perform "un-childlike" acts of violence is both symptomatic of the moral darkening of humanity and an indictment of prelapsarian American society (most straightforwardly the audience's present). It also represents a call on the white hero to restore them to their "ideal" state of innocence.

When Neville passes on the cure derived directly from his blood, his self-sacrifice ensures the rejuvenation of humanity and symbolically reinvigorates the white institutional male. A foregrounded shot of the blood and vial, with the infected children massed in the background, clearly connotes his role in their survival; the orphaned children now have a symbolic "father." As Claire Sisco King similarly observes, "a new family is born . . . from the broken body of a 'tragic man.'"[29] Neville's sacrificial death also renders him a Christ figure, which Nama argues foreshadows "the narcissistic self-pity of white male martyrdom . . . that became a signature feature" in post-Vietnam Hollywood films.[30] Indeed, Neville is repeatedly associated with Christ, as when Dutch early responds to Neville's declaration of immunity: "Christ, you could save the world."[31] For any viewer still finding such symbolism too subtle, Heston has Neville assume the Christ pose in death, his blood spreading across the fountain's water to signal the potency and purity of Neville's "160-proof Anglo Saxon" blood. Neville's cure and sacrifice deliver children to a supposed, ideal prelapsarian state of "childhood" and a reinvigorated

Figure 11.4.   *Omega Man*, 1971, Seltzer Productions.

prelapsarian "new" world; an equally nostalgic construction of prelapsarian "America." Humanity's future, imagined as an undiscovered and untouched Eden collectively by Neville and Dutch, symbolically lies outside the decayed city. Yet while children are typically supposedly dependent on the symbolic return of the "father," Neville equally needs the children to restore whiteness and patriarchy as sacrificial *and* foundational. For example, the archetypically innocent little girl, by placing his military cap in front of his cruciform body, symbolically anoints the white male Christ figure as militarized, muscular, and institutional. In so doing, *she* repairs patriarchal failings and restores institutional underpinning for society's survival.

Omega Man also ambiguously—albeit less coherently or earnestly than *TWTFTD*—explores the (im)possibility of interracial coupling and miscegenation. It first decentralizes race through Neville's rather unlikely coupling with Lisa, who swiftly (and unpersuasively) disavows her black militant attitude—although not her stereotypically sassy black sexuality—upon the seductions of the white institutional male. Yet neither does either party fear the potential product of their liaison, a mixed-race child, in contrast to *TWTFTD*, even later laughing after Lisa amusedly tosses away a pack of birth control pills she finds in a derelict pharmacy.[32] The film at least acknowledges the functional possibility of miscegenation. Neville also subjects Richie (Eric Laneuville) to a series of transfusions of his "160-proof old Anglo Saxon" blood to cure him. With Neville's blood, Richie symbolically represents the couple's racially mixed child. Thus, Nama argues *Omega Man* builds "an aura of scientific authority around the curative properties of white Anglo-Saxon blood;" "a means to cure and repopulate a diseased and dying world." However, this too readily dismisses Neville's numerously declared dual complicity in its "disease and dying," both for the plague and as unable to avert it; and the successful fusion of Neville and Richie's blood—arguably whitened, but also successfully hybridizing black and white—who likewise develops the capacity to cure. It also ignores the ongoing ambivalence of whiteness in the film, both deadening and heroic, diseased and curative, with Neville—like the even whiter Family—similarly considered dangerous and complicit.

Whiteness and blackness are, however, problematically associated with starkly different relations to futurity and hope in *Omega Man*. Late adolescence, and particularly the liminal statuses of white Dutch (whose youth is signified in his unspoken unsuitability as a prospective mate for Lisa) and black Richie, is ambivalently represented. The apocalypse derails their respective comings of age but renders their respective unchildlike "knowingness" differently. The young white male is ultimately reincorporated into the ideology he questions post-apocalypse, assuming provenance of Neville's cure and the role of the white father, but the young black male is sacrificed to confirm the Family's barbarity and mobilize the symbolic restoration of white patriarchy through sacrificial death. *Omega Man* here seemingly communicates the ultimate futility and impossibility of miscegenation and interracial romance; the black child cured by white blood is murdered and Lisa "turns" (and therefore ends the film "white," sporting the whitened hair and skin of the Family) and betrays Neville; symbolically erasing blackness and extinguishing difference within the survivor group. Nama and Gallagher consider the film thus respectively "reflect[s] America's history of hypersurveillance of racial boundaries" and the "limitations of racial equality."[33] In this respect, Neville's sacrifice thus rescues conservative notions of "childhood" endangered by Otherness, including Richie's blackness. Yet the disavowal of difference is associated with the evil of the Family, who kill the cured Richie as a consequence.

Moreover, the black teenager becomes a "knowing" figure who, rather than sacralizing the institutional white "father," challenges and disrupts the reinvigoration of white patriarchy.[34] Richie explicitly questions Neville's motives, his association with the corrupted old world order, and his utility and relevance in this new world. Richie recognizes Neville is Matthias's violent mirror, identifying their shared association with blighted, monstrous urbanity, and declaring that neither belongs in the "new" world. Neville as violent father-savior has no place in a world in which, although founded on sacrificial institutional male whiteness, he is deemed redundant, even "hostile." Thus, child figures in *Omega Man* surprisingly occupy a range of complex positions that complicate the status of the white institutional male; the "innocent" blond child anoints the white male father as foundational, and the sacrificial black child recognizes his redundancy. While the (again unrepresented) post-apocalyptic future is located in white children, Richie identifies Neville's supposedly pure "160-proof Anglo-Saxon" blood as perhaps even as diseased as that of the also-white Family, significantly compromising the white patriarch's final redemption and province over the future.

"POST-RACIALITY," THE FUTURE AS WHITE, *AND* FOUNDATIONAL RACIAL DIFFERENCE: THE INCOHERENCE OF *I AM LEGEND* (2007)

Conventional understandings and constructions of the post-apocalyptic significance of childhood also seemingly dominate *I Am Legend*; children divinely figured and silent. The film, numbered amongst a recent resurgence in Hollywood post-apocalyptic films, likewise apparently showcases sacrificial blackness and paternal redemption to safeguard the survival of a symbolic white child. *I Am Legend*, which most avowedly reworks *Omega Man*, stars Will Smith as military scientist Robert Neville, the apparent sole human survivor of a viral plague that wipes out much of the world's population and turns the remainder into mindlessly violent "vampire-zombies." *I Am Legend* evokes 9/11 by relocating Neville to an eerily empty New York, as well as its aftermath, by cultivating anxieties about *living with* a persistent threat of terror. Set three years later, the film depicts Neville's struggle for survival and search for a cure, battling isolation, psychic disintegration, and survivor's guilt as much as the "vampire-zombie" Darkseekers that control the city by night. Traumatic memory flashbacks cumulatively reveal the harrowing evacuation death of Neville's wife and daughter; *Omega Man*'s figurative father rendered *actual*, linking professional to paternal guilt. Neville thoroughly doubts his "protective" capacity, professionally shattered through his failed lead in averting apocalyptic plague and paternally so by his daughter's death. The first scene at Neville's now empty home confirms the symbolic linking of his professional protective role with his status as father. A *Time* magazine cover on his fridge, on which a uniformed Neville is hailed as "*Savior: Soldier, Scientist,*" first obscures Neville in a family photo, and in *also* appending a question mark over his uniformed body, Neville not only questions his professional identity but effectively *erases* himself as father.

The film's (re)location to New York also invokes *TWTFTD*, with mannequins similarly arranged in a DVD store to simulate and reinvoke consumer society and practices. However, unlike Burton, Neville constructs a postracial world where "consumption" is privileged over race; even though he only engages white mannequins he is ostensibly blind to their "racial" difference.[35] This postracial ideal is thereafter personified by two other survivors, a younger Latin woman (Alice Braga) and an "adopted" white boy (Charlie Tahan). Neville will ultimately sacrifice himself to protect them and a cure, passed on before he kills himself and the attacking Darkseekers with a grenade. In *I Am Legend*, the future-identified child is again white and silent—although this time traumatically indicative of innocence lost in the apoca-

Figure 11.5. *I Am Legend*, 2007, Warner Brothers.

lypse. The black child is also again sacrificial, with Neville's daughter post-
humously facilitating Neville's redemption and thereby safeguarding the
white child.

Disrupted fatherhood is first cautiously restored when, after awaking
from an otherwise suicidal revenge act where Anna rescues him, Neville
hallucinates the return of his family. Likewise signaling his trauma, the camera, offering his psychological perspective, first shows his wife and daughter
in his kitchen before a shot from his optical point-of-view breaks the delu-
sion, as Neville "discovers" the unknown woman and child. By associating
them with his wife and daughter his hallucination establishes another ad hoc
family *and* foregrounds the opportunity to redeem the prior paternal failure
to save his daughter. Neville's self-sacrifice to save humanity, represented by
a fledgling survivors' colony envisioned by Anna, resurrects the symbolic
father as also savior. By rendering Neville as a Christ figure, *I Am Legend*
ostensibly restores normative notions of masculinity by privileging militarized masculinity, individualism, and a Christological worldview, and recov-
ers institutional masculinities as foundational in the reinvigoration of "America." In also saving this "second family," he establishes a benevolent pater-
nalist relationship with Anna and Ethan. Sacrificial death finally reunites the
father with his family, an emphasis foregrounded in a final, predeath look at
another photograph of his family *with Neville reintegrated.* Thus, Neville's
sacrifice doubly assuages "protective" professional and paternal guilt
through redemptive male sacrifice. Yet, as in *Omega Man*, children numerously *resurrect* fatherhood, with the symbolic "second child" and the deceased daughter repairing patriarchal and paternal failings. After awkwardly
adjusting to the presence of a "second family," Neville's gentle placement of
Ethan into his daughter's bed significantly acknowledges the loss of his
daughter, but in the symbolic restoration of the child to the bedroom Ethan
also revives the familial home and restores him as father—in Anna's eyes
and the audience's. Prior to this moment, childhood in *I Am Legend* is not
only conventionally sacralized, but enshrined and frozen. Not only has Neville's lost daughter's bedroom remained untouched, but he leaves a baby's
unused room completely undisturbed in an apartment he scouts for food and
provisions.[36]

The divine and pure prelapsarian child lies at the center of American
idealized cultural images of the child, with children in film often also representative of nostalgic notions of a prelapsarian state.[37] However, this is both
reiterated and complicated in *I Am Legend*. The black child, Neville's daughter, Marley, is divinely figured through her posthumous *and* prophetic redemption of the father, channeled through her repeated use of butterfly symbols, invoking her purity and alignment with nature, as well as post-apocalyptic hopes for transformation and new life. She makes butterfly symbols
prior to the apocalypse and symbolic "call" on Neville to listen to her entreat-

Figure 11.6.   *I Am Legend*, 2007, Warner Brothers.

ies to save Ethan and Anna, the figurative mother, who wears a butterfly tattoo (which signals her divinity rather than Neville's).[38] Anna and Ethan, the hope for the future to be shepherded to safety, are in this sense the "holy mother and child," notably coming from Maryland and heading north to the envisioned mountainous rural survivor's colony at Bethel, Vermont.[39] However, akin to *Omega Man*, the "holy child" is also consistently—and unsettlingly—armed post-apocalypse.

The ad hoc family gives the appearance of a post-racial American post-apocalyptic imaginary. Nama argues blackness in post-9/11 SF cinema functions "to promote an image of a racially integrated America" through "multicultural fantasies" that function to subordinate race in the service of nation and/or displace it onto the alien-monster Other.[40] Meanwhile, Brayton claims that *I Am Legend* proffers diversity "working" to eradicate a more threatening Other to "revive" the nation, resonating with post-9/11 political anxieties.[41] As in *Omega Man*, Neville's sacrifice supposedly culminates in the establishment of a "new" world through reinvigorated nostalgic notions of "childhood" and "America"; this time evidenced in the briefly depicted village-nation colony as an ideal image of the rural American foundational township.[42] However, the American "village-nation" is restored through a surviving white child, sacrificial blackness, and the symbolic destruction of the Darkseekers in Neville's final suicidal explosion. Anna hands the vial given by Neville over to a faceless white male authority (only his hands are shown). In Anna's transfer of the cure, *I Am Legend* thus recenters "whiteness," the cure not only controlled by unseen white male hands, but America's post-apocalyptic future and hope located in a white child. Paternal sacrifice finalizes the resurrection of the father, seemingly ensures a "postracial" future and the restoration of the nation as white and patriarchal, and founded on sacrificial blackness—including the death of the black child—and female subordination.

In Neville's sacrificial death and Anna's delivery of the cure into white hands, the film seemingly resolves social and cultural anxieties about the threat *of and to* difference, already disavowed through Neville's mannequins, including by prominent blackness. However, although Neville symbolically destroys the Darkseekers, their actual annihilation is merely elided. In contrast to dominant critical opinion, *I Am Legend* ultimately positions a female Darkseeker—the embodiment of otherwise horrific difference—as a redeemer, of Neville *and* humanity, as Neville recognizes: "The cure's in her blood."[43] While King observes the cure is derived from the female Other, she overlooks that it is *also* a hybrid with Neville's blood; an implicit avowal of complementary difference that complicates Nama's assertions about Hollywood science fiction's strict policing of racial difference.[44] The future also paradoxically incorporates the Other and thus the survival of difference, however disavowed. Indeed, the cure represents not only the survival of difference in America's future, but difference *as* foundational. While whiteness arguably thrives on the symbolic death of difference, *it cannot be eradicated.* Despite the idealized "postracial" construction, represented by the mannequins and a "second family," *I Am Legend* offers an ambivalent and decidedly multiracial "postracial" future, founded both in the surviving white child *and* a hybridized cure derived from the blood of a sacrificial black hero and a female vampire-zombie. These contrasting though equivalent survivals of whiteness *and* racial "otherness" finally expose the persistence of and attendant anxieties related to racial difference in America's present, exacerbated by demographic shifts away from white dominance and the subsequent ascension of Barack Obama into the presidency (which had supposedly signaled America's "postracial" reality).

Figure 11.7. *I Am Legend*, 2007, Warner Brothers.

CONCLUSION

Despite ranging from the late classical period to a recent Hollywood block-buster, child figures in these "final man" post-apocalyptic films belie their relative invisibility or marginality, even their absence. Indeed, despite the seeming conventionality of representations of "the child" and children, par-ticularly in the latter two films, children in these post-apocalyptic fictions not only hold fluid, complex meanings, but are *appropriately* revelatory figures. Children reveal the complexity, persistent *and* persisting cultural ambiva-lence of representations of race and sexuality, the ongoing tension between the disavowal and recognition of racial difference, and varying prospects for an interracial future, romance, and miscegenation. These "final man" films offer an often incoherent and uncertain admixture of child figures, including innocent children, divine and pure children, militarized children, sacrificial black children, future-identified white children, absent children, and know-ing children (that temporarily unsettle white male hegemony). More than timeless symbols of futurity, survival, and hope, child figures in post-apoca-lyptic contexts variously expose contemporary *and* persistent American ra-cial anxieties and preoccupations, including about the displacement of the (white) father, threats to white hegemony through the prominence of cultural and racial Others, and the supposed realities of postraciality in contemporary America.

I Am Legend and *Omega Man* superficially reinforce the symbolic order and conservative social regimes through the redemption of symbolic and actual fathers. Yet in *Omega Man*, white male hegemony is both anointed by the innocent child and disrupted by the black teenager's knowing identifica-tion of the patriarchal figure's monstrosity and redundancy, thereby compro-mising his final sacrificial restoration. And in *I Am Legend*, the survival and restoration of whiteness is not only supported by sacrificial blackness, in-cluding a divinely figured child, but ultimately founded on otherwise dis-avowed difference. Indeed, the persistence of racial anxieties in these post-apocalyptic narratives is most signaled through the telling omission of any real vision of the establishment of a new world—America's future either largely unrepresented or ideologically incoherent. America's Edenic return/future goes entirely unrepresented in *Omega Man* and the village-nation is only briefly (and ambivalently) depicted in *I Am Legend*—and the result of a belated reshoot following negative test audience responses to a more ambiva-lent original ending, in which the reality of the colony remains uncertain.[45] *TWTFTD* takes this further yet, completely refiguring American "civiliza-tion" by decentering white patriarchy and masculinity's dominance, and with a child at best a prospective, uncertain hope. The film's embrace of an ambiguous future was routinely read as a narrative failing upon its release, but it may more significantly acknowledge the falsity of too readily resolving

America's racial anxieties through the panacea of classical Hollywood narration. Indeed, if children and the child narratively embody futurity, *TWTFTD* radically suggests the child may not even figure in, much less symbolize, America's imagined post-apocalyptic future—and the (absent) child be all the more meaningful for it.

NOTES

1. For more on Hollywood and spectacular destruction, see Steve Neale, *Genre and Hollywood* (London: Routledge, 2000). For examinations of the persistent fascination with "witnessing," respectively, the destruction of New York and Los Angeles, see the following: Max Page, "The Future of New York's Destruction: Fantasies, Fictions, and Premonitions after 9/11," in *The New Blackwell Companion to the City*, ed. Gary Bridge and Sophie Watson (Chichester: Wiley-Blackwell, 2011); Mike Davis, *Ecology of Fear: Los Angeles and the Imagination of Disaster* (New York: Metropolitan Books, 1998).

2. Roslyn Weaver, *Apocalypse in Australian Fiction and Film: A Critical Study* (Jefferson, NC: McFarland, 2011), 14–15.

3. This expression repurposes Clover's (1992) influential designation of the "final girl" in slasher horror. Each film also showcases (self-conscious) star performances—chronologically—in Harry Belafonte's singing and political persona, Charlton Heston's star body and performance aesthetic, and Will Smith's star body.

4. The apocalyptic disaster in each is only represented in partial, decontextualized fragments, either protagonist flashbacks or found media snippets, with the focus of each film on life post-apocalypse. As per Weaver's finding on secular apocalypses' divergence from biblical antecedents, each film overemphasizes disaster and judgment, largely—though arguably tellingly—omitting any real vision of the establishment of a new world.

5. Mick Broderick, "Surviving Armageddon: Beyond the Imagination of Disaster," *Science Fiction Studies* 20, no. 3 (1993), www.depauw.edu/sfs/backissues/61/broderick61art.htm.

6. See also Laura Copier, "Preposterous Revelations: Visions of Apocalypse and Martyrdom in Hollywood Cinema, 1980–2000" (Doctoral diss., University of Amsterdam, 2008), 42–43. Copier claims Hollywood apocalypse narratives often offer "traditional" representations of gender and authority and tales of male redemption associated with "masculine ideals" of self-mastery and power.

7. Adilifu Nama, *Black Space: Imagining Race in Science Fiction Film* (Austin: University of Texas Press, 2008).

8. Debbie Olson and Andrew Scahill, eds., *Lost and Othered Children in Contemporary Cinema* (Lanham, MD: Lexington Books, 2012), ix.

9. Glen Donnar, "Gendering Apocalypse and Selling (in)Security: Redeeming Father, Performing Consumption and Securing the Home in *I Am Legend*," in *Apocalypse: Imagining the End* (Oxford: Interdisciplinary Press, 2013); "Terrified Men, Monstrous Masculinities: Representing and Recuperating American Masculinities in Contemporary Hollywood 'Terror Threat' Films" (PhD Thesis, RMIT University, 2013).

10. Debbie Olson and Giselle Rampaul, "Representations of Childhood in the Media," in *The Routledge International Handbook of Children, Adolescents and Media*, ed. Dafna Lemish (London & New York: Routledge, 2013), 23.

11. Karen Lury, *The Child in Film: Tears, Fears and Fairytales* (London: I.B. Tauris, 2010).

12. Belafonte, like Will Smith, was an iconic black crossover star, albeit one more explicitly aligned with black activism and civil rights.

13. Class and race immediately mark Burton's relationship with the mannequins. When he first carries the female mannequin out and into his car, the film offers a light-hearted satire of racial fears of predatory black male sexual behavior. And as he labors in work clothes to restore

the "civilization" that oppressed him, the white mannequins lounge in evening dress and watch over his work.

14. Susan Courtney, *Hollywood and Fantasies of Miscegenation: Spectacular Narratives of Gender and Race, 1903–1967* (Princeton & Oxford: Princeton University Press, 2005).

15. Nama, *Black Space: Imagining Race in Science Fiction Film.*

16. Stéphanie Larrieux, *"The World, the Flesh, and the Devil*: The Politics of Race, Gender, and Power in Post-Apocalyptic Hollywood Cinema," *Quarterly Review of Film and Video* 27, no. 2 (2010): 142.

17. Sarah quietly observes Burton for weeks before his mannequin "homicide." Race and sex immediately constrains and circumscribes their relationship with Sarah—in shock—saying, "Don't touch me," and shrinking back against the wall. Burton, clearly offended, replies, "Don't worry, I won't touch you," before they fall back on pre-apocalypse social roles to re-establish civilities.

18. Larrieux, *"The World, the Flesh, and the Devil*: The Politics of Race, Gender, and Power in Post-Apocalyptic Hollywood Cinema"; Courtney, *Hollywood and Fantasies of Miscegenation: Spectacular Narratives of Gender and Race, 1903–1967*. Burton as "barber" is just one of multiple race-identified "service roles" Burton performs, including as valet, waiter, cook, and nightclub entertainer.

19. The tension of persisting norms and roles erupts into (symbolic) violence when Burton angrily throws the white male mannequin off his balcony. The camera earlier approximates the mannequin's point-of-view to communicate Burton's continued feelings of black invisibility: "You look at me but you don't see me. You don't see me and you wouldn't care if you did."

20. Paul Williams, *Race, Ethnicity and Nuclear War: Representations of Nuclear Weapons and Post-Apocalyptic Worlds* (Liverpool: Liverpool University Press, 2011).

21. Larrieux, *"The World, the Flesh, and the Devil*: The Politics of Race, Gender, and Power in Post-Apocalyptic Hollywood Cinema."

22. Olson and Rampaul, "Representations of Childhood in the Media," 24–25.

23. The film is the second cinematic adaptation of Richard Matheson's influential vampire/last man 1954 novel, *I Am Legend*. Matheson's novel was numerously adapted for the screen throughout the 1960s and early 1970s. The novel addresses post–WWII atomic fears, race relations, and white cultural anxieties, particularly in relation to changes in urban populations.

24. Nama, *Black Space: Imagining Race in Science Fiction Film*. See also, Mark Gallagher, "Omega Men: Late 1960s and Early 1970s Action Heroes," in *Action Figures* (New York: Palgrave Macmillan, 2006).

25. Along with Nama, see the following: Gallagher, "Omega Men: Late 1960s and Early 1970s Action Heroes"; Janani Subramanian, "Alienating Identification Black Identity in *the Brother from Another Planet* and *I Am Legend*," *Science Fiction Film and Television* 3, no. 1 (2010).

26. For example, Matthias's now-white black militant lieutenant is castigated for his continued use of the rhetoric of black power and adherence to the "old hatreds."

27. Gallagher, "Omega Men: Late 1960s and Early 1970s Action Heroes," 85.

28. Olson and Rampaul, "Representations of Childhood in the Media," 24–25.

29. Claire Sisco King, *Washed in Blood: Male Sacrifice, Trauma, and the Cinema* (New Brunswick, NJ: Rutgers University Press, 2012), 154.

30. Nama, *Black Space: Imagining Race in Science Fiction Film*, 51.

31. Matthias even martyrs Neville with a spear. An earlier coproduction, *The Last Man on Earth* (USA/Italy, 1964, Ubaldo Ragona and Sidney Salkow), with a script originally drafted by Matheson, is the first adaptation to make the protagonist a scientist and deploy Christ-figure iconography.

32. Lisa and Neville's laughter at the folly of "control" perhaps also criticizes perceived feminist weakening of patriarchal institutions and sexual codes. Yet Lisa also parodies sexual politics, ironically enacting pre-1960s domestic sexual codes by playfully asking whether she can borrow Neville's credit cards to go shopping.

33. Nama, *Black Space: Imagining Race in Science Fiction Film*, 43; Gallagher, "Omega Men: Late 1960s and Early 1970s Action Heroes," 106.

34. Nama, *Black Space: Imagining Race in Science Fiction Film*, 49.

35. Postraciality is simplistically perceived to be a feature of Smith's screen persona. For an extended, more critical consideration of Smith's relation to race, see Donnar, "Terrified Men, Monstrous Masculinities: Representing and Recuperating American Masculinities in Contemporary Hollywood 'Terror Threat' Films." The prospect of sex (and children) also only resides in the lifeless ideal of commoditized and sexualized (white) mannequin "bodies"—even after the arrival of a female survivor. Neville's fetishization of these inanimate bodies is especially evident when he spies a "sexy" female mannequin perusing the adult section, signaling her availability and his sublimated desires.

36. While Neville's martyrdom marks his Christ-figuration, many scholars mistakenly claim the cure is derived solely from his blood.

37. Debbie Olson, "Little Burton Blue: Tim Burton and the Product(ion) of Color in the Fairy Tale Films *The Nightmare before Christmas* (1993) and *The Corpse Bride* (2005)," in *Portrayals of Children in Popular Culture: Fleeting Images*, ed. Vibiana Cvetkovic and Debbie Olson (Lanham, MD: Lexington Books, 2013), 184–85.

38. For more on the overall ambivalence of butterflies, both associated with the final emergence of a reborn "America" and visually identified with the lead Darkseeker *as* a butterfly, see Donnar, "Terrified Men, Monstrous Masculinities: Representing and Recuperating American Masculinities in Contemporary Hollywood 'Terror Threat' Films."

39. Perhaps this more properly renders Neville as Joseph rather than Christ; that is, defending the cure rather than being the cure.

40. Nama, *Black Space: Imagining Race in Science Fiction Film*, 40–41.

41. Brayton, "The Racial Politics of Disaster and Dystopia in *I Am Legend*," 74–75.

42. Humanity's continuation again requires fleeing the city, overrun by the racial/ideological Other, for the countryside.

43. Females, initially demonized in the film, are numerously redefined as *redeemers*. They (including his dog, Samantha) numerously rescue Neville, carry the cure—by blood, faith, and hand—and facilitate his heroism. For more on this underexamined aspect of the film, see Donnar, Op Cit.

44. King, *Washed in Blood: Male Sacrifice, Trauma, and the Cinema.*

45. For a detailed consideration of the significance of the two endings, see Donnar, "Gendering Apocalypse and Selling (in)Security: Redeeming Father, Performing Consumption and Securing the Home in *I Am Legend*."

BIBLIOGRAPHY

Brayton, Sean. "The Racial Politics of Disaster and Dystopia in *I Am Legend*." *The Velvet Light Trap* 67 (Spring 2011): 66–76.

Broderick, Mick. "Surviving Armageddon: Beyond the Imagination of Disaster." *Science Fiction Studies* 20, no. 3 (1993). www.depauw.edu/sfs/backissues/61/broderick61art.htm.

Copier, Laura. "Preposterous Revelations: Visions of Apocalypse and Martyrdom in Hollywood Cinema, 1980–2000." Doctoral diss., University of Amsterdam, 2008.

Courtney, Susan. *Hollywood and Fantasies of Miscegenation: Spectacular Narratives of Gender and Race, 1903–1967*. Princeton & Oxford: Princeton University Press, 2005.

Davis, Mike. *Ecology of Fear: Los Angeles and the Imagination of Disaster*. New York: Metropolitan Books, 1998.

Donnar, Glen. "Terrified Men, Monstrous Masculinities: Representing and Recuperating American Masculinities in Contemporary Hollywood 'Terror Threat' Films." PhD Thesis, RMIT University, 2013.

———. "Gendering Apocalypse and Selling (in)Security: Redeeming Father, Performing Consumption and Securing the Home in *I Am Legend*." In *Apocalypse: Imagining the End*. Oxford: Interdisciplinary Press, 2013.

Gallagher, Mark. "Omega Men: Late 1960s and Early 1970s Action Heroes." In *Action Figures*, 81–111. New York: Palgrave Macmillan, 2006.

King, Claire Sisco. *Washed in Blood: Male Sacrifice, Trauma, and the Cinema*. New Brunswick, NJ: Rutgers University Press, 2012.

Larrieux, Stéphanie. *"The World, the Flesh, and the Devil*: The Politics of Race, Gender, and Power in Post-Apocalyptic Hollywood Cinema." *Quarterly Review of Film and Video* 27, no. 2 (2010): 133–43.

Lury, Karen. *The Child in Film: Tears, Fears and Fairytales*. London: I.B. Tauris, 2010.

Nama, Adilifu. *Black Space: Imagining Race in Science Fiction Film*. Austin: University of Texas Press, 2008.

Neale, Steve. *Genre and Hollywood*. London: Routledge, 2000.

Olson, Debbie. "Little Burton Blue: Tim Burton and the Product(ion) of Color in the Fairy Tale Films *The Nightmare before Christmas* (1993) and *The Corpse Bride* (2005)." In *Portrayals of Children in Popular Culture: Fleeting Images*, edited by Vibiana Cvetkovic and Debbie Olson, 183–93. Lanham, MD: Lexington Books, 2013.

Olson, Debbie, and Giselle Rampaul. "Representations of Childhood in the Media." In *The Routledge International Handbook of Children, Adolescents and Media*, edited by Dafna Lemish, 23–30. London & New York: Routledge, 2013.

Olson, Debbie, and Andrew Scahill, eds. *Lost and Othered Children in Contemporary Cinema*. Lanham, MD: Lexington Books, 2012.

Page, Max. "The Future of New York's Destruction: Fantasies, Fictions, and Premonitions after 9/11." In *The New Blackwell Companion to the City*, edited by Gary Bridge and Sophie Watson, 305–16. Chichester: Wiley-Blackwell, 2011.

Subramanian, Janani. "Alienating Identification Black Identity in *The Brother from Another Planet* and *I Am Legend*." *Science Fiction Film and Television* 3, no. 1 (2010): 37–56.

Weaver, Roslyn. *Apocalypse in Australian Fiction and Film: A Critical Study*. Jefferson, NC: McFarland, 2011.

Williams, Paul. *Race, Ethnicity and Nuclear War: Representations of Nuclear Weapons and Post-Apocalyptic Worlds*. Liverpool: Liverpool University Press, 2011.

Chapter Twelve

"Not the Little Blonde Innocent You Picture"

Race and "Innocent" Girlhoods in The Hunger Games *Fandom*

Cassandra L. Jones

A study published in the *Journal of Personality and Social Psychology* in February 2014, "The Essence of Innocence: Consequences of Dehumanizing Black Children" came to disturbing conclusions that many in the black community had long known to be true: that innocence, a protection afforded to children that typically gives them the benefit of the doubt when it comes to criminality, is not granted to black children in equal measure as it is given to white children. While the study focuses on black boys in contexts in which they are dehumanized and points to a decided gap in the research as concerns African American girls, it certainly calls attention to the importance of examining the various discourses concerning blackness, girlhood, and innocence in American culture. These varying discourses about black girlhood can be found circulating in and around the film adaptation of *The Hunger Games* and a highly publicized series of racist tweets in which fans responded to seeing Rue as a black girl.

The figure of Rue in the 2012 film adaptation of *The Hunger Games* is the height of "innocence." Depicted as a wood nymph whose knowledge of the land allows her to effectively conceal herself and utilize creatures to defend herself when necessary, she is starkly contrasted with the gang of "career tributes" who actively hunt their prey. Rue's defensive strategy marks her as virtuous in a corrupt world. Her death in the Games highlights the cruelty of a government who demands the yearly deaths of its children, and inspires the outlying districts to rise in rebellion. Despite the film's representation of black girlhood as one of both purity and power, any reading of race and gender must also take account of the curious fan response in the weeks leading up to the film's release.

Upon viewing the film's trailer, some fans took to the Internet with disappointment, shock, and even outrage that Rue had been cast in the film as an African American girl. Despite the character's "dark skin" in the novel, it was not the translation of her skin tone from dark to light that incensed fans. Indeed, it was the blackness of this young figure whose death inspires a revolution that several fans were not able to accept. Tweets such as "call me racist but when I found out rue was black her death wasn't as sad" (Jashper Paras, Twitter post, March 26, 2012. http://twitter.com/jashperparas) reveals that Rue's death, once portrayed by a literal, rather than figurative black body, is no longer worthy of the audience's empathy.

What this moment exposes is a snapshot of contemporary racism in the "postracial" present. While this fresh-faced, delicate young girl might otherwise be read as "angelic," particularly when thrust into the post-apocalyptic landscape of the battlefield, these tweets reveal how actor Amandla Stenberg's blackness limits readings of her hegemonic femininity and age as innocent, inspiring, or even grievable. Using Judith Butler's notion of the grievable life, this chapter examines the competing discourses of race, gender, and age at work in the film and the online fan responses to expose how racism impacts our ability to accord full humanity to the black body, even when that body is swathed in discourses of innocence.

The Hunger Games tells the story of Katniss Everdeen, a sixteen-year-old girl who lives in District 12 of Panem. After a civil war between the wealthy Capitol and the poorer, outlying districts which had completely destroyed the most distant, District 13, the Hunger Games were instituted as a punishment and a reminder of the power of the Capitol. Each year, two tributes from each district, a boy and a girl between the ages of twelve and eighteen, are required to participate in a televised fight to the death. While some districts, like 12, are reluctant for anyone to participate and run a lottery to choose, other districts have "career tributes," children who have trained all their lives for participation in the Games and gladly volunteer. Fighting in a specially designed arena filled with deadly genetically altered flora and fauna and run by a Games Master who can add other "challenges" along the way, the tributes are at war both with each other and the environment.

Living with her younger sister and mother, Katniss acts as the primary caregiver to the family, illegally hunting animals outside of the borders of the district and trading with black market vendors for food and other supplies in the starving district. Katniss is particularly close with her twelve-year-old sister Primrose. When Prim's name is called in the Reaping, the lottery in which tributes are drawn from a pool, Katniss immediately volunteers as tribute and joins the Hunger Games in her sister's stead.

The tributes are transported to the Games in the Capitol, where the Hunger Games are a highly anticipated and highly rated source of entertainment for its citizens. In the Capitol, they are groomed and clothed, richly fed, and, in a nod to reality shows and their construction of good and evil characters and edited story lines, are instructed in how to best construct their in-game identities. Each tribute is provided with a stylist, a public relations consultant, and a mentor, a "winner" of an earlier Games from their district, and paraded through a press junket to introduce themselves and their specific abilities to the viewing Capitol audience.

While preparing for the Games, Katniss meets Rue, a small, gentle, African American girl who very much reminds her of Prim. This girl later saves her life inside the Games arena when Katniss is driven up a tree by a group of career tributes. Knocking down a hive of genetically engineered wasps that Rue points out allows the two to escape further into the arena and form an alliance. Rue, a Harvester from District 11, a farming district, has skills overlooked by the other tributes. She is small and nimble, thus able to navigate trees with ease and minimal detection. Her knowledge of the mockingjay, a genetically engineered animal who imitates sounds and songs, allows Rue to communicate with Katniss across distances without speaking, while her intimate knowledge of plant life is useful in healing Katniss's wounds.

Unfortunately, the alliance is broken when Rue is killed by another tribute. As Rue lies dying, Katniss sings to her, and, after she dies, covers her body with white flowers in a gesture of mourning and defiance. She holds up three fingers in District 12's gesture of farewell to Rue. Simultaneously broadcast in each of the districts, the gesture is mirrored by viewers in District 11 gathered to watch on a screen in the city center. The loss of Rue's life, the loving way in which Katniss mourns her even while in a battle to the death, the gesture of farewell and unity in grief immediately set off a riot in which the police are attacked and district offices connecting them to the Capitol are destroyed. In these moments, the power of Rue's death is revealed.

If we are to understand the depiction of Rue in the film as innocent and therefore a figure worthy of grief, we must first unpack the term "innocent." Despite contemporary debates about the "mean girl," Western culture continues to draw on constructions of childhood as innocent that emerged in the late eighteenth and early nineteenth centuries. As Robin Bernstein notes, these innocent children were understood as "sinless, absent of sexual feelings, and oblivious to worldly concerns." This view emerged from various philosophical traditions, "including Lockean tabula rasa and the Rousseauian youth who was at essence an uncorrupted element of nature." Indeed, childhood innocence encompassed not simply the absence of sexual feeling, but also the ability to redeem adults with their holiness.[1] In fact, children were seen not just as innocent, but rather as the embodiment of innocence itself. This construction replaced previous Calvinist constructions of childhood as inherently sinful with the idea of childhood as a time of innocence. This notion of embodied innocence was also imbued with race. As Bernstein notes, this "angelic" childhood was raced and indeed, that race was white.

An example of this is Little Eva of *Uncle Tom's Cabin*, the "emblematic child-angel of the nineteenth century."[2] Her innocence was (racially) marked by her "golden-brown" hair, "deep blue eyes," her fondness for the color white in clothing, the "blizzard of white of her funeral," and the flowers that filled the room. Piety, purity, and delicateness all mark her figure and count-less other "heroines of sentimental fiction" in the nineteenth century as inno-cent.

Where Little Eva's innocence and whiteness are tightly bound, Rue, both in the novel and in the film are black, yet remain marked as innocent by similar tropes. *The Hunger Games* film draws on this history of innocence in its attempt to showcase political cruelty. Stenberg's soft voice, demure car-riage, and the blue dress with puffy sleeves, white socks, and matching Mary Janes she wears while being interviewed before the Games, all highlight her delicate, sensitive nature. The defensive strategies she employs in training and the actual Games place Rue as a morally pure figure unwilling to use violence. She functions in stark contrast to the lustful violence of the career tributes, whose hearts have been hardened by their training. Indeed, her knowledge of the healing power of plants and the special skills of animals position her as one who appreciates and celebrates life rather than looking to destroy it. This as well marks her moral purity and symbolic innocence. And, just as in Little Eva's funeral, Katniss covers Rue's lifeless body with white flowers, symbolically emphasizing the purity of her spirit. It is this very innocence that makes her such an important figure in the film. It is her innocence marked in these ways that underscores the cruelty of the Capitol's regime. Rue's fictional death makes her a martyr that serves as the catalyst for a society-wide civil rights movement.

Innocence and the death of innocent figures can be powerful political symbols, particularly when innocence means needing "protection from harsh adult-like treatment."[3] Although, innocence has historically been marked as white, as evidenced by Little Eva, there have been historical moments in which that innocence has extended to black girls. In 1963, at the moment of the September 15 bombing of the 16th Street Baptist Church in Birmingham, Alabama, in which four girls were killed and many were injured, media accounts of the event focused primarily on the deceased, highlighting their innocence and employing it in service of the aims of the civil rights move-ment. The murder of Cynthia Wesley, fourteen; Denise McNair, eleven; Carol Robertson, fourteen; and Addie Mae Collins, fourteen, in the bombing was discussed in such a way as to emphasize their blamelessness, increasing the sense of urgency surrounding the need for federal civil rights legislation.

We can see this rhetorical positioning quite clearly in the coverage of the attack by the *New York Times*. Unlike other journalists covering the story, Claude Sitton's article did not focus on the "hysterics" of the black residents after the attack, but rather included the detail that "The four girls killed in the blast had just heard Mrs. Ella C. Demand, their teacher, complete the Sunday school lesson for the day. The subject was 'The Love That Forgives.'" Playing on sympathetic Americans' shock that a church should be bombed, on a Sunday no less, Sitton provides a picture of the girls as pious and pure, learning of the power of love and forgiveness at almost the very moment of their death. Additionally, Sitton describes the position of their bodies as "huddled together beneath a pile of masonry debris."[4] Emphasizing a sense of fear in their last moments, Sitton stresses the innocence of these girls in their Sunday best and juxtaposes it with the cruelty of the perpetrators of the crime.

A piece written by the United Press International and run by the *Washington Post* was even more sentimental in its coverage of the attack. It focused equally on the destruction of innocent lives as much it did on the sacred site of the church, letting the destruction of the church itself stand in for the loss of human life. While the article does not provide exact details about the positions of the bodies, the author chooses instead to paint an image of bloodied and destroyed nursery space: "Parts of brightly painted children's furniture were strewn about in one Sunday School room, and blood stained the floors." Quotes such as "The only stained glass window in the church that remained in its frame showed Christ leading a group of little children. The face of Christ was blown out" help to confer the black girls with an angelic quality, associated as they are here with a caring Christ. This quote simultaneously depicts the bombers both in opposition to the love of Jesus and as cruelly and coldly destructive.

This same cruelty and sense of horror is evoked in an article covering the ongoing FBI investigation nearly one year later in the *Saturday Evening Post*:

> In all the hatred and fear and violence that has marked the present racial upheaval in America, no single incident has so shocked the conscience of the country as the bombing of Birmingham's 16th Street Baptist Church last September 15. The explosion under the church stairway at 10:22 that morning hurled rubble for blocks, injured 19 people and killed instantly four young Negro girls inside the church. The wanton, brutal crime sickened America on both sides of the Mason-Dixon line and gave new impetus to the drive for civil-rights legislation. As nothing else had done—or perhaps could do—it epitomized the ugliness of racial conflict.[5]

McMillan emphasizes the power of this moment and the urgent need for federal intervention in a situation growing increasingly dire by the turn. Indeed, Martin Luther King, Jr., himself called attention to these girls' deaths to highlight the cruelty of a government who had turned a blind eye to the previous twenty-one bombings of African American property in Birmingham: "the blood of four little children . . . is on your hands. Your irresponsible and misguided actions have created in Birmingham and Alabama the atmosphere that has induced continued violence and now murder" (Six Dead). Indeed, the portrayal of these girls as innocent victims was a powerful moment in the civil rights struggle. And yet, if the discourses of girlish innocence were so strongly associated with whiteness, both then, and as I argue, now, how did these girls come to find themselves associated with this quality?

The time and location of their murder, Sunday morning in a church, seems to play a key factor in the attribution of innocence to the Birmingham four. The *Washington Post* article's emphasis on the church as the site of the tragedy seems to suggest the desecration of the church is as important, or perhaps even more important, than the death of the children. The race of the children is certainly erased as the reader is asked to consider, not the image of the black girls' mangled bodies, but the image of an almost certainly white stained-glass Jesus, his head blown off by the blast. Indeed, multiple articles depict the church as a site of peace (and peaceful blacks within it), while the space outside the church is depicted as a site of chaos (and chaotic, "hysterical" uncontrolled blacks). Indeed, these girls were certainly not the first children to be killed by whites in the South, yet the sensational aspect of their murder in a church on a day of service served to raise the profile of the attack while journalists heightened the horror for readers by emphasizing the girls' innocence.

Lest we think that sympathetic reporters were inclined to speak about all black children during the civil rights movement in this way, attributing equal amounts of innocence, we might briefly examine the Children's Crusade earlier that year and also in Birmingham. Widely reported as the largest segregation protest Birmingham had ever seen, the May 2, 1963, march was composed primarily of teens and children, boys and girls, some as young as five years old. Reports of the exact number of marchers varied between four hundred and eight hundred, but what is certain is that many of the reports tend to reveal a construction of black childhood that is more in line with that of the recently published study, "The Essence of Innocence" and the tweets in which a black Rue is a Rue that cannot be grieved; that is to say, a construction of black childhood without innocence.

Robert Gordon's coverage of the children's march on May 3, 1963, "Waves of Young Negroes March in Birmingham Segregation Protest," curiously focuses on the large numbers of protestors, leaving the ages of the protestors largely unremarked upon. Aside from the title, the article uses the word "youth" or "young" only four times and leaves the most salacious detail, that protestors as young as five years old were participating, to the very last. Indeed, Gordon mentions not just the children marching, but highlights additional (adult) protestors in front of downtown businesses carrying signs reading, "No Dignity, No Dollars" and "Segregation Sold Here." The conflation of the two groups reconfigures the marchers not as children, but as adult-like. As Philip Atiba Goff's recent study claims, black children are often dehumanized and in those situations, "children can be treated with adult severity."[6]

This may seem an odd reading when so many have remarked upon the infantilization of African Americans that so frequently appears in constructions of blackness. To be sure, constructions of marginalized groups are often contradictory. Black women, for instance, might be depicted as either the asexual mammy or a hypersexual Jezebel figure. But, perhaps these ideas may not be as contradictory as they appear. It is the infantilization of blackness that refuses to acknowledge a difference in age between the children marching and the adults protesting in front of the stores. It is important to note, however, that the infantilization of blacks is only useful in promoting an image of docility. When confronted with the politically agitating black figure, this slippage between youth and adulthood no longer signals that docility, nor does it invoke the discourse of the beneficent slave master or the need to protect African Americans from themselves. The protesting black figure, be it child or adult, does not "deserve" protection. In this sense, the slippage between child and adult in the case of political confrontation serves to limit the conference of innocence upon black children's bodies.

The black figure associated with political protest, and its ability to block access to innocence, is, perhaps, one of the reasons fans responded with such virulently racist tweets despite the secondary visual and aural work to construct Rue as a symbol of innocence and virtue in *The Hunger Games* film. Rue is, after all, a key figure whose death acts as a flashpoint that initiates the revolution depicted in the rest of the series. When faced with the visualization of Rue as an innocent, yet revolutionary, black girl, these fans were unable to accept what seemed to be contradictory messages. They tweeted their disappointment claiming that the film was both "ruined" and that they had lost interest in seeing it: "why does rue have to be black not gonna lie kinda ruined the movie" (Maggie Mcdonnell, Twitter post, March 26, 2012. http://twitter.com/maggie_mcd11), and "I was pumped about the Hunger Games. Until I learned a black girl was playing Rue" (John Knox IV, Twitter post, March 26, 2012. http://twitter.com/johnnyknoxIV).

Perhaps the most troubling of the tweets were Jashper Paras's (Paras, Twitter post) and Alana Paul's tweet (Alana Paul, Twitter post, March 26, 2012. http://twitter.com/sw4Q), "Awkward moment when Rue is some black girl and not the little blonde innocent you picture." What these two tweets reveal is the power of white privilege and the way in which Amandla Stenberg's race, functions as marked, blocking Paras's empathy for the character. Her life is no longer as meaningful as it once was. His grief for this fictional character is no longer as deeply felt. Paul's tweet demonstrates she initially imagined Rue as a "little blonde innocent." While she does not specifically mention a lack of empathy for Rue, Paul's use of the word "innocent" in contrast to Amandla Stenberg's blackness reveals a deeper message about who is afforded innocence in American culture.

Writing of how we value life in times of war in order to justify state-sanctioned killing, Butler asserts that war divides "populations into those who are grievable and those who are not."[7] It is our inability to recognize lives politically, nationally, or ideologically different from our own that causes us to "feel horror in the face of certain losses but indifference or even righteousness in light of others.[8] The lives cannot be mourned because they are not recognized as lives at all. "An ungrievable life is one that cannot be mourned because it has never lived, that is, it has never counted as a life at all."[9] Although Butler is speaking of nationalism during war, the notion of the grievable life extends beyond the frame of war and is a useful tool for unpacking these tweets to consider how race, childhood, and innocence converge in American culture, leading some lives to be construed as more grievable than others.

Indeed, this dovetails with Goff and colleagues' argument concerning the link between dehumanization and sanctioned violence. Building on the "Negro-ape metaphor" that has historically constructed not just blackness as animalistic, but blacks themselves as animals, their study revealed that white participants who were subliminally exposed to images of apes before being shown a video of police beating a black man were more likely to endorse that beating, "despite the extremity of the violence." When the suspect was white or they had not been primed by the ape image, participants did not endorse the beating.[10] Just as in war, the enemy is dehumanized so as to facilitate the violence meted against him, so too does dehumanization play a role in lack of attribution of innocence in their study of black boys.

When we add the dimension of gender to this equation, we can trace additional ways in which the black child's body is refused innocence, in this case sexual innocence. While nineteenth-century innocent (white) girlhood was depicted as the absence of sexual feeling, black girls are not afforded this same notion. However, just as there is a slippage between adult and child in the case of the protesting black figure, a similar conflation of black womanhood and girlhood occurs when it comes to sexual innocence. As Dionne P. Stevens suggests, "The good, innocent, virginal girl continues to be an idealized image of womanhood associated with white females, but unattainable for African American females."[11] Indeed, Patricia Hill Collins, bell hooks, and many other scholars have discussed the controlling image of the Jezebel as a key figure of discrimination against black women that highlights perceptions of black women's sexuality as deviant. In cases of sexual assault, in which women's complicity is always questioned, ("she was asking for it by wearing a short skirt," etc.), the sexually insatiable Jezebel results in a construction of black women as inherently un-rapeable. Sex with a black woman, according to this stereotype, is never forcible no matter the circumstances.

Toni Irving's study of rape cases in Philadelphia from 1995 to 2000 demonstrates how this circulating discourse has devastating consequences for black women. In this five-year-period, two thousand rape cases of low-income black women were ignored by the Sex Crimes Unit of the Philadelphia police department , which used the noncriminal code 2701 "investigation of person" to overlook cases in which the victim was "perceived to be lying."[12] The majority of the cases given these throwaway codes "tended to be poor, transient women, with histories of drug abuse or petty criminal records."[13] In the eyes of the Philadelphia Sex Crimes Unit, these women, by virtue of their race, class, and personal history, were not seen as credible witnesses and as a result were denied access to justice. As Irving notes, "That poor black women's experiences are excluded from the legal register positions them as persons without legitimate sexual identities, not unlike their status during slavery.[14]

However, it is not just black women who suffer from the controlling image of the sexually available Jezebel when it comes to establishing their credibility as a victim. We must also consider the case of seven-year-old Jesine Williams. The conflation of black girlhood and womanhood allowed assumptions about the sexual availability of black women to extend to young Jesine as well. Abducted while playing outside her babysitter's house, Williams was driven to a park, raped, and then pushed out of the car in the snow. Found by a female stranger and taken to the house of Dorothea Arrington, Jesine recounted the details of the rape and identified her assailant as Jasper Washington, a man her aunt used to date, to Arrington and police officer Sheila Pressley. Pressley later wrote up the report as a case of a lost child, made no mention of rape allegations, and then dropped Williams off at a neighbor's house because her mother was not at home.

As Irving notes, "Jesine's case reveals the legitimating aims that politically construct black females from girlhood as sexual subjects outside the scope of the kinds of experiences that stand as normative."[15] Despite her lack of problematic history that tainted the perception of the other women's status as credible victims, what we can see here is how, as a result of circulating discourses of black women's hypersexuality, Jesine had access to neither credibility, nor to the virtuous (sexual) "innocence" that is frequently associated with girlhood in American culture. In fact, in his own defense in the press, her attacker made of use of these discourses, claiming that "[Jesine] kept lying on a lot of people."[16] As a result of these discourses, Jesine's victimhood is discredited, made unrecognizable, because her life itself is unrecognizable as a life within the confines of white, middle-class, hetero-normative discourses. Her life is ungrievable. She is one of the "'subjects' who are not quite recognizable as subjects . . . 'lives' that are not quite—or, indeed, are never—recognized as lives.[17] Indeed, Irving herself seconds this claim, asserting that this policing procedure "highlights a race- and class-based frame through which sexual assault victims' lives are viewed as outside of a recognizable human community."[18]

The report of the "lost child" also indicates the lack of grievability of Jesine Williams's life based on her race and class in the eyes of the law. According to Butler, war leads "to a specific exploitation of targeted populations, of lives that are not quite lives, cast as 'destructible' and 'ungrievable.' Such populations are 'lose-able,' or can be forfeited, precisely because they are framed as already being lost or forfeited; they are cast as threats to human life as we know it rather than as living populations."[19] Living in a neighborhood made up of so-called million dollar blocks ("blocks where enough people from the same street are imprisoned such that the total cost of their incarceration exceeds one million dollars"), as a poor, black girl, Jesine was already seen as a lost cause.[20] Her neighborhood, which in contemporary conservative rhetoric is constructed as a drain on society that threatens the very fabric of the country, places her as a not-quite subject whose life is already "lose-able." As a result, she has diminished claims to justice and is framed as existing outside of a recognizably human life. Thus, we see the devastating result of these discourses surrounding black women and girls' sexuality.

While Rue is not a victim of sexual assault in the book or the film, Jesine William's story and this construction of black women's and girls' lives as outside of "a recognizable human community" certainly help to explain why when Jashper Paras "found out rue was black her death wasn't as sad" (Paras, Twitter post). In addition, when faced with this history of systemic denial of full subjectivity and access justice, we see how telling it is that Alana Paul's tweet unites childhood innocence, and its attendant lack of sexual awareness or feeling, with whiteness.

This association of "innocence" with whiteness is not the only tweet through which we might trace how Stenberg's race "spoils" the reading of Rue and, subsequently, the film for these fans. Indeed, we see evidence of this lack of attributed (sexual) innocence in EJ Santiago's tweet: HOW IN THE WORLD ARE THEY GOING TO MAKE RUE A FREAKIN BLACK BITCH IN THE MOVIE ?!?!?!??! lolol not to be racist buuuuut…I'm angry now ;o" (EJ Santiago, Twitter post, March 26, 2012. http://twitter.com/frea-kinej). His use of the phrase "black bitch" to describe a twelve-year-old

African American girl demonstrates the ways in which black girls are not afforded childhood innocence, a status which denotes their lives as worthy of protection as well as access to justice when wronged.[21] Her skin color precedes her and the conflation of black girlhood and womanhood under the sign of the Jezebel has already granted her a status aged enough to be considered a "bitch." In order to more fully understand how this lack of attributed innocence denies Stenberg the status of a grievable life, we must unpack the term "bitch."

It is important to note that "bitch" and, particularly, "black bitch" have multiple meanings. While the standard derogatory use of "bitch" signals the dismissal of a woman through claims of an overly aggressive nature, perhaps that the woman acts too much like a man in the assertion of her (nonsexual) desire,[22] "black bitch" also carries with it connotations about reputed sexual voraciousness and availability of black women. Discussing the evolution of controlling images of and sexual scripts for black women, both Patricia Hill Collins and Dionne P. Stevens point to the "gangster bitch" or the "black bitch" as the representational inheritor of the earlier Jezebel. The black bitch is devious and manipulates men with her sexuality.[23] The sexualized black bitch is typified by the female hustler, "a materialistic woman who is willing to sell, rent, or use her sexuality to get whatever she wants."[24] Indeed, as Collins notes, these images of objectified black women appear increasingly across media platforms, particularly in contemporary music videos in which legions of nameless, scantily clad women "dance, strut, and serve as visually appealing props for the rapper in question."[25] Rarely acknowledged in these videos as individuals, these women are reduced to their bodies and the bodies themselves are interchangeable, becoming the latest in "a history of the display of nameless, naked Black female bodies in Western society, from the display of enslaved African women on the auction block under chattel slavery to representations of Black female bodies in contemporary film and music videos."[26]

This namelessness of black women recalls the language of Alana Paul's tweet, in which "some black girl" is playing Rue as opposed "the little blonde innocent" Paul had imagined. Her use of the word "some" refuses to individuate Stenberg, whereas the imaginary blonde Rue is identified both by the use of multiple adjectives to describe her ("little," "blonde," and "innocent") and as an individual in Paul's use of the article "*the* (little blonde innocent)."

It is this anonymity, this inability or refusal to individuate Stenberg, in a culture that highly values individualism, that again demonstrates how Stenberg, and now by extension, Rue, is unrecognizable as a subject and is, therefore, ungrievable. The grievability of a life is dependent upon the ability of mourners to individuate that life and provide testimony to it. At the same time, mourning highlights the connections within a community as mourners testify to the ties forged as the result of a life lived. Grief is an act that both "bring[s] to the fore . . . relational ties,"[27] revealing how we are connected to one another and that represents a transformation of self as the result of the loss of that specific connection, marking both a sense of communal identity and individuation within that community. However, Stenberg/Rue is denied this connection in both Paul's tweet in which she is simply "some black girl" and Jashper Para's tweet in which, as the result of her blackness "her death wasn't as sad." Again, these tweets reveal that her life, by virtue of her race and the social meanings attached to that race, is not a life recognized as such and therefore carries less importance. She is not "the little blonde innocent," but rather is "some black girl," and the stunning difference between the value of these two lives creates the "awkward moment" to which Alana Paul refers.

These various tweets concerning Stenberg's casting and the fans' inability to enjoy the film or feel the depth of Rue's loss as keenly reveal the contours of a specific aspect of contemporary racism in which African American girls are denied[28] the innocence associated with whiteness. It is this inability to associate innocence with black girlhood which diminishes the fans' ability to grieve her and therefore experience the full power of her death within the film. As a life ungrievable, hers, like many of other black children, is a life that is expendable without remorse or contemplation. I have primarily explored the aspects of innocence related to the protesting black figure, sexual innocence, and slippage between constructions of the black child and adult, but it would also be worthwhile to consider how these tweets reflect aspects of criminal innocence also denied to African Americans as the result of systemic racism. To do so would reveal how discourses of innocence and criminality impact the lives of young men like Trayvon Martin, Kimani Gray, and Jordan Davis as well as how we interpret and manage the losses of these young lives.

NOTES

1. Bernstein, 4.
2. Bernstein, 4.
3. Goff et al., 527.
4. Sitton.
5. McMillan, 15.
6. Goff et al., 527.
7. Butler, 38.
8. Butler, *Frames of War*, 41–42.
9. Butler, 38.
10. Goff et al., 527.
11. Stevens, 4.
12. Irving, 106.
13. McCoy and Fazlollah, qtd. in Irving, 106.
14. Irving, 104.
15. Irving, 107.
16. Fazollah, qtd. in Irving, 107.

17. Butler, *Frames of War*, 4.
18. Irving, 104.
19. Butler, *Frames of War*, 31.
20. Irving, 101.
21. Goff et al., 527.
22. However, Patricia Hill Collins also identifies positive connotations to the word "bitch" in which a "Black bitch," such as Pam Grier, uses her "looks, sexuality, and intellect, and/or aggression in service to African American communities."
23. Collins, *Black Sexual Politics*, 126.
24. Collins, *Black Sexual Politics*, 127.
25. Collins, *Black Sexual Politics*, 128.
26. Collins, *Black Sexual Politics*, 128–129.
27. Butler, *Precarious Life*, 32.
28. While I have used language like denial in this chapter, I do not wish to suggest that the cure for this social illness is to simply attribute innocence to black girls as well as white girls, effectively ending this state of denial. Childhood innocence, in which children are seen as devoid of sexual feeling or curiosity, leads to its own set of issues, not the least of which is the moral panic around the sexualization of children/teens and the contemporary replication of nineteenth-century fears about the intrusion of working-class sexuality into middle-class cultural landscapes.

BIBLIOGRAPHY

Bernstein, Robin. *Racial Innocence: Performing American Childhood from Slavery to Civil Rights*. New York: New York University Press, 2011. Print.

Butler, Judith. *Frames of War: When Is Life Grievable?* London: Verso, 2009. Print.

_____. *Precarious Life: The Powers of Mourning and Violence*. London: Verso, 2006. Print.

Collins, Patricia Hill. *Black Feminist Thought: Knowledge, Consciousness, and the Politics of Empowerment*. 2nd Ed. New York: Routledge, 2000. Print.

_____. *Black Sexual Politics: African Americans, Gender, and the New Racism*. New York: Routledge, 2005. Print.

Egan, R. Danielle, and Gail Louise Hawkes. "Sexuality, Youth, and the Perils of Endangered Innocence: How History Can Help Us Get Past the Panic," *Gender and Education* 24, 3 (2012): 269–284. Print.

Giroux, Henry A. *Stealing Innocence: Youth, Corporate Power, and the Politics of Culture*. London: Palgrave Mcmillan, 2000.

Goff, Philip Atiba, et al. "The Essence of Innocence: Consequences of Dehumanizing Black Children," *Journal of Personality and Social Psychology* 106, 4 (2014): 526–545. *EBSCO*. Web. 3 April 2014.

Gordon, Robert. "Waves of Young Negroes March in Birmingham Segregation Protest" *The Washington Post*. 3 May 1963. Web. 1 April 2014.

Hendrick, Harry. "Constructions and Reconstructions of British Childhood: An Interpretive Survey, 1800 to the Present" *Constructing and Reconstructing Childhood: Contemporary Issues in the Sociological Study of Childhood*, eds. Allison James and Alan Prout. London: UK Falmer Press, 2005. 33–60. Print.

Irving, Toni. "Decoding Black Women: Policing Practices and Rape Prosecution on the Streets of Philadelphia," *National Women's Association Journal* 20, 2 (2008): 100–120. Print.

Kitzinger, Jenny. "Who are you kidding? Children, Power, and the Struggle against Sexual Abuse" *Constructing and Reconstructing Childhood: Contemporary Issues in the Sociological Study of Childhood*, eds. Allison James and Alan Prout. London: UK Falmer Press, 2005, 161–186. Print.

Knox IV, John. Twitter post, March 26, 2012. http://twitter.com/johnnyknowiv.

Mcdonnell, Maggie. Twitter post, March 26, 2012. http://twitter.com/maggie_mcd11.

McMillan, George. "The Birmingham Bomber." *Saturday Evening Post*. 6/6/1964, 237, 22: 15–19. 5p.

Paras, Jashper. Twitter post, March 26, 2012. http://twitter.com/jashperparas.

Paul, Alana. Twitter post, March 26, 2012. http://twitter.com/sw4q.

Santiago, EJ. Twitter post, March 26, 2012. http://twitter.com/freakinej.

Sitton, Claude. "Birmingham Bomb Kills 4 Negro Girls in Church; Riots Flare; 2 Boys Slain." *New York Times*. Web. 12 Mar 2014.

Stephens, Dionne P., and Layli D. Phillips. "Freaks, Gold Diggers, Divas, and Dykes: The Sociohistorical Development of Adolescent African American Women's Sexual Scripts," *Sexuality and Culture* 7, 1 (2003): 3–47. Print.

Stewart, Dodai. "Racist *Hunger Games* Fans Are Very Disappointed" *Jezebel*, ed. Jessica Coen. 26 March 2012. Web. 2 Nov. 2013.

The Hunger Games. Directed by Gary Ross. 2012. Santa Monica, CA: Lionsgate, 2012. DVD.

Index

About the Contributors

Eduardo Barros-Grela is associate professor in the Department of English at A Coruna University (Spain), where he teaches American studies and cultural studies. He is a graduate of the State University of New York (MA and PhD). In 2002–2003, he worked as a funded research fellow at the Humanities Institute (New York) and then was hired as a professor at California State University (2003–2007). His academic interests include space in cultural studies, posthuman aesthetics, *in*organic bodies and spaces, visual studies, and the dialectics of representation and performance. His publications include works on American studies (*American Secrets: The Politics and Poetics of Secrecy in the Literature and Culture of the United States*), film ("Heterotopia Meets Autopia: David Lynch's Aesthetics of Californian Spatialities"), ecocriticism ("Imaginary Representations and Cultural Performances of Ecocriticism"), cultural studies ("Performances of Uncertainty in Spaces of Contingency: Aesthetic Confinement and Mechanisms of Silencing in Paul Auster, Haruki Murakami, and Park Chan-wook" and "Chicano Visualities: A Multicultural Rewriting of Californian Spatialities"), and literature ("Dystopian Scenarios in Heterotopic Spaces: Paul Auster's *Man in the Dark*").

María Bobadilla Pérez is assistant professor in the Department of Specific Didactics at A Coruna University (Spain), where she teaches English language teaching and literature. She received a PhD in languages and literature at the State University of New York (2004) and has a PhD in the same area from the Universidad Complutense of Madrid (2006). Her academic interests include gender studies, nineteenth-century English literature, visual studies, and ESL teaching methodologies. She has published on gender and literature studies (*Woman and Education in the Victorian Novel: The Governess as a*

Model in Jane Eyre), Latino literature *(Latino Literature in the United States: The Construction of Identity through Memory*), and critical theory *(Postmodernism and its Consequences over Theoretical and Practical Feminism: Susan Bordo and Judith Butler*).

Tarah Brookfield is associate professor in history and youth and children's studies at Wilfrid Laurier University (Ontario, Canada). Her research focuses on women and youth's peace activism in the Cold War era, and society's fears and conception of nuclear war. She is the author of *Cold War Comforts: Canadian Women, Child Safety, and Global Insecurity* (Wilfrid Laurier University Press, 2012).

Jennifer Brown completed her PhD in English literature in Trinity College, Dublin, Ireland, in 2010. She has been a teacher of English language and literature for nine years, teaching in Ireland, Spain, and Italy. She has presented at the International Gothic Association conference and published reviews with the *Irish Journal of Gothic and Horror Studies*. She is the author of *Cannibalism in Literature and Film* (Palgrave Macmillan, 2012) and is currently an independent scholar.

Glen Donnar is lecturer in the School of Media and Communication at RMIT University in Melbourne, Australia. He has published diversely on popular cultural representations of gender, genre, terror, monstrosity, and disaster in American film and television, including on 9/11, the JFK assassination, and post-apocalyptic film.

Aryak Guha is assistant professor in English in Sree Chaitanya College, West Bengal, India. Dr. Guha obtained his doctoral degree working on the popular English comic book series "Amar Chitra Katha" ("Immortal Picture Tales" [a literal, and I'm afraid a bit prosaic, translation]) published from Mumbai, India, since 1967. His interests include comic books, popular print illustration and visual arts, sociology/cultural history of childhood, and post-colonial literature.

Mark Heimermann is a doctoral candidate in the English department at the University of Wisconsin–Milwaukee and serves on the executive committee of the International Comic Arts Forum. His research interests include comics studies, contemporary literature, the grotesque, and representations of childhood.

James M. Hodapp is assistant professor in the English department at American University of Beirut. He received his PhD from University of Maryland in 2014 and his primary research fields are postcolonial studies,

African literature, and world cinema. His work explores alternative genealogies for reading seminal postcolonial texts by challenging the accepted wisdom of non-Western texts as responses. He has also written scholarly articles on African literature, graphic novels, global pedagogy, and gender.

Frank Jacob is assistant professor (tenure track) of world history at the City University of New York, QCC. He received an MA from Würzburg University in 2010 and a PhD from Erlangen University in 2012. Dr. Jacob worked as assistant professor of modern history at Würzburg University (2013–2014) and lectured courses in modern history and Japanese studies at Düsseldorf University and Erlangen University before. He is the editor of the journal *Global Humanities*, *Journal of East Asian History*, and the series *Comparative Studies from a Global Perspective*. Dr. Jacob has widely published on Japanese, German, and global history. One of his recent books is called *Japanism, Pan-Asianism Terrorism* (Academica Press, 2014).

Cassandra L. Jones is assistant professor of African American studies at the University of South Carolina Upstate. Her research examines the intersection of race, technology, and speculative fiction, particularly the work of Octavia Butler. She frequently teaches courses on Afrofuturism and the Black imagination.

Betül Ateşçi Koçak is a PhD student in Advanced English Studies: Languages and Cultures in Contact Department at Universidad de Salamanca. Her thesis focuses on traumatic spaces in post-9/11 fiction. Her research interests range from Turkish and American literature and culture, trauma studies, senses of places, heterotopias, and non-places.

Eric D. Miller, PhD, is associate professor of psychology at Kent State University (East Liverpool Campus) in Ohio. His primary research and scholarly focus has examined how adults cope with and adjust to loss and other adverse events. He has published many papers on this topic and is the author of the textbook *The Psychology of Adjustment and Coping* (BVT Publishing). Dr. Miller also edited the book *Stories of Complicated Grief: A Critical Anthology* (NASW Press) and served as co-editor (along with John H. Harvey) of the book *Loss and Trauma: General and Close Relationship Perspectives* (Taylor & Francis/Brunner-Routledge).

Debbie Olson, PhD, is lecturer at University of Texas at Arlington. Her research interests include images of African and African American children in film and popular media, West African film and literature, race and identity politics, transnationalism, cultural studies, video gaming, and New Hollywood cinema. She is editor-in-chief of *Red Feather Journal: An Internation-*

al Journal of Children's Popular Culture (www.redfeatherjournal.org), co-editor of *Lost and Othered Children in Contemporary Cinema* (2012) and *Portrayals of Children in Popular Culture: Fleeting Images* (2012), and editor of *The Child in the Films of Alfred Hitchcock*. Her articles have appeared in *The Black Imagination: Science Fiction and Futurism* (2011), *The Tube Has Spoken: Reality TV as Film and History* (2009) and *Facts, Fiction, and African Creative Imaginations* (2009), and many others. She is series editor for Lexington Books' Children and Youth in Popular Culture Series.

Joseph Wiinikka-Lydon is a doctoral candidate at Emory University's Graduate Division of Religion in Ethics and Society. He is currently a visiting instructor of religion at The University of the South.